SEPTEMBER 11
CONSEQUENCES FOR CANADA

September 11
Consequences for Canada

KENT ROACH

McGill-Queen's University Press
Montreal & Kingston · London · Ithaca

© McGill-Queen's University Press 2003
ISBN 0-7735-2584-X (cloth)
ISBN 0-7735-2585-8 (paper)

Legal deposit second quarter 2003
Bibliothèque nationale du Québec

Printed in Canada on acid-free paper.

McGill-Queen's University Press acknowledges the financial support
of the Government of Canada through the Book Publishing Industry
Development Program (BPIDP) for its activities. It also acknowledges
the support of the Canada Council for the Arts for its publishing
program.

National Library of Canada Cataloguing in Publication

Roach, Kent, 1961–
    September 11: consequences for Canada / Kent Roach.

Includes index.
ISBN 0-7735-2584-X (bnd)
ISBN 0-7735-2585-8 (pbk)

1. September 11 Terrorist Attacks, 2001. 2. Terrorism–Political
aspects–Canada. 3. Terrorism–Prevention–Government policy–
Canada. 4. National security–Canada. I. Title.

FC635.R62 2003   971.064'8   C2003-900787-1
FI034.2.R62 2003

Typeset in Sabon 10/13
by Caractéra inc., Quebec City

To Jan

Contents

SEPTEMBER 11
CONSEQUENCES FOR CANADA

I

September 11, 2001

The September 11 terrorist attacks on the United States had immediate consequences for Canada. Alexander Filipov, a Regina-born engineer, had switched his reservation at the last minute to be on American Airlines Flight 11. This flight was the first 767 aircraft driven into the massive twin towers of the World Trade Center. Another Canadian, former NHL hockey player Garnet "Ace" Bailey, was on United Airlines Flight 175 as it smashed into the south tower. Twenty-two other Canadians were among the 2,823 people killed in the subsequent collapse of both towers. The Canadians were in the World Trade Center for a variety of reasons. Some had business appointments; others were working at the New York offices of their firms. Some had moved to New York for employment opportunities, and a few were visitors to the city. David Barkway, a managing director of BMO Nesbitt Burns in Toronto, had a business appointment at the 105th-floor office of the bond-trading firm Cantor Fitzgerald. He paged his Toronto office asking for help but was never heard from again. He left a two-year-old son and a wife pregnant with their second child. Christine Egan, a nurse, had accompanied her younger brother Michael Egan to his office to view the city. She was to meet an old schoolmate in the lobby at 9.30 AM, but both brother and sister perished. No Canadians were involved in the crashes of a third hijacked aircraft into the Pentagon in Washington or of a fourth in Pennsylvania, after passengers attempted to seize the aircraft from the hijackers.[1]

Canada had experienced terrorism before. To much public approval, the *War Measures Act* had been proclaimed in force at 4.00 AM on October 16, 1970, in response to the kidnapping of British diplomat James Cross by one cell of the Front de Libération du Québec (FLQ) and the kidnapping of Quebec Cabinet minister Pierre Laporte by another cell. The Cabinet declared the FLQ to be an unlawful association, and the police arrested close to 500 people on suspicion they were guilty of the new offences of being a member or supporter of the FLQ. These repressive measures did not prevent Laporte's subsequent murder. Those involved with his kidnapping and death were eventually apprehended and convicted of murder, kidnapping, and other crimes that existed before the October Crisis. Cross was recovered in late December and his kidnappers allowed to take a plane to Cuba.[2] In an eerie coincidence, Canadian newspapers on the morning of September 11, 2001, featured a story about the arrest in New York City of a man who had hijacked an Air Canada flight in 1971. When the plane landed safely in Havana, two other hijacked aircraft were already on the ground.[3] Terrorism took a more deadly turn with the 1985 bombing of an Air India flight from Vancouver, killing all 329 passengers on board. Still, Canadians, like the rest of the world, had never experienced suicide hijackings of the scale of the September 11 attacks.

Within forty-five minutes of the attacks on the World Trade Center and the Pentagon, Canadian officials decided that airports from Vancouver to St John's would accept 224 planes destined for the United States. A Canadian official later told the *Los Angeles Times*: "This government took a big risk that day. Nobody knew if there would be more attacks."[4] Once American officials had decided to close their airspace, there was little else that Canada could do as it accepted only those aircraft that did not have enough fuel to return to their point of departure. Some of the planes were deliberately diverted to remote, less-populous parts of Canada. A Korean 747 airliner was allowed to land in Whitehorse, Yukon, even though it was thought to be high-jacked. Gander, Newfoundland, with a population of 10,000, accommodated over 6000 people in thirty-eight aircraft in the three days before full air service was resumed. Stranded passengers in Halifax were housed in a Canadian military base.

Many stories emerged of warm Canadian hospitality and new friendships. Passengers who stayed at Gander later established scholarships for local residents, and some made return trips to see new friends.[5] Stephen Jay Gould, the famed Harvard scientist who was soon to die of cancer, wrote that while stranded with 9000 others in Halifax, "I heard not a single harsh word, saw not the slightest gesture of frustration, and felt nothing but pure and honest welcome ... And so Canada, although you are not my home or native land, we will always share this bond of your unstinting hospitality to people who descended upon you as frightened strangers and received nothing but solace and solidarity in your embrace of goodness."[6] Another American passenger on the last of forty-two planes diverted to Halifax commented that she was "humbled by the empathy and support of the Halifax community ... I would thank the military personnel and support staff and airport staff for their many kindnesses and frequently the response would be 'Glad to do it. We're neighbours.'"[7]

Along with much of the world, Canada declared a national day of mourning after September 11. More than 100,000 people attended a memorial service on Parliament Hill. Prime Minister Chrétien told the audience: "We reel before the blunt and terrible reality of the evil we have just witnessed." Addressing the American ambassador to Canada, Chrétien added: "Our friendship has no limit. Generation after generation, we have travelled many difficult miles together. Side by side, we have lived through many dark times, always firm in our shared resolve to vanquish any threat to freedom and justice. And together, with our allies, we will defy and defeat the threat that terrorism poses to all civilized nations. Mr. Ambassador, we will be with the U.S. every step of the way. As friends, as neighbours, as family." Ambassador Paul Cellucci replied that he had "been touched, at times overwhelmed, by the outpouring of support." The tragedy "has brought us together as never before. It has, once again, shown us that the differences that divide us are far, far less important than the ties that bind us."[8] As one American analyst stated: "For millions of Canadians, Americans are friends, family and business partners. The choice between international terrorists and helping a neighbour was simple, and most Canadians made it without equivocation or calculation of national interest."[9] Canadians, as individuals, were deeply affected by the September 11 terrorist attacks and responded generously and compassionately to the suffering of their neighbours.

But the relationship between the governments of Canada and the United States has never been easy. Soon after the attacks, reports surfaced that as many as five of the terrorists entered the United States from Canada, as had Ahmed Ressam, an al-Qaeda terrorist caught at the border in 1999 with a Canadian passport and explosives to bomb the Los Angeles International Airport. These reports were quickly found to be erroneous,[10] but the impression that Canada was a terrorist haven lingered. Late in September 2001 the *Christian Science Monitor* commented that Canada, "the giant, genial nation – known for its crimson-clad Mounties and great comedians – has also become an entry point and staging ground for Osama bin Laden's terrorist 'sleeper cells.'"[11] Although the *New York Times* stated that Canada had altered many of its security policies in an "attempt to reassure the United States that Canada is not a sanctuary for terrorists," it still reported in 2002 "that Canada's liberal refugee and immigration policies are of particular concern."[12]

A Toronto memorial service for the thousands of victims of September 11 was marred when one of its coordinators, an American minister who was also the president of Republicans Abroad, "spoke at length about Christianity being the only salvation." To applause from the audience, a Toronto lawyer criticized these remarks as insensitive to the non-Christians in the audience.[13] This would not be the last time that differing Canadian and American sensitivities to multiculturalism would clash. Canada would subsequently protest American border policies that targeted Canadian citizens born in the Middle East and other Muslim countries for particular attention. Stories mounted of Canadians, mainly from these groups, being poorly treated by American officials. There were also some hurtful but apparently deliberate slights.[14] In his dramatic address to a joint session of Congress on September 20, 2001, President Bush failed to mention the Canadians who died in the attacks or Canada's warm reception for the hundreds of American-bound flights, even though he mentioned fifteen other countries. He subsequently thanked Canada, but suspicions lingered that Canada's response to September 11 was not appreciated enough by the American government.

There were also concerns that Canada was trying too hard to please the American government in its new war against terrorism and that the long-term consequence of September 11 would be an erosion of Canadian independence and difference from the United States. Shortly after September 11, Canadian leaders pledged their support for American-led military operations against the Taliban and al-Qaeda in Afghanistan, even if it meant that some innocent people would be hurt.[15] This early support was backed up by Canada's largest military contribution since the Korean War, involving nearly 3000 troops and including a 750 Light Infantry Battle Group that operated as part of a U.S. Army Task Force. It remained in Afghanistan for only six months because of resource constraints. Canadian military participation in Afghanistan was controversial. Some argued that placing Canadian troops under de facto American control harmed not only

Canada's sovereignty but also its reputation for peace-keeping and respect for international law. They also supported Canada's autonomy from a new American Northern Command with a mandate to defend all of North America by land, air, and sea.[16] Others, however, argued that Canadian participation in American military operations in the defence of North America, missile defence, and in a possible invasion of Iraq was necessary. For them, the experience in Afghanistan demonstrated the urgent need for Canada to spend much more money on the military.[17] The degree of Canadian participation in the war against Afghanistan did not overly impress the United States, as the American ambassador repeatedly called on Canada to spend more on its military, but it was not lost on Osama bin Laden. The al-Qaeda leader, who is believed to have planned the September 11 attacks and apparently survived the massive bombings of al-Qaeda strongholds in Afghanistan, noted that Canada, along with Great Britain, France, Italy, Germany, and Australia, had joined the United States in its attack on Afghanistan. With reference to terrorist bombings on October 12, 2002, that killed over 180 people in Bali, Indonesia, including many Australians and two Canadians, bin Laden chillingly threatened revenge on all of America's allies.[18]

Four Canadian soldiers did not return home from Afghanistan. They were killed by "friendly fire" from an American "top gun" pilot. The pilot, who had taken "go pills," or amphetamines, during his long flight mission, had observed ground fire from the Canadians' routine live-fire exercises outside Kandahar, an Allied stronghold. He was flying at high speed and altitude and was told to hold fire. Still, the pilot, who had been nicknamed "psycho" because of his aggressiveness, declared self-defence, descended, and released his 250 kilogram laser-guided bomb on the Canadians, only to be told 32 seconds later that the ground fire came from "friendlies." The pilot and his wingman were subsequently charged with involuntary manslaughter, but also received substantial support from their home state of Illinois. *The New York Times* reported: "The case has been a national obsession in Canada, and a source of continuing friction between the Bush administration and the Canadian government."[19]

There was less controversy in Canada when it was discovered that elite Canadian special forces had given captives to the Americans for detention and interrogation at Guantanamo Bay, Cuba, in probable violation of the Geneva Conventions. There was almost no controversy when the Canadian Navy subsequently handed over captured al-Qaeda suspects to the Americans.[20] The Americans continued to detain and interrogate 600 captives from Afghanistan at Guantanamo Bay. The captives included Omar Khadr, a Canadian teenager who had apparently thrown a grenade that killed an American soldier during hostilities near the Afghanistan-Pakistan border. The Canadian government expressed concerns about Khadr's youth and lack of access to Canadian consular officials.[21] Nevertheless, he remained in American custody at Guantanamo Bay without being accorded the rights of a prisoner of war not to be interrogated or the rights of an accused charged with a crime.[22] If Khadr is eventually charged, he may face the death penalty, since the United States is one of the few countries in the world that still executes juvenile offenders.

The Canadian government made efforts on the home front to respond to the threat of terrorism and to satisfy both American and United Nations expectations. A little more than a month after September 11, it introduced a massive and hastily drafted *Anti-terrorism Act* (Bill C-36). The bill included new legal concepts such as investigative hearings, preventive arrests, broad motive-based crimes for participation in or support for terrorist groups at home or abroad, as well as new powers to list terrorist groups, deprive them of charitable status, and take their property. There were fears that the bill, as introduced, would define some anti-globalization protests and illegal strikes as terrorist activities. A broad coalition of civil libertarians, lawyers, unions, Aboriginal people, the refugee community, anti-globalization protesters, and groups representing Muslim and Arab Canadians all expressed fears about the breadth of the bill. Before it became law in December 2001, Bill C-36 was amended to respond to some of the criticisms, but concerns remain about the necessity and breadth of the new anti-terrorism law.

September 11 also revived criticism that the Supreme Court of Canada had engaged in judicial activism by ruling that fugitives generally could not be returned for trial to the United States without assurances that the death penalty would not be applied. Would this decision mean that Canada could not return an al-Qaeda operative to the United States without such assurance? Criticisms of the Supreme Court were renewed when, in January 2002, it ruled that the same reasoning applied to prevent the deportation of suspected terrorists to face a substantial risk of torture.[23] Would this decision mean that Canada could not return a terrorist to a country such as Jordan or Saudi Arabia which might use torture in interrogations? Arguments were made that it was the elected government of Canada, not the independent courts, that should make decisions affecting Canadian security and foreign relations. At the same time, the Court would not commit itself to an absolute rule that extradition or deportation of a terrorist to face the death penalty or torture would never be constitutional. Would the Court condone the torture of terrorists in some cases, as Harvard law professor Alan Dershowitz argued it should, if necessary to prevent another September 11?[24] Many judges, including Chief Justice Beverley McLachlin, recognized that September 11 would place pressures on the courts to readjust the balance between liberty and security, but also that the courts might have to take unpopular stands in terrorism cases.[25]

After passing the *Anti-terrorism Act*, the government introduced another massive bill, the *Public Safety Act*, but it was withdrawn after criticisms that it would give ministers dangerous new powers to declare military security zones around places of protest such as the 2002 G8 meeting in Kananaskis, Alberta. The bill also provided for greater controls over airport security and dangerous biological and explosive materials, and it increased efforts to make nuclear plants and pipelines more secure from possible terrorist attacks. Biological terrorism became an issue after post-September 11 mailings of anthrax in the United States resulted in five deaths. In January 2002 Canadians were reminded of the insecurity of their water supplies as a judicial inquiry concluded that budget cuts leading to less monitoring of water quality had contributed to the death of seven people in Walkerton, Ontario, in 2000 because of accidental *E. coli* contamination.[26] If water could be accidentally poisoned without the government responding, what would ensure that the government could prevent or respond to the deliberate poisoning of water, air, or food? The *Public Safety Act* was reintroduced with new restrictions on some ministerial powers, but it has yet to be enacted. Canada's legislative and administrative response to the terrifying prospect of biological and nuclear terrorism and its preparation for emergencies such as September 11 lags behind the American response, which includes a new agency for "homeland security," the vaccination of a million military and health-care personnel, and plans to provide free smallpox vaccinations for all Americans who want them.[27]

Although the *Public Safety Act* was not pushed forward, a separate bill dealing with exchange of information about airline passenger lists was quietly passed to ensure compliance with new American security requirements. In December 2001 the Supreme Court unanimously ruled that Canadian travellers did not have a reasonable expectation of privacy in their customs declaration forms to outweigh the government's interests in determining whether they were on vacation while receiving unemployment insurance.[28] Elinor Caplan, the minister responsible for customs, has defended "advance passenger information" as a "major investigative tool" that "puts investigators hard on the trail of suspected killers and terrorists" and "significantly increases our ability to track pedophiles, find criminals trying to enter our country, identify potential drug smugglers, and protect the health of Canadians."[29] The federal privacy commissioner, George Radwanski, however, questioned the use of advance airline passenger lists for general law enforcement purposes. He strenuously opposed plans to keep a "big brother" database on the foreign travels of Canadians over the past six years. Supported by a legal opinion from retired Supreme Court of Canada Justice Gérard La Forest that allowing government agencies access to detailed, travel-related information of millions of innocent Canadians would violate the Charter, Radwanski raised concerns about the "unprecedented creation of government dossiers of personal information about all citizens." He also took exception to the idea that those who oppose the database are "indifferent to terrorism, murder and armed crime, drug smuggling, pedophilia, the plight of children, even plagues."[30] As in other countries, there were concerns that new powers in the war against terrorism were spreading to wars against other serious crimes and that privacy was being sacrificed in the new quest for security.

In December 2001 the federal government allocated almost $8 billion in spending on security in its self-proclaimed "security budget." The new spending was devoted to policing, the military, increased airport security, and border and immigration controls, but not to matters such as health care that many Canadians saw as a more immediate threat to their personal security. The budget focused on more police officers, security officials, immigration officials, and border guards. Much less money was devoted to responses that might prevent or respond to nuclear and biological terrorism or deliberate or accidental contamination of food and water supplies. The 2001 security budget made it seem as though terrorism was the only threat to the security of Canadians. Even with respect to a possible repeat of September 11, it is not clear that Canadians were getting their money's worth for a new security tax of $24 per round airline trip. A year after

September 11, the chair of a Canadian Senate committee worried that box cutters similar to those used by terrorists could still be placed on aircraft at Canada's busiest airport. Armed marshals were placed on some flights, especially those into Washington, but not all baggage was screened for bombs. Air Canada pilots demanded that better security doors be installed on their cockpits or that they be given taser guns.[31]

The immediate concern for many Canadians after September 11 was not distant events in Afghanistan, new legislation, or even aviation security, but ensuring that the almost $2 billion in trade that crosses the American-Canadian border every day continued to flow. The American *Patriot Act*,[32] enacted with overwhelming support in Congress in October 2001, did not allay concerns about increased border delays and bottlenecks. It provided for the tripling of border guards and customs and immigration officials on the "northern border," one many Americans believed was a threat to their security. Such a mobilization at the American border would have inconvenienced the people who make a total of almost 200 million crossings every year. It might have harmed the American economy, but it would certainly have devastated the Canadian economy, which relies on exports to the United States. In December 2001 broad framework agreements were signed between Canada and the United States calling for increased collaboration in identifying security risks and facilitating the flow of low-risk goods and people over the border. The "smart border" agreements went beyond safer and more efficient flows of goods and people, however, and led to the initialing of a "safe third country" agreement between Canada and the United States. This agreement prohibited most refugees from applying to Canada if they reached the United States first. It may have responded to American concerns about Canada's "liberal" refugee policies, but it did not ensure free trade – as witnessed by bitter trade disputes that raged over American softwood lumber tariffs and farm subsidies.

The border agreements did not ease frictions between the two governments. Canada protested that Canadian citizens born in the Middle East and Muslim countries were being singled out for photographing, fingerprinting, and registration in the United States. The Canadian government temporarily issued a travel advisory to Canadian citizens born in these countries about the American practices. The Americans responded that such practices were not automatically tied to place of birth and did not constitute racial profiling. Speaking at Niagara Falls, New York, United States Attorney General John Ashcroft warned

that "no country is exempt from the war against terrorism" and that
the National Security Entry and Exit Registration System, which had
already fingerprinted and photographed 14,000 people, including
1400 Canadians, would continue to operate. Some Canadians protested the system as racial and religious profiling. Rohinton Mistry, a
prominent Canadian author who was born in India, cancelled his
American book tour because of the way he had been treated in
American airports.[33]

September 11 had consequences for the tenor of Canadian democracy. There was a widespread outcry after a University of British
Columbia professor, Sunera Thobani, criticized American foreign
policy shortly after September 11 as "bloodthirsty" and "vengeful."
She also raised concerns about Canadian complicity with the American-
led war in Afghanistan and a possible war against Iraq. The negative
reaction to Thobani's speech at an academic conference included police
investigations into whether she should be charged criminally with
wilfully promoting hatred against Americans; denunciations of her
speech by both the prime minister of Canada and the premier of British
Columbia; and arguments in the media that it was somehow inappropriate for her, as an immigrant to Canada, to make such harsh criticisms of either Canada or the United States. Nevertheless, many
Canadians agreed with Thobani that American foreign policy was one
of the causes of September 11.[34] Even Prime Minister Chrétien was
later prepared to relate September 11 to global disparities of power
and wealth, but his comments on the first anniversary of September
11 that the "Western world is getting too rich in relations to the poor
world" were greeted with criticisms that he was being "anti-American"
and blaming the victim for the crimes of September 11.[35]

The Thobani and Chrétien comments relating September 11 to
broader issues of American foreign policy and global justice prompted
debates about Canadian nationalism and Canada's place in the world.
Veteran journalist Robert Fulford argued that the Thobani speech was
a symptom of a more general anti-Americanism that was an unacceptable part of Canadian nationalism and a denial of the many values
Canada shares with the United States.[36] Historian Michael Bliss went
further: he predicted that September 11 was "the end of Canadian
nationalism" and was "driving us faster along the road we had already
chosen, the road of continental integration."[37] In the immediate aftermath of September 11, many Canadians seemed prepared to sacrifice

sovereignty for continued security and prosperity. Former foreign affairs minister Lloyd Axworthy expressed concerns that September 11 may have started a "slippery slope" that will erode "Canada's ability to speak with an independent and considered voice" on a range of matters.[38] The notorious picture of Canadian troops roughly handing over detainees at Kandahar Airport to the Americans for possible detention in the open-air cages of Camp X-Ray in Guantanamo Bay, Cuba, may symbolize a shift towards greater integration with the United States at the expense of civil liberties, respect for international law, and sovereign foreign, immigration, and military policies. At the very least, the aftermath of September 11 has prompted fundamental debates about the nature of Canadian law, democracy, sovereignty, and security.

LAMENT FOR A NATION?

In my more pessimistic moments, I find myself thinking of George Grant's *Lament for a Nation*,[39] in which he declares Canadian sovereignty and a distinctive Canadian democracy to be dead. That book was written in response to Canada's decision to accept nuclear arms in the wake of the Cuban Missile Crisis of October 1962. Although September 11 was traumatic, the Cuban crisis was even more so. Canadians feared they would be caught in the middle of an impending nuclear war between the United States and the Soviet Union. Nevertheless, Prime Minister Diefenbaker refused to cooperate with the Americans or accept nuclear weapons. He persisted even after his minister of defence resigned and he was strongly criticized by the American government. Diefenbaker lost the 1963 election to Lester Pearson, who had decided that Canada must accept nuclear arms. Grant argued that Diefenbaker's error was his failure to recognize "that a branch-plant society could not possibly show independence over an issue on which the American government was seriously determined."[40] Diefenbaker's defeat, he said, was "the defeat of Canadian nationalism" and, indeed, the death of the Canada. In his view, Canada could remain distinct from the United States only by resisting involvement in the new American empire, including the war in Vietnam. Canada had to develop those aspects of its political culture that were both more conservative and more socialist than the liberalism and faith in limited government and modern progress shared by Democrats and Republicans south of the border.

There was some support for Grant's arguments that the Cuban Missile Crisis revealed Canada as no longer a fully sovereign nation. When Diefenbaker hesitated to place Canadian forces on full alert during the crisis, the military, acting in coordination with the Americans, did so in any event. Michael Bliss has suggested that the fact that Canadian officials, without consulting the prime minister, decided to accept stranded aircraft when American airspace was closed on September 11, 2001, similarly underlines that, "in a real North American crisis," Canadian "sovereignty is an illusion." He questioned whether Canada can afford to have "more liberal immigration and security procedures than the United States ... If Americans implement ethnic 'profiling' as a sensible security procedure, can we refuse to do the same?"[41] Certainly on some issues, Canada has followed the American lead in the war against terrorism. In February 2002 the *New York Times* concluded that "Canada has thoroughly overhauled its security policy since the Sept. 11 attacks on the United States, tightening coordination with Washington in military, intelligence and law enforcement matters while easing its traditional concerns over privacy and other civil liberties." It quoted a senior Bush administration official that the Canadians "have done a lot, yes, but at the same time, they have a lot to do, and they know it."[42] There are legitimate fears that September 11 is driving Canada towards Americanized criminal justice, immigration, and military and foreign policies that depart from such Canadian values as multiculturalism, peacekeeping, and respect for international laws and institutions.

In my more optimistic moments, however, I believe that it is unwise to lament a Canada that was lost on that surreal morning of September 11. Grant was premature in declaring Canadian sovereignty to be dead once Diefenbaker was defeated and the government accepted nuclear weapons.[43] Indeed, Grant's death notice for Canada was the start of a new Canadian nationalism. Prime Ministers Pearson and Trudeau subsequently took stands on a variety of issues, including Vietnam and nuclear disarmament, which were very unpopular with both Democratic and Republican administrations to the south. The history of Canadian relations with the United States has been one of continual pushes towards continental integration and pulls towards sovereign nationalism. The shock of September 11 tilted the balance towards integration, but it also provided Canada with opportunities to reaffirm its differences from the United States. Realizing this potential, however, will take more imagination and will than we have generally seen since September 11.

SEPTEMBER 11 AND OTHER CHALLENGES TO LAW, DEMOCRACY, SOVEREIGNTY, AND SECURITY

Within the short span of less than two years, how do we assess Canada's response to September 11 and situate the new challenges faced by Canada into a larger context of recent challenges for Canadian law, democracy, sovereignty, and security? Although the challenges of September 11 are particularly dramatic and intense, one of the arguments of this book is that they are not fundamentally different from those we have faced in the past. In other words, September 11 did not change everything. Rather, it accelerated a number of pre-existing challenges already faced by Canada. This is an important message, given the many apocalyptic statements that have been made about September 11.

Before September 11, we were already in the habit of expanding our criminal law in a symbolic attempt to respond to well-publicized crimes that threatened Canadians' sense of security. The 1990s had seen an expansion and toughening of the criminal law in more or less direct response to a number of well-publicized murders, including the massacre of fourteen women at École Polytechnique in Montreal and murders in biker gang wars. As in the United States, there has been a tendency to "govern through crime."[44] Complex issues such as crimes against women and minorities, and now terrorism, have been dealt with in a symbolic and punitive manner through the enactment of tougher criminal laws, including new offences that denounce conduct that was already criminal.[45] Both before and after September 11, Canadian governments have prided themselves on advancing equality and victims' rights by enacting more criminal laws, despite the absence of evidence that criminal laws make real such laudable rights. Canadians have relied on the criminal law in a desperate and frequently vain quest for an increased sense of security and an understandable desire to express concern for those victimized by crime. September 11 only continued this trend.

The difficulty for Canadian courts as they make decisions with regard to terrorism mirrors the larger phenomenon of Canadian courts being put on trial and held up to increased public and political scrutiny of their decisions.[46] The pressure placed on our courts by governments and the public, most of whom, it seems, would prefer that their Supreme Court be elected,[47] makes it vitally important that courts exercise their role independently and fearlessly. At the same time, however, some recent deferential developments in jurisprudence under the *Canadian Charter of Rights and Freedoms*,[48] as well as the historical records of courts in times of wars and other crises, should make us uneasy with the arguments of the former minister of justice Anne McLellan that the *Anti-terrorism Act* was acceptable because it was consistent with the Charter. The fact that most of the legislation may be Charter proof, in the sense that it will not be struck down by the courts, does not mean that it was necessary, wise, or even just. September 11 continued a trend of Canadian courts being put on trial and of governments Charter proofing questionable laws.

Before September 11, not all was well with Canadian democracy. Since the protests against the World Trade Organization in Seattle, similar Canadian protests against globalization, poverty, and the treatment of Aboriginal people have often been greeted with intimidating police presences and other security measures that are not conducive to a robust democracy that invites dissent.[49] Many expressed legitimate fears that the *Anti-terrorism Act* as first introduced could be used against illegal protests that disrupted essential public or private services. The subsequently introduced *Public Safety Act* was dubbed the "Kananaskis Act" because of the ability it would have given the minister of defence to declare the already isolated site of the G8 summit an off-limits military security zone.[50] Since September 11 there has been an increased temptation to brand the most strident of Canada's dissenters as terrorists. Nevertheless, such dissenters were already seen as dangerous before September 11. Efforts to curb democratic debate, including debate about the causes and consequences of terrorism, are unfortunate. As a nation that regularly debates secession in a democratic manner, Canada should be a shining example of a free and democratic society. Robust democracy at home and abroad will not always prevent terrorism, but it will reaffirm the illegitimacy of violence in the pursuit of political ends.

Since September 11, terrorism has been linked with Canada's immigration and refugee policies, even though none of the September 11 terrorists entered the United States through Canada. Concerns about systemic discrimination in the criminal justice system and linkages between criminal justice and immigration are not, however, new. There was evidence of the profiling and over-incarceration of Aboriginal people and African Canadians long before September 11. Similarly, the immigration system was already being used to achieve punitive objectives such as the deportation of permanent residents convicted of crimes.[51] Both before and after September 11, Canada faced the danger of Americanized criminal justice policies in which underclasses and groups stereotypically associated with crime were exposed to heightened state surveillance and incarceration.[52] Although the federal government was eager to defend the *Anti-terrorism Act* as legislation that promoted human rights and protected racial and religious minorities from hate crimes, it resisted calls to commit itself in the act to non-discrimination in the administration of the many new powers given to police and prosecutors. This refusal has led to fears that new and existing security powers could be used, as they have been in the United States, to target or profile people simply because they are perceived to be of the same race, religion, or country of birth as the September 11 terrorists. The government's claims that the act advances human rights ring hollow, and the proposed legislation was opposed by many groups which feared that their human rights would be harmed by the new anti-terrorism law. The fallout from September 11 has presented new threats to equality, but even before September 11 there was a need for Canadians to renew their commitment to non-discrimination in the administration of all our laws.

Well before September 11 the forces of globalization and continental integration were buffeting Canadians. Nationalists had long expressed fears for the preservation of Canadian sovereignty, but these concerns increased in the wake of the 1988 *Free Trade Agreement* and the hollowing out of Canadian governments and corporations during much of the 1990s.[53] Canadian nationalism was not particularly healthy before September 11. Some influential Canadians had lost confidence in Canada's future as a humane and peaceful alternative to the United States. There was much envy of American prosperity, importance, and low taxation rates and increasing interest in American practices of privatized public goods, including health and education. The greater integration of the Canadian economy into the American economy and the need for a free flow of goods across the border make Canada vulnerable to American demands about security and attempts to link security concerns with broader issues of Canadian foreign, military, immigration, refugee, and criminal justice policy. These demands in turn reduce Canadian confidence in the wisdom of maintaining distinctive policies on these fronts. There are real concerns that Canada has not done enough since September 11 to preserve a sovereign foreign policy, with its traditional post-Second World War commitments to peacekeeping, respect for international law, and a generous refugee policy. Still, Canadian sovereignty was under siege long before September 11.

The horrible events of September 11 and their non-stop media coverage made Canadians feel more insecure. But Canadians had plenty of reasons to feel insecure before that fateful day. Governmental cuts in the 1990s affected a range of government services that contributed to the security of Canadians. The seven deaths in the summer of 2000 from the *E. coli* in Walkerton's water supply made many Canadians worry about the safety of their food and water. Other fears relate to nuclear and aviation safety, our reliance on computer systems and power grids, and the declining quality of Canada's health care system and its air and water. The prospect after September 11 that terrorists could poison our water and air, crash our planes, hack our computers, and blow up our nuclear reactors only added to the existing risk of accidents with respect to such materials. Although the world certainly seemed more dangerous to Canadians after September 11, it also seemed quite risky before that time.[54] The challenge is to respond rationally to the many risks we face and to integrate the threat of terrorism with other risks in modern society.

CONCLUSION

This book has two main goals. The first is to provide a critical assessment of the consequences of September 11 for Canada. To this end, I will examine post-September 11 developments in Canadian law and democracy and in its immigration, military, foreign, and security policies. Much of the focus will be on Bill C-36, *the Anti-terrorism Act*, because it remains Canada's prime legislative response to September 11 and the one that has been subjected to the most public debate. The government's claims that this new law is needed to prevent terrorism and that it will advance human rights will be critically assessed in light of evidence that many of it most controversial provisions were not used during the first year of the law's existence[55] and the fears of many groups that the law will infringe their human rights. The government's claims that the new law is consistent with the Charter will also be examined. Although the act violates a wide range of Charter rights, the courts may well find that these limitations are reasonable. The successful Charter-proofing of the new law reflects the ambiguous nature of the Charter in both guaranteeing rights and legitimating limitations on rights. This ambiguity is underlined by the fact that courts have refused to commit themselves to never send a suspected terrorist from Canada to face torture or the death penalty.

Looking beyond the *Anti-terrorism Act*, I will suggest that the Canadian government has been too quick to allow the imperative of keeping the border open and secure to be linked with more contentious issues of foreign, military, and immigration policy. Such linkages can undermine sovereignty and adversely affect Canada's international reputation. They may not even succeed in keeping the border open for trade. Canada can, as it is doing with respect to American softwood lumber tariffs, use existing trade mechanisms to keep the border open. Ceding sovereignty in the hope of free trade and security is not, however, the answer. Canada should not resist sensible cooperation with the United States on common border and security issues, but it should not rush towards measures that will adversely affect Canada's ability to devise its own independent policies. Since September 11, Canada has placed its enviable reputation for peacekeeping, a generous refugee policy, and respect for international law and institutions in jeopardy.

The second goal of this book is to provide a sense of how Canada's anti-terrorism policies should evolve in the future. Although September 11 has, in the short-term, hastened Canada's integration with the United States, it need not do so. It could result in renewed Canadian nationalism and a more measured and moderate Canadian response to terrorism. The Canadian approach to terrorism could place less emphasis on the criminal sanction and military force than the American approach and more emphasis on respect for international law, robust democracy, non-discrimination, and a welcoming multiculturalism. The Canadian approach could also integrate terrorism into the broader context of other threats to human security. Terrorism should be integrated into a broader human security agenda that includes better protection of food and water safety, nuclear and biological safety, public health, and emergency response.[56] Attempts to increase the security of places and materials vulnerable to terrorism may protect Canadians not only from catastrophic terrorism but also from the greater risk of accidents and natural disasters. A broader security agenda that targets places and systems may avoid some of the threats to equality, liberty, and privacy that occur when people are targeted as potential terrorists. It may also avoid some of the conflicts with courts that should vigorously protect civil liberties and equality, even at the risk of public opposition.

Abroad, concerns about terrorism should be integrated into broader concerns about achieving human security, arms control, keeping the peace, and building democracies. Canadian policy should resist efforts to link the need for an open and secure border with broader issues of Canada's sovereign foreign, military, and immigration policy. Canada's interests are not necessarily America's interests. Canada is in a good position to help separate legitimate concerns about terrorism and security from more controversial aspects of American foreign policy. A broader security agenda will not be achieved by enacting more criminal laws and giving the police greater powers, as was done with the *Anti-terrorism Act*. It will not be achieved by spending the massive amounts required to ensure that the Canadian Forces can fight in combat with the high-tech American military. It will not be achieved by heavy-handed policies at home and abroad that may only increase grievances and produce more terrorists. Without more imagination and will, however, Canada may continue to fall into the slipstream of America's war against terrorism.

2

Criminalizing Terrorism

The main legislative response to September 11 in Canada was Bill C-36, the massive *Anti-terrorism Act*. This legislation weighs in at 186 pages of bilingual text and added a new part to the *Criminal Code* entitled "Terrorism." For the first time, the code defined terrorism. It also criminalized many forms of financing and facilitating terrorism, including participation in and support for terrorist organizations. The bill was produced with record speed. Its main parts were drafted between September 11 and October 13, with the crucial definition of terrorism discussed right up to the last minute before the bill was introduced in Parliament on October 15, 2001.[1] Some amendments were made subsequently in response to concerns that illegal political protests and strikes and the expression of religious or political beliefs could be defined as terrorism. Controversial new powers of preventive arrest and investigative hearings were also subject to a renewable five-year review, or "sunset clause." After a truncated debate on third reading, the act was passed by the House of Commons on November 29, 2001, by a 189 to 47 vote and later approved without amendments by the Senate. It was proclaimed in force on December 24, 2001, in time to be included in Canada's report to the United Nations on the steps it had taken to fight terrorism in light of September 11. It represents a massive and permanent change to Canadian criminal law with respect to terrorism. Many pages were added to Canada's criminal laws, but almost none of the new provisions were used during the first year that the *Anti-terrorism Act* was in force.[2] The new law has symbolic and political value as a response to September 11, but old criminal and immigration laws still provided important legal powers to respond to terrorist threats.

THE LEGAL NEED FOR NEW TERRORISM LAWS

Throughout the debates on the bill, Minister of Justice Anne McLellan stressed that new criminal laws were necessary to prevent terrorism. In her November 20 appearance before the Justice Committee, she argued:

Perhaps the greatest gap in the current laws is created by the necessity of preventing terrorist acts. Our laws must reflect fully our intention to prevent terrorist activity and, currently, they do not.

Under our current laws, we can convict terrorists who actually engage in acts of violence if we are able to identify and apprehend them after their acts have been committed.

However, I think we all agree that Canadians have a right to expect their government to do everything it can to prevent such horrific acts as those of September 11 from happening in the first place ...

The Criminal Code offences in c-36 will allow us to convict those who facilitate, participate in and direct terrorist activity and these must include preventive measures which are applicable whether or not the ultimate terrorist acts are carried out.[3]

A person unschooled in the criminal law might assume from these remarks that the existing criminal law was powerless to apprehend the September 11 terrorists until they were on the planes, when, as the minister of justice reminded us, it was too late. But a moment's reflection should reveal the inaccuracy of such a belief. The so-called twentieth hijacker, Zacarias Moussaoui, was in custody before September 11 and stands charged with conspiring and attempting a number of serious crimes, including hijacking and murder. Indeed, he may well have pled guilty to these charges but for his concern that the death penalty under American law might be applied. Similar charges could have been laid in Canada had Moussaoui or the September 11 terrorists planned their attacks in Canada.

What the September 11 terrorists did was already a crime long before they stepped on the planes. Agreements or conspiracies among two or more persons to commit murder or to hijack a plane are themselves serious crimes, even though "there may be changes of operation, personnel, or victims" before the completed crime can be committed and even though the ultimate crime may be committed outside Canada.[4] The fact that some of the terrorists might not have known the full details of the crime would not relieve them of criminal responsibility.[5]

Attempts to commit crimes are also serious crimes. If the intent to commit a crime is clear, a person may be guilty even though a "considerable period of time"[6] would have to elapse before the completed offence could be committed. A person need not even have committed an act that is criminal in order to be guilty of an attempted crime. Taking flying lessons with the intent to crash a jetliner into a building could be a sufficient basis for a conviction for attempted murder, a crime that carries a maximum of life imprisonment. The *Criminal Code* also prohibits counselling or assisting others to commit crimes. There is little reason to think that Canadian courts would not have sensibly interpreted existing criminal law to apply to apprehended acts of violent terrorism.

Had the September 11 terrorists planned their crimes in Canada and had law enforcement officials been aware of their activities, the existing law would have allowed them to be charged and convicted of serious crimes before they boarded the aircraft. They likely would have been guilty of conspiracy to hijack the plane, conspiracy to murder, attempted hijacking, or attempted murder when they were still planning their suicide missions. Such offences already carry high maximum penalties, including life imprisonment. The failure of September 11 was one of law enforcement, not of the criminal law.

THE POLITICAL NEED FOR NEW TERRORISM LAWS

The legal argument that much of the *Anti-terrorism Act* was not necessary to apprehend known terrorists before they commit acts of violence misses the political reality that new criminal laws in response to September 11 were "inevitable"[7] and "should come as no surprise."[8] Over the last decade, Parliament has added new crimes every year to what is already an overflowing *Criminal Code*. Crimes such as criminal harassment or stalking, child pornography, procuring an underage prostitute, and gang offences have been added to the code not so much because of a legal or technical need to expand the ambit of the criminal law, but because of a political need to denounce such harms. Bill c-36 falls into this pattern of "reactive and ad hoc" criminal law reform that senior Department of Justice official Stanley Cohen recognized in 1996 when he observed: "Distressing events, especially well-publicized events, galvanize politicians and policy makers to legislative action. After the fact reform often implies that the law is, or at least has been, powerless to prevent such occurrences – which is not correct – but ultimately there are limits to the ability of the formal law to deter or prevent crime."[9]

This increased tendency to amend the criminal law to respond to well-publicized tragedies and to "govern through crime"[10] follows American patterns of making crime a top political issue. For example, Stockwell Day, when he was leader of the opposition, tried to make child pornography a "Willie Horton" type issue in the 2000 federal election, but without the success enjoyed by American politicians who often attempt to make their opponents seem "soft on crime." With or without such dramatic politicization, the *Criminal Code* is becoming an increasingly important focal point of Canadian politics. It is relatively simple and cheap to amend the code, compared with other strategies that may help prevent crime or repair its harm. The political and populist lure of adding to the *Criminal Code* has simply been irresistible.

This tendency to "govern through crime," and the consequent "criminalization of politics," would have raised alarm bells with the likes of George Grant, who argued that Canadian democracy should take a different path from American democracy and that the possibilities of genuine conservatism and socialism were what really distinguished Canada from the United States.[11] Our panicked politicization of and constant bolstering of the *Criminal Code* does not display either a tory's confident faith in the traditional criminal law as a secure bulwark against disorder or a socialist's sense that the criminal law has only a limited role in responding to the social, economic, and political injustices and grievances of the day.[12] It also does not display a liberal's belief in the importance of restraint in the use of society's strongest and most coercive instrument. The expansion of the criminal law is not principled; it is political, symbolic, and somewhat cynical.

To understand the pressures brought to bear on contemporary Canadian criminal law, one need only look at the law of first-degree murder. First-degree murder is our most serious crime, and it includes murders that are committed in the course of a short list of other serious offences. This list includes some of the heinous crimes committed by the September 11 terrorists – hijacking an airplane, kidnapping, forcible confinement, and hostage taking. This short list of crimes has been getting longer. In 1997 two new offences were added in response to well-publicized crimes. Parliament added the new offence of criminal harassment[13] after a number of high-profile and tragic cases in which women were murdered by their former partners. It also added organized crime bombings to the list after the death of an eleven-year-old boy in a bombing in a biker gang war.[14] In 2001 Parliament added the offence of intimidating a justice system participant or a journalist investigating organized crime after the shooting of crime journalist Michel Auger.[15] The law of first-degree murder has been expanded through piecemeal changes driven by politics, media attention, advocacy by interest groups representing victims and the police, and a desire to denounce horrible acts of violence.

This pattern was repeated as Parliament once again expanded the crime of first-degree murder after September 11 by providing that deaths caused while committing or attempting to commit new terrorism offences will also be punished as first-degree murder.[16] It was not enough to rely on the fact that planned and deliberate murders, and murders committed during kidnappings and hijackings, would already be classified as first-degree murder under the existing criminal law. It was necessary to include terrorist acts. My point is not so much to criticize these additions to the law of first-degree murder,[17] but to note that they reflect a "narrative" and even "memorial" style in the criminal law based on a greater awareness of the harm suffered by victims of particular crimes. Legislation is becoming more embedded in particular narratives and political aspirations.[18] The rationale for these *Criminal Code* amendments rests on the felt need to recognize tragic cases, not the more abstract issues of coherence within the code or respect for fundamental principles of criminal law. Although it is relatively simple and satisfying to add to the *Criminal Code*, it is much more difficult to repeal new parts that were added in haste or during a time when the emotional impact of horrific crimes was intense. The many new crimes of terrorism added to our *Criminal Code* in the immediate aftermath of September 11 fit a pattern of the criminal law being amended to memorialize terrible crimes.

THE CRIMINALIZATION OF POLITICAL OR RELIGIOUS MOTIVES

The new narrative and memorial style in the criminal law helps explain why the *Anti-terrorism Act* requires the prosecutor to prove beyond a reasonable doubt that a terrorist activity was committed "in whole or in part for a political, religious or ideological purpose, objective or cause."[19] In essence, this requirement demands proof of motive as an essential element of a crime, something that is generally not necessary in criminal law. Only a few years ago the Supreme Court affirmed the traditional principle that "it does not matter to society, in its efforts to secure social peace and order, what an accused's motive was, but only what the accused intended to do."[20] The traditional principles of criminal law are based on whether the accused knew or intended that his actions would cause death, as opposed to the broader motive or rationale for such violence. The accused's motive has been legally irrelevant for a long time. But the accused's motive sometimes does matter to society. The motives of the hijackers mattered very much in the immediate aftermath of September 11. The irrelevance of motive as a matter of legal principle does not mean it is not a politically salient factor. A democratic criminal code can criminalize motive.

It does not follow that a democratic criminal code in a liberal and multicultural society should criminalize motive, especially motive based on political or religious beliefs. Parliament has resisted the temptation to criminalize motive before with respect to crimes against female genital mutilation, even though these crimes were often motivated by religious beliefs.[21] Parliament denounced intentional violence regardless of its motivation and did not risk being seen as denouncing particular religious beliefs. The government's decision to include motive as an element of the new terrorism offences was criticized by a number of groups who feared that the law would be used to target those who held political or religious views that were deemed to be "extreme" or "unusual." The government responded to these criticisms with an amendment providing that "the expression of a political, religious or ideological thought, belief or opinion" would not constitute a terrorist activity, unless it fell under one of the other broad definitions of terrorist activities.[22] This amendment probably makes the criminalization of motive safe from Charter challenge. The expression of extreme religious and political views will not itself generally constitute terrorism.[23] A conclusion that the inclusion of religious or political motive is Charter proof, however, does not mean it was necessary or wise.

The inclusion of religious or political motive was not necessary to distinguish terrorism from other crime.[24] It can also be criticized from the perspective of both due process and crime control. The requirement of proof of political or religious motive raises the risk of an acquittal if the prosecutor cannot prove the appropriate motive beyond a reasonable doubt. Why should we acquit a person of a crime if his or her motives are unknown or cannot be classified as political, ideological, or religious?[25] The motive requirement undercuts the notion of a liberal criminal law that inquires only into the mind of the accused, as opposed to his or her heart. The requirement for proof of political or religious motive will make the politics and religion of suspects a fundamental issue in terrorism trials. Unlike in the United States, where proof of political and religious motive is not required to make out a terrorism charge, judges will not be able to shut down evidence about the accused's politics or religion on the grounds that it is irrelevant. Canadian judges will have difficulty echoing the words of one American judge in the bail hearing of al-Qaeda suspects, "We don't convict people for their thoughts or what they read."[26] Terrorism trials in Canada will be political and religious trials.

The requirement of proof of political or religious motive will also affect police investigations. The police now have a legal duty to collect evidence about the political and religious beliefs of those they suspect will commit crimes related to terrorism. If they do not do so, they will not be doing their job of collecting evidence that the prosecution will need to establish a crime of terrorism. The police are not experts in politics and religion. They may not understand unconventional political beliefs or the religious beliefs of minorities. They may blur the line between terrorism and radical political or religious dissent.[27] The police may target those whose politics and religion they find to be extreme, or those who are associated with terrorism by means of widely held stereotypes.

Why would the government risk losing convictions and alienating minority communities by insisting on criminalizing religious or political motive? A possible explanation is a desire to denounce not only the crimes of the September 11 terrorists but also their anti-Western political and religious motives. Anne McLellan explained the need to broaden the definition of terrorism in the mandate of the Canadian Security Intelligence Service (CSIS) to include religiously motivated violence on the basis that "as we have seen, terrorists may be driven by motives other than the purely political."[28] Although no manifesto explaining the rationale for the events of September 11 has been issued and there is evidence that the terrorists did not live their lives in America as devout Muslims, it is widely believed that their suicide mission was motivated by what is commonly called Islamic fanaticism. The motive section of the bill responds to these perceptions and denounces such political or religious beliefs as extreme and criminal.

But this association comes uncomfortably close to "stereotypes about Muslims [that are] all present in the back of many people's minds."[29] Indeed, the equation of Islam with extremism or fanaticism and with religious and political violence may itself constitute one of the stereotypes that are implicitly invoked by the extraordinary inclusion of motive as an essential element of Canada's new crimes of terrorism.

It is unfortunate that we did not have enough confidence to rely on the traditional criminal law principle that motives never justify crimes. Instead, we criminalized political and religious motives by making them an essential part of the many new crimes of terrorism. In some cases, this inclusion might make it more difficult to obtain convictions. In all cases, it will require the police to collect and the prosecutor to call evidence about the accused's religion or politics. The *Anti-terrorism Act* also criminalizes motive in the new hate crime of mischief to religious property, "if the commission of the mischief is motivated by bias, prejudice or hate based on religion, race, colour or national or ethnic origin."[30] Without this new motive-based hate crime, these crimes would be covered by existing laws against mischief and by provisions stipulating that a hate motive is an aggravating factor that should increase the accused's sentence.[31] It could perhaps be argued that a conviction for simple mischief to property does not adequately denounce the harm of hate-motivated damage to a mosque or a synagogue. But this argument is not available with respect to the ultimate terrorist crime: murder. Our most serious crime, murder, can adequately denounce murders committed with religious or political motivation. Murder is murder. Its blameworthiness is neither enhanced nor excused by political or religious motives.

The requirement of proof of political or religious motive for the new crimes of terrorism confirms that, as with the case of first-degree murder, we are changing our *Criminal Code* to recognize and respond to particular cases, and not on the basis of general principles. We ignored criminal law principles because we wanted to denounce Islamic fanaticism, even though the existing criminal law would never allow the accused's religious or political beliefs to excuse the commission of murder or any other crime. A criminal code that says that no motive can excuse crimes can be a potential agent for agreement on conduct that we all – whatever our political and religious beliefs – can agree is unacceptable.[32] A criminal code that denounces certain religious or political motives as extreme and criminal, however, runs the risk of alienating our diverse and multicultural citizenry.

A BROAD DEFINITION OF TERRORISM

Before September 11 it was difficult to agree on a definition of terrorism. The last time the Canadian *Criminal Code* referred to terrorism was in its infamous section 98 enacted in response to the post-First World War Red Scare, including the Winnipeg General Strike. This provision was widely criticized for infringing civil liberties and was repealed in 1936. Terrorism was not defined during the invocation of the *War Measures Act* in 1970. Instead, the Front de Libération du Québec and other groups that advocated the use of force or the commission of crime as a means of accomplishing governmental change within Canada were declared to be unlawful associations. As we will see, the definition of terrorism in the *Anti-terrorism Act* is much broader than the definition of unlawful associations used during the October Crisis. In many ways, this expansion reflects globalization. Terrorism is now defined not only as attempts to use crime to change the government of Canada but governments in other countries as well. The definition of terrorism has also been broadened to include politically motivated attempts to disrupt essential public or private services.

Some have argued that Canada's attempt to define terrorism is an important contribution to a regime of international criminal law and respect for human rights. My colleague Patrick Macklem has written that terrorism has been "a crime without a name" and that "after September 11 it's time to give terrorism a name."[33] In my view, the terrorism we saw on September 11 already had a name in our domestic criminal law: murder. Our existing law took a strong position that rejected any hint of moral relativism or what Irwin Cotler has called the "moral and legal shibboleth" that "one person's terrorist is another person's freedom fighter."[34] No political motive or cause excused murder. At the level of international law, the matter is admittedly more complex, but it is possible that the September 11 attacks already had a name: crimes against humanity.[35]

The Supreme Court of Canada has recognized that "there is no single definition [of terrorism] that is accepted internationally. The absence of an authoritative definition means that, at least at the margins, 'the term is open to politicized manipulation, conjecture and polemical interpretation.'"[36] Because of the difficulties of defining terrorism, it is not included in the mandate of the new International Criminal Court. Even after September 11, the international community has failed to reach agreement on how to define terrorism for a proposed comprehensive anti-terrorism convention.[37] Some countries, especially from the Third World, expressed concerns that national liberation movements should not be defined as terrorism. Nelson Mandela told the United Nations that "terrorism is a relative term ... You become a terrorist if your aims and objectives fail."[38] Other countries, including the United States, argued that state terrorism committed by armed forces against civilians should not be defined as terrorism. As one commentator concluded: "The search for a definition of terrorism in some ways resembles the quest for the Holy Grail."[39] It is not surprising that there was no agreement on including terrorism in the mandate of the new international court. Moreover, it is doubtful that, in the weeks of shock and sorrow after September 11, Canadian officials suddenly gained wisdom or ingenuity in defining terrorism that was not available before.

It would be wrong to suggest that there have not been some international agreements about what constitutes terrorism. The 1999 International Convention on the Suppression of the Financing of Terrorism, for example, defines terrorism as "any act intended to cause death or serious bodily injury to a civilian ... when the purpose of such act, by its nature or context, is to intimidate a population or to compel a government or an international organization to do or abstain from doing any act." In a case decided after September 11, the Supreme Court read this definition of terrorism into an undefined reference to terrorism in the *Immigration Act*. Although it was careful to indicate that Parliament could enact a different definition, the Court stated that this international definition of terrorism "catches the essence of what the world understands by 'terrorism.'" This definition focuses on serious violence against civilians which is intended to intimidate a population or compel governments and international organizations to act. As will be discussed below, Parliament in the *Anti-terrorism Act* has enacted a much broader definition of terrorism that includes attempts to intimidate a population with regard to its economic security; to compel persons to act in a certain way; and to cause serious disruption to essential public or private services. Concern about the scope, or breadth, of Canada's new definition of terrorism is not limited to civil libertarians and defence lawyers. Reid Morden, a former director of CSIS, has observed that Canada's definition of terrorism is broader than that found in comparable British and American legislation and runs "an even greater risk of catching legal dissent than the regime which existed under the *War Measures Act*."[40]

The new definition of terrorist activities in the *Anti-Terrorism Act* is complex, but important to understand, because it is incorporated in many new offences applying to the financing and facilitation of terrorist activities. Terrorism is now defined in the *Criminal Code* to cover acts of domestic and international terrorism committed both inside and outside Canada. This broad scope may reflect the nature of global terrorism, but it goes beyond the previous emphasis during the October Crisis on domestic terrorism. It means that assistance, including financial assistance, for acts committed far away from Canada may be prosecuted as crimes of terrorism in Canada. People in Canada who send support for rebels resisting a foreign dictatorship could be caught by this definition of terrorism. The only exemption is for "armed conflict ... in accordance with customary international law or conventional international law" and "the activities undertaken by military forces of a state in the exercise of their official duties, to the extent that those activities are governed by other rules of international law." It is unclear whether this exemption adequately responds to concerns that support for revolutions against dictatorships and other unjust regimes in foreign countries could be classified as support for terrorist activities. The Supreme Court has taken notice that "Nelson Mandela's African National Congress was, during the apartheid era, routinely labelled a terrorist organization, not only by the South African government but by much of the international community."[41] The ANC committed crimes that might be defined as terrorism. It definitely did not constitute the military forces of the state, and it is not crystal clear that the ANC was at all times engaged in an armed conflict in accordance with international law. International law may have evolved since that time to recognize armed struggle against apartheid as legal, but the answer is not yet clear. In any event, other borderline cases in which Canadians send money to finance struggles in foreign lands are liable to investigation and prosecution as acts of terrorism. At the same time, state terrorism committed by armed forces will not be terrorism unless it violates the uncertain rules of international law.

The first part of Canada's new five-page definition of terrorism has ten subparagraphs incorporating various offences in the *Criminal Code* that apply to offences committed outside Canada, but have some connection with Canada. These crimes are designated as terrorist crimes, but only to the extent that they implement twelve international conventions against various acts of terrorism, including the unlawful seizure of aircraft, crimes against internationally protected persons, the taking of hostages, crimes in relation to nuclear materials, terrorist bombings, and the financing of terrorism. The complex drafting of this provision was influenced by Canada's desire to demonstrate that it was implementing the international conventions it had signed against terrorism. The government also argued that the rushed legislative schedule for the entire act was necessary to comply with a United Nations Security Council resolution requiring countries to report back by the end of December 2001 on the implementation of the resolution.[42] For better or for worse, amendments to Canada's *Criminal Code* were being driven by the need to comply with international standards and schedules.

The first part of the definition of terrorism is complex and confusing and may result in much litigation. In the *Finta*[43] case, a closely divided Supreme Court disagreed over which provisions in a similarly worded war crimes offence simply granted jurisdiction to Canadian courts to try crimes committed outside Canada and which defined essential elements of the offence that the prosecutor had to prove in order to establish that the accused was sufficiently blameworthy to be guilty. Under the *Anti-terrorism Act*, Canadian courts will likely have to make the same fine distinctions between which parts of this complex definition grant jurisdiction and which are fault elements that the prosecutor must establish. This part of the definition of terrorism may even be too complex to administer. After the *Finta* case, the government concluded that it was too difficult to prosecute war criminals and, instead, focused on using the immigration system to remove war crimes suspects from Canada. So too may the government often rely on immigration proceedings to remove people from Canada who have supported crimes of terrorism committed outside Canada.

The second part of Canada's new definition of terrorism is more important and will be applied against those charged with domestic terrorism. It is modelled on the broad and "elastic" definition of terrorism in the United Kingdom's *Anti-terrorism Act*, 2000.[44] As we have seen, the prosecutor under this definition must establish that acts committed inside or outside Canada were committed "in whole or in part for a political, religious or ideological purpose, objective or cause." The requirement for proof of such motive was defended on the basis that it helps to ensure that "ordinary crimes" are not prosecuted as terrorist crimes. The separation of terrorism from other crimes, however, would have been accomplished by the separate requirements of proof of intention to intimidate the public with regard to security or to compel certain actions. The American *Patriot Act*, anti-terrorism legislation that is not known for its leniency, does not require proof of political or religious motive for terrorist crimes.

After having establishing that the act was done for a religious or political cause, Canadian prosecutors must next establish that the acts were committed with the intention of intimidating the public with regard to its security or compelling persons, organizations, or governments in or outside Canada to do, or refrain from doing, any act. This requirement is even broader than the British act, which is restricted to attempts to influence governments or to intimidate the public. The broader Canadian definition defines security to include economic security[45] and applies to attempts to compel not only domestic and international governments and organizations but also "persons," including corporations. Politically motivated crimes that are designed to compel corporations or individuals to change their behaviour, or that threaten economic security, could constitute a terrorist activity under the broad Canadian definition of terrorist activities. It goes well beyond the traditional scope of anti-terrorism measures that have been directed against the subversion of governments and the intimidation of the public. Given that politically motivated attempts to change corporate behaviour and threaten economic security could be classified as terrorism, it is not surprising that some in the anti-corporate globalization movement felt targeted by the *Anti-terrorism Act*.

Once the prosecutor has established the accused's religious or political motive and intent to intimidate or compel, the next task is to show that the activities were intended to cause certain kinds of harm. They include the intentional causing of death or serious bodily harm by the use of violence, so as to cover traditional acts of terrorism such as bombing and assassination. They also include the intentional endangerment of life or risk to the health or safety of the public. These acts cover biological or nuclear terrorism, as well as attempts to poison water, air, and food supplies, even if they did not succeed in causing death or serious bodily harm. Property damage is also included, but only if it will result in harm or danger to life or in serious risks to public health or safety. This approach is more restrained than that taken in the British legislation, which applies to all politically or religiously motivated property destruction.

Strikes and Protests Disrupting Essential Services as Terrorism?

The restrained Canadian approach to property damage was, however, eclipsed by a final provision defining as a terrorist activity the intentional causing of serious interference with or disruption "of an essential service, facility or system, whether public or private." The prohibited harm goes beyond threats to life, bodily integrity, or health and safety to include the disruption of essential services, such as electricity, gas, roads, computer and communication systems, and all other essential public and private services. Here the Canadian law was breaking new ground because the British legislation defined only the disruption of electronic systems as terrorism. The broader Canadian definition could cover a staggeringly wide number of activities that might otherwise be considered only property crimes, and sometimes not even crimes at all. The act accommodated the privatization of essential services by providing that acts of terrorism could be committed against corporations, a matter that was re-enforced by the inclusion of threats to economic security.

As originally introduced, this broad provision had an exemption for "lawful advocacy, protest, dissent, or stoppage of work" that was not intended to endanger life or public health and safety. A huge problem, as many civil libertarians, labour activists, and anti-globalization protesters pointed out, was the use of the word "lawful." A significant amount of protest and dissent is unlawful in the sense that it violates trespass, labour relations, or minor criminal laws. This flawed exemption, along with the broad definition of terrorism to cover activities directed against corporations and economic security, lent support to fears that the bill would target the type of unlawful anti-globalization protests seen at Seattle and Quebec City, illegal strikes by nurses, or Aboriginal blockades of roads.

As we will see in chapter 3, this overbroad definition of terrorism was the focal point for a broad coalition of civil society groups that mobilized to oppose parts of the government's anti-terrorism bill. After extensive public criticism, the government amended the bill to remove the qualifier that the protests or strikes must be "lawful." Now, the fact that a politically motivated disruption of essential public or private services would violate the *Criminal Code*, provincial trespass laws, or even municipal bylaws will not automatically render it a terrorist activity. At the same time, however, the exemption for protests and strikes is not absolute. Serious disruptions of essential public or private services, whether unlawful or lawful, that are intended to result in death, serious bodily harm, danger to life, or serious risk to public health and safety would still fall under the definition of terrorism. The intent requirement here is important, so a striking nurses' union could argue that its intent was not to cause serious risk to public health or danger to life, but, rather, to secure concessions from the government or the employer. At the same time, however, a court might find intention to endanger life or public health if it was proven that essential workers knew with a high degree of certainty that their disruption of essential services would have such effects.

Threats and Incomplete Crimes of Terrorism

The definition of terrorism now included in the *Criminal Code* would be quite broad even if it applied only to completed acts. Parliament has, however, gone on to define terrorism as a "threat ... to commit any such act or omission." The line between a threat and an expression of a strong political or religious idea can be a fine one. Is a religiously or politically inspired prediction or wish about the collapse of corrupt or sinful societies also a threat to commit terrorism? This decision would be difficult for judges to make. In the first instance, the judgment call will be made by the police, who may be less mindful of freedom of expression and freedom of religion than judges. Even if the person is ultimately acquitted, irreparable damage to his or her social and economic position may be done. And it is not only the person making threatening statements who may be charged. Those who provide that person with the forum to make such threats could also be charged with facilitating terrorism. Those who provide property or financing to that person could be charged with one of the many offences relating to the financing of terrorism. Organizations that the person partici-pates in may have their property forfeited and their charitable status revoked. They may be officially listed by the Cabinet as a terrorist organization. The *Anti-terrorism Act* casts a very broad net.

The police do not have to wait until an act of terrorism has been committed to charge a person, and a person can be convicted for agreeing to, attempting, or assisting terrorism, or for helping a terrorist to escape. This expansion of the criminal law is quite sensible and valuable when applied to ordinary criminal offences such as murder and hijacking. It helps explain why the ordinary criminal law provides important tools to combat terrorism. But the *Anti-terrorism Act* is not ordinary criminal law. As we will see, the new law has a series of offences that make illegal activities such as financing, facilitating, or instructing terrorism, or participating in a terrorist organization, all acts of preparation that occur well before any terrorist act is actually committed. Parliament has instructed the courts that people can be convicted for planning, counselling, or assisting others to commit acts which themselves are only acts of planning, counselling, and assistance. Canadian courts have avoided expanding the ordinary criminal law in this way. For example, they have rejected attempted prosecutions of far-removed crimes such as counselling someone to counsel an offence or attempting to conspire to commit an offence.[46] Nevertheless, it is doubtful that the courts can refuse to do so under the *Anti-terrorism Act* because Parliament has clearly provided for such expansions of criminal liability. The net of criminal liability has been widened in complex and undesirable ways.[47]

In short, the complex and lengthy definition of terrorism now found in our *Criminal Code* remains very broad. Domestically, disruptions of essential public and private services, or protests and strikes that are intended to endanger public health and safety, could be treated as terrorism. Threats of terrorism are themselves a terrorist crime. Internationally, those who would send money and other forms of assistance in foreign struggles may be convicted of various crimes of supporting terrorism. The definition of terrorism that was quickly drafted and placed in our *Criminal Code* after September 11 goes far beyond international definitions of terrorism that focus on serious violence against civilians. Nevertheless, this flawed definition of terrorism will likely be with us for some time because the legislation is permanent.

THE CABINET'S LIST OF TERRORIST GROUPS

The new *Anti-terrorism Act* defines terrorist groups as well as terrorist activities. This defining is not an academic exercise, since there are many new offences that prohibit support for or participation in a terrorist group. A terrorist group is defined broadly as "an entity that has one of its purposes or activities facilitating or carrying out any terrorist activity" and "includes an association of such entities." An entity can include "persons" as well as groups. A terrorist group need not have engaged in acts of terrorism; it may only be associated with others that have committed terrorism or that may facilitate the commission of terrorism in the future. Under the ordinary criminal law, assisting a crime is itself a crime, but liability is based on what an individual does and knows. The *Anti-terrorism Act* extends this concept to groups and raises serious issues about guilt by association with groups.

An even more problematic alternative definition is that a terrorist group is "a listed entity." How does one become a listed entity? The federal Cabinet decides that it is satisfied "that there are reasonable grounds to believe that a) the entity has knowingly carried out, attempted to carry out, participated in or facilitated a terrorist activity; or b) the entity is knowingly acting on behalf of, at the direction of or in association with an entity referred to in paragraph (a)." There is no judicial oversight before the Cabinet makes its decision to add to its list of terrorists, even though the Supreme Court has recognized the importance of prior judicial review to prevent unreasonable invasion of privacy, something that will surely occur when an individual or group is publicly listed by the government as a terrorist.[48] There are limited grounds for judicial review after the Cabinet has added a group to its list. After-the-fact judicial review, however, may be too late for a group that has been erroneously placed on the official list of terrorist organizations. They will have been stigmatized as a terrorist group and people will be afraid that they may be charged with terrorism offences if they participate or give money to the organization.

The provision for judicial review after a group has been listed as a terrorist group is quite weak. A judge of the Federal Court will determine whether the listing decision "is reasonable on the basis of the information available to the judge," without all that information necessarily being disclosed or even summarized for the group seeking judicial review of the Cabinet's decision.[49] The idea that the Cabinet, as opposed to the courts, can decide which group is terrorist goes back to the 1970 invocation of the *War Measures Act*, when the Cabinet declared the FLQ to be an illegal organization. One difference now is that the Cabinet does not have to declare an emergency to list a group as a terrorist organization. The Cabinet did not immediately make use of its new listing power, but in July 2002 it listed al-Qaeda and six other related groups. The government was criticized for not including other groups from the Middle East. In late November 2002 it listed Hamas, a Gaza-based group that had claimed responsibility for suicide bombings in Israel. The solicitor general explained the government's caution on the basis that "being listed under Bill C-36 ... is a very, very serious matter. They can have their assets seized and frozen and association with those groups is considered to be a crime."[50] After further public criticism, lobbying, and threats of litigation by B'nai B'rith, the Cabinet in December 2002 added the political wing of the Lebanese-based group Hezbollah to its list of terrorists. This addition brought the Cabinet's list of terrorist groups to sixteen, but did not end the political controversy. Lebanon complained that the Cabinet's decision was based on a mistranslation of a speech of a Hezbollah leader that was thought to endorse suicide bombing. The executive director of the National Council on Canada-Arab Relations called on the Cabinet to list groups that fundraise for Israeli settlements, and the B'nai B'rith called for the listing of more groups associated with suicide bombings on the basis that they were worse than Hezbollah.[51] The Cabinet's list of terrorist groups is expanding, and the content of the list has become the subject of political lobbying and controversy.

Once an organization has been listed by the Cabinet as a terrorist group, the government will likely argue that it need not prove beyond a reasonable doubt at a criminal trial that the group is actually a terrorist group. The *Anti-terrorism Act* suggests that it may be enough for the government simply to point to the fact that the group is on the Cabinet's list. The group will, of course, have no hearing before being listed by the Cabinet, and only limited rights of judicial review of the Cabinet's decision after the fact. The courts may even uphold the Cabinet's decision to add a group to its list of terrorists without disclosing or even summarizing the government's evidence to the group listed. The role of the independent judiciary in determining whether a group is terrorist may be precluded by the Cabinet's decision to list a group as a terrorist group. As happened during the October Crisis, the government will usurp judicial powers by deciding which organizations are illegal terrorist groups.

THE NEW TERRORISM OFFENCES

The new offences in the *Anti-terrorism Act* were defended by the government as a means to disable and dismantle terrorist organizations before they could commit terrible acts of violence such as those seen on September 11. The act accomplishes this goal by criminalizing a broad range of involvement with terrorist groups. Although these offences would be useful and perhaps appropriate to dismantle a terrorist organization such as al-Qaeda, they could have a more chilling effect if they were used against groups providing assistance to rebels abroad or to domestic groups that may disrupt essential services with the possible intent to endanger public health or safety. As we will see, the leaders of such groups could not only be prosecuted for instructing terrorism but could also find their landlords, bankers, followers, and friends prosecuted for financing terrorism, participating in a terrorist organization, facilitating terrorism, or harbouring terrorists. In addition, the organization itself could be listed as a terrorist organization and have its charitable status revoked and its property confiscated. The act seems designed to make terrorists "outlaws" and to allow those associated with terrorists to be prosecuted for assistance and services they provide to terrorists. Much will depend on whom the government aims the heavy guns of the *Anti-terrorist Act* against.

New Offences of Financing Terrorism

Under the act, it is an offence to wilfully provide or collect property intending or knowing that it will be used in whole or in part for the commission of terrorist activities. To its credit, this offence requires that the accused must subjectively know that the property will be used for terrorism.[52] People who support an organization, but who have "no idea the money they are donating – or a portion of it, at least – is being diverted to finance political or religious violence" should not be convicted. This restriction may rightfully protect the morally innocent financier of terrorism, but it may also make it more difficult for authorities to prosecute those who finance terrorism.[53] Once a group has been listed by Cabinet as a terrorist organization, it will be more difficult for people to claim that they did not know that their donations would be used in whole or in part for terrorism.

It is also an offence to provide property or "financial or other related services" intending or knowing that they will be used to facilitate or carry out any terrorist activity or simply knowing that they will be used by or will benefit a terrorist group.[54] This latter formulation requires no nexus to a terrorist activity and could punish a person who knowingly benefits terrorists for up to ten years. As my colleague Kevin Davis has observed, this offence becomes more problematic as the connection to actual acts of terrorism becomes more remote. "On the one hand, it does not seem farfetched to target a person who sells a cropduster to a known terrorist. On the other hand, it does seem a bit farfetched to convict a restaurant owner simply for serving food and drink to known terrorists" or even "for serving customers who he knows are in the habit of making contributions to terrorist groups."[55] It is also an offence to "possess property intending or knowing that it will be used, directly or indirectly, in whole or part, for the purpose of facilitating or carrying out a terrorist activity."[56] This offence could apply to those who have committed no overt acts, but simply possess property knowing it will be used to facilitate terrorism.

It is also an offence for any person in Canada and any Canadian outside Canada to knowingly deal with property owned or controlled by a terrorist group or to provide any financial or related services in respect of terrorist property.[57] The focus is on terrorists, as opposed to terrorist activities. Landlords or vendors of property could be imprisoned for up to ten years for renting or selling property to those they know are members of a terrorist group or are controlled by a terrorist group. Given the breadth of this offence, it would be very important that the prosecutor establish beyond a reasonable doubt that the accused knew that the group was a terrorist group. The government, however, could argue that the Cabinet's decision to list the group as a terrorist group should suffice. This process would allow the government both to prosecute the crime and to act as a judge about whether any particular organization was a terrorist group. This offence is supplemented by a mandatory duty on all persons in Canada and every Canadian outside Canada to disclose to the commissioner of the RCMP and to the director of CSIS any property in their possession or control they know is owned or controlled by, or on behalf of, a terrorist group.[58] Such mandatory duties constitute an exception to the general principles that individuals have no legal duties to assist the state in criminal investigations.

The new financing offences are backed up by provisions for the forfeiture of property. These provisions go beyond the existing criminal law to allow the forfeiture of property owned by terrorists, even though it has not been, and will not be, used for terrorist crimes.[59] There is no necessity for a criminal conviction that requires proof beyond a reasonable doubt. All that is required is proof on a balance of probabilities before a judge of the Federal Court. A terrorist's house can be forfeited, even though it was never used for terrorism. The judge is given the unenviable task of determining the impact of the forfeiture of the home on the person's family and whether a child or spouse living in the house with the terrorist "appears innocent of any complicity or collusion in the terrorist activity."[60] This provision could legalize actions that will punish not only terrorists but their families, too, and it presents another example of how the broad provisions of the *Anti-terrorist Act* come uncomfortably close to punishing guilt by association. Alan Dershowitz, the Harvard law professor who has been consulted by the Canadian government on terrorism issues, has defended collective punishment, including the destruction of Palestinian homes after suicide bombings, on the basis that "even if some people who do not support terrorism feel some economic impact, that seems to be a small moral price to pay – especially since they expect to reap the benefits of the terrorism – for saving many innocent lives."[61] This is a "utilitarian ends justify the means" argument that ignores the injustice of punishing people who did not participate in the crime of terrorism.

In a practical sense, these new financing offences and forfeiture provisions are some of the most important parts of the *Anti-terrorism Act*. Although it may be difficult to deter a suicide bomber, these offences are directed at third parties who provide funds, property, and services to terrorists or who share property with terrorists. The actions of such third parties may be more amenable to deterrence by stiff and certain criminal sanctions, but the state must be careful not to punish on the basis of guilt by association. Most of the new financing provisions can be justified as necessary to comply with Canada's obligations under the 1999 United Nations Convention for the Suppression of the Financing of Terrorism and the post-September 11 UN resolutions relating to the financing of terrorism. The new financing offences could be used, as the government promised, to disrupt and disable terrorist organizations before they commit acts of terrorist violence. The ability to charge not only terrorists but their bankers and landlords with terrorism offences could be a strong law enforcement tool, and an appropriate one, too, when applied to groups that plan on committing serious violence.

There are, however, problems of sheer breadth. The Canadian law applies to funds, property, and services that may not be related to acts of terrorism. The new financing offences could apply to those who provide medical or legal services to terrorists. They are also tied to a definition of terrorism that goes beyond the commission of serious violence and a definition of a terrorist group that includes everyone on the Cabinet's list. To their credit, the financing offences generally require that the accused know they are dealing with terrorists and intend to assist them, and that a person without this guilty knowledge should be acquitted. This qualification, however, is not the same as protection against investigation and charges. The breadth of the financing offences and the forfeiture procedures give police and prosecutors a lot of discretion, while often limiting the discretion of judges. The police will be able to lay charges, or threaten to lay charges, against people involved in a wide variety of financial transactions with suspected terrorists. The costs of such broad offences may "fall disproportionately on members of specific ethnocultural groups" who may find their ability to engage in "ordinary commercial transactions" or charitable activities to be impaired.[62]

New Offences of Facilitating Terrorism

Although the financing offences and forfeiture provisions give police new tools to disrupt and disable terrorist networks, the case is less clear in relation to the other five new terrorist crimes of facilitating terrorism. All these offences incorporate the definition of terrorist activity discussed above, and some also incorporate the definition of terrorist groups. All five offences criminalize activities both before and after the actual commission of terrorism which might otherwise have to be prosecuted under the ordinary criminal law relating to attempted crimes, conspiracy to commit crimes, counselling crimes, or being an accessory after the fact. They either simply duplicate the existing law or expand the relatively well-defined limits of criminal liability. Like the financing offences, but unlike most criminal offences, all the new terrorism offences require the consent of a provincial or federal attorney general to be prosecuted. This requirement will restrain individual police officers from launching terrorism prosecutions on their own initiative. It also extends federal powers by giving the federal attorney general power to prosecute terrorism offences in the *Criminal Code*. This authority could result in a federal terrorist prosecution in the face of a provincial decision not to prosecute.

The broadest new offence makes it an indictable offence punishable by up to ten years' imprisonment if a person "knowingly participates in or contributes to, directly or indirectly, any activity of a terrorist group for the purpose of enhancing the ability of any terrorist group to facilitate or carry out a terrorist activity."[63] This offence stops short of demands made by the official opposition, the Canadian Alliance, that membership in terrorist organizations be itself illegal. This was the approach taken during the 1970 October Crisis, when membership in the FLQ was itself a crime. The decision to make participation, as opposed to membership, in an organization an offence was taken from organized crime legislation, and it avoids a possible Charter challenge

on the basis that a crime of membership violates freedom of association. Nevertheless, the offence of participation in a terrorist group is
in some sense even broader than a membership crime. It can catch
people associated with, but not an actual member of, a terrorist group.

Participation and contribution includes providing or receiving
"training," "providing or offering to provide a skill or expertise for
the benefit of, at the direction of, or in association with a terrorist
group," and "entering or remaining in any country for the benefit of,
at the direction of or in association with a terrorist group." This last
clause criminalizes a "sleeper" who enters a country at the direction
of a terrorist group but who does nothing. It has been criticized for
establishing "guilt by association wherever you are in the world and
whatever you are doing."[64] It is broader than a new offence under
American law of providing material support for terrorists which has
been used to charge an alleged al-Qaeda sleeper cell near Buffalo, New
York. The Canadian offence may be committed whether or not the
accused's participation or contribution actually enhances the ability of
a terrorist group to carry out a terrorist activity. The broad new
participation offence includes many forms of association with a terrorist group, something that is underlined by the direction to courts
to consider whether a person "frequently associates with any of the
persons who constitute the terrorist group" or uses words or symbols
associated with the terrorist group. The regulations enacted during the
October Crisis similarly made attendance at any meeting, as well as
speaking publicly in advocacy for a terrorist group, evidence in support
of a conviction.[65] During the October Crisis and in the months after
September 11, Canadian criminal law moved uncomfortably in the
direction of guilt by association.

In reply, it can be argued with some justification that the new
offences will apply only if people know they are associating with
terrorists and intend to enhance their ability to engage in terrorism.
There is, however, one offence that seems to lack such a fault requirement. It provides that everyone who "knowingly facilitates a terrorist
activity" is guilty of an indictable offence punishable by up to fourteen
years' imprisonment. So far, so good. Even the regular criminal law
punishes those who intentionally assist others to commit crimes. The
fault requirement of the new facilitating terrorism offence is, however,
qualified by providing that it is not necessary for the facilitator to know
that a particular terrorist activity is facilitated.[66] "Reading the legislation in its best possible light," this clause may mean "that the facilitator

need not know which terrorist activity is being assisted."[67] A drafter of the act has argued that this approach was necessary "to capture the person who is prepared to assist a 'martyrdom operation' without knowing the specific objective."[68] The legislation, however, goes even further to provide that it is not necessary that "any particular terrorist activity was foreseen or planned at the time it was facilitated." This wording goes beyond watering down the fault element to obliterating it. It seems impossible to knowingly facilitate a terrorist activity when you do not know that "any particular terrorist activity was foreseen or planned at the time it was facilitated." If any fault is required on behalf of the accused to obtain a conviction, it would seem to be failing to take reasonable care to ensure that what was being facilitated was actually a terrorist activity.[69] The accused would still, however, be convicted and punished for knowing facilitation of a terrorist activity when, in fact, the person did not know about the terrorist activity.

Another provision makes it an offence to knowingly instruct any person to carry out any activity that benefits a terrorist group "for the purpose of enhancing the ability of any terrorist group to facilitate or carry out a terrorist activity."[70] This offence can include instructions to carry out activities that are themselves legal, such as instructions to obtain food, shelter, funds, or medicine that may enhance the ability of any terrorist group to carry out terrorist activities.[71] The only restraint on this very broad offence is that the accused must knowingly instruct the activities for the purpose of enhancing the ability of any terrorist group to facilitate or carry out terrorist activities.

A less broad new offence applies to those who instruct a person to carry out a terrorist activity.[72] This new offence would cover the same ground as the old offence of counselling a crime and would apply to terrorist masterminds such as Osama bin Laden. Nevertheless, the government could not resist broadening even this offence to provide that it is not necessary for the accused to instruct a particular person to carry out the terrorist activity or to know the identity of the person instructed. General instructions to political or religious groups or the public-at-large to commit a terrorist activity could fall under this new offence.[73] Even if such instructions were an "expression of a political, religious or ideological thought, belief or opinion," they would not be exempted from criminal liability because they would fall under the broad definition of the criminal offence of instructing terrorism.

The final new offence applies to "everyone who knowingly harbours or conceals any person who he or she knows to be a person who has carried out or is likely to carry out a terrorist activity, for the purpose of enabling the person to facilitate or carry out any terrorist activity." It requires that the accused know that a person has done or is likely to do a terrorist activity and that the accused has provided assistance towards that end. This requirement is more restrictive than the American *Patriot Act*,[74] which applies to those who ought to know that they are assisting a terrorist. As we will discuss in greater detail in chapter 4, it remains to be seen whether the courts will require subjective knowledge that the person assisted is a terrorist as a constitutional requirement for all terrorism offences – yet such a subjective fault level is appropriate, especially given the breadth of the new terrorism offences.

Other New Offences

Parliament's work was not done even after it added all these new financing and facilitation of terrorism offences. It also created an important new offence punishable by life imprisonment for those who deliver, place, discharge, or detonate an explosive or lethal device (including biological agents, toxins, or radioactive material) into a place of public use or into a public or private infrastructure system distributing services such as water, energy, and communications for the benefit of the public.[75] This offence applies to modern terrorist techniques, designed to cause terror in cities, such as "dirty" bombs with radioactive material or biological material, as well as attempts to poison the water supply or bring down hydro or telephone lines. These are all serious harms, and it is appropriate that they be targeted in a new offence, even though, as we will see in chapter 7, there may be more effective means than reliance on the criminal sanction to prevent them. This new offence is also noteworthy because it demonstrates that the reference in the definition of terrorist activities to the disruption of essential services could have been more precisely defined with less fear of catching strikes and acts of protest.

A new offence of hate-motivated mischief to religious property was also included in the law.[76] It recognizes the close connection between many acts of terrorism and hate crimes. As we will see in chapter 3, the new hate crime provision, along with other new provisions providing for the deletion of hate crimes from the internet, were important features of the government's defence of the entire *Anti-terrorism Act* as being supportive of both human rights and the Charter. This new hate crime requires proof of a hate motive as an essential element of the offence and marks a departure in Canadian criminal law from using hate only as an aggravating factor at sentencing.[77] It applies only to places of religious worship and requires the prosecutor to establish that the crime was "motivated by bias, prejudice or hate based on religion, race, colour or national or ethnic origin," but not by other grounds of hate already recognized under Canadian sentencing and constitutional law. Again, this provision demonstrates how the *Anti-terrorism Act* responded to particular concerns arising from September 11 at the expense of consistency with more general legal principles.

INCREASED PUNISHMENT

Minister of Justice Anne McLellan stressed that one of the main purposes of the *Anti-terrorism Act* was to impose tougher penalties on terrorists. The basis for her apparent belief that tougher penalties would deter the type of terrorists who caused such destruction on September 11 was not clear. Nevertheless, the act provides for increased and mandatory consecutive sentences for all terrorism offences and increased periods of ineligibility for parole. It also deems the commission of an offence for terrorism purposes to be an aggravating factor at sentencing. This approach accords with a trend to increased legislative direction on issues of punishment that, until recently, had been left to the sentencing discretion of trial judges. The government resisted the temptation to enact mandatory minimum sentences for terrorism offences, even though such sentences would have been Charter proof, given the Supreme Court's recent deference to Parliament on whether mandatory sentences constitute cruel and unusual punishment.[78] Even stiff mandatory minimum penalties would, however, be unlikely to deter most terrorists.

NEW INVESTIGATIVE POWERS

Canada's new *Anti-terrorism Act* gives the police new powers to investigate terrorism.[79] They are now able to engage in electronic surveillance with respect to terrorist offences for up to a year, as opposed to the normal sixty-day period, and they do not have to demonstrate that less-intrusive investigative procedures are unlikely to succeed. They also do not have to inform a person subject to such surveillance for up to three years.[80] All these changes are based on earlier legislation applying to organized crime – a connection that raises the issue of how new police powers spread. The experience in other countries is that new police and prosecutorial powers enacted in response to terrorism have a tendency to spread throughout the criminal law.[81]

The new electronic surveillance provision can be defended on the basis that it requires judicial authorization and supervision. Concerns have been raised, however, about the high approval rate by the courts of wiretap applications from the police. Random studies of search warrants issued by lower judicial officials suggest that as many as one-half of warrants may be improperly issued.[82] Finally, public support for invasions of privacy even in the immediate aftermath of September 11 was not particularly high. In one poll, only 29 per cent of respondents agreed that intelligence and law enforcement agents should be able to monitor their telephone calls without their knowledge.[83] The new law, of course, allows judges to authorize this activity for up to three years.

The most novel of the new police powers – preventive arrest and investigative hearings – were criticized by civil libertarians and defence lawyers as unprecedented departures from traditional principles, but defended by the government as consistent with the Charter and necessary to prevent terrorism. Both powers require the consent of the attorney general and, except in exigent circumstances, prior judicial authorization. As we will discuss in chapter 4, these new police powers have been drafted with the Charter in mind and are likely consistent with it. Nevertheless, the short public debate that preceded the enactment of the law featured many criticisms of these new powers. The government made some concessions and, in late November, introduced amendments that require yearly reports about the use of preventive arrests and investigative hearings. It is not clear whether these yearly reports will simply report raw numbers or provide enough qualitative information to serve as an accountability mechanism for these novel powers. In any event, it appears that the first reports will be quite short, as senior department of justice official admit they are not aware of the use of the powers of preventive arrest or investigative hearings during the first year of the new law's operation.[84] This lack of use also raises the question of whether these new police powers should be allowed to expire, or "sunset." A late amendment to the law provides that the new powers will expire in five years' time unless Parliament again authorizes their use.[85]

Preventive Arrests

The preventive arrest provision in the *Anti-terrorism Act* is not clearly labelled as such but is contained in a section with the innocuous title "recognizance with conditions."[86] Nevertheless, it provides for preventive arrest when a police officer has reasonable grounds to believe that a terrorist activity will be carried out and reasonable grounds to suspect that the imposition of a recognizance with conditions (a peace bond in which a person agrees to abide by certain conditions) or an arrest is necessary to prevent the carrying out of a terrorist activity. Thus, the police officer needs to have only suspicion on reasonable grounds about the individual who is subject to preventive arrest. These broad grounds are a departure from the ordinary criminal law, which requires police officers to have reasonable and probable grounds to arrest a person.[87]

A person subject to preventive arrest must be brought before the judge as soon as possible, and within a maximum of twenty-four hours. After the arrest, the judge is given the discretion to adjourn hearings for up to forty-eight hours, thereby extending the period of preventive arrest on suspicion to a possible seventy-two hours – a period considerably shorter than the seven days allowed under legislation in the United Kingdom. It is also substantially shorter than that wanted by a sample of Canadians who were polled in late September 2001. At that time, 53 per cent of respondents approved of indefinite detention of those suspected of being involved in terrorist activities, a practice that would go beyond the draconian provisions of internal security laws found in Singapore and Malaysia and a six-month period of detention enacted in emergency regulations in Indonesia after the Bali bombings.[88] Although many Canadians remained reluctant to allow the police to listen to their private calls or emails in the immediate aftermath of September 11, many had no trouble with the idea that suspected terrorists should be permanently locked up.

The effects of a preventive arrest may last much longer than seventy-two hours. If the judge is satisfied that there are reasonable grounds to suspect that the arrestee will commit a terrorist activity, the judge may require that person to enter into a recognizance or peace bond that requires him to be of good behaviour and not to possess weapons or explosives for a period up to twelve months. The judge may also require other reasonable conditions, such as non-association with suspected terrorists. A person who refuses to enter into such a recognizance may be jailed for up to twelve months, and a person who violates a condition of a recognizance or peace bond is guilty of an offence punishable by up to two years' imprisonment. Those subject to preventive arrest on suspicion may find themselves caught up in the law for some time.

The new power to impose recognizances or peace bonds on a suspected terrorist builds on peace bond provisions in the *Criminal Code* which were repeatedly expanded in the 1990s to respond to fears about serious crime. The code now allows peace bonds to be imposed where there are reasonable grounds to fear sexual assaults or criminal organization offences.[89] These new provisions were enacted in response to both horrific crimes and a controversial Charter ruling striking down a vagrancy offence that prevented all convicted offenders from loitering in public parks for the rest of their lives.[90] The new "peace bonds for terrorists" demonstrate again how the criminal law builds on itself, using previous expansions to justify further expansions. It also follows the pattern of new criminal laws being fashioned as a response to particular crimes, and not on the basis of overarching principles. Finally, the plethora of peace bond provisions now found in the *Criminal Code* demonstrates an increased willingness to use the costly and coercive apparatus of the criminal law in an attempt to respond to the risk, and even the fear, of horrific crimes. Unfortunately, there is little evidence suggesting that peace bonds will stop terrorists. They could, however, result in the imprisonment of a suspected terrorist who refuses to accept or abide by peace bond restrictions on otherwise lawful activities.

Investigative Hearings

The *Anti-terrorism Act* also introduces the new and controversial concept of investigative hearings into Canadian criminal law. As with preventive arrests, the prior consent of the attorney general is required. The police have to establish to a judge that there are reasonable grounds to believe that a terrorism offence has or will be committed, that the subject has direct and material information relating to the offence, and that reasonable efforts have been made to obtain such information. The judge can then order the person to answer questions and provide documents. A person subject to an investigative hearing may well fear subsequent prosecutions under the many broad new offences relating to the financing and facilitation of terrorism. Unlike in the United States, however, such a person cannot "take the Fifth" and refuse to incriminate himself unless the prosecutor grants him immunity from subsequent prosecution. Rather, the new Canadian law provides: "No person shall be excused from answering a question or producing a thing ... on the ground that the answer or thing may incriminate the person or subject the person to any proceeding or penalty."[91] It also grants those required to speak at an investigative hearing only a limited form of immunity from the compelled statements or evidence derived from them from being used against them in subsequent prosecutions. If the person refuses to talk at an investigative hearing, the judge must decide what to do. The new legislation provides no specific guidance, but options include the use of contempt powers or subsequent prosecutions for disobeying a court order. Although it is not clearly stated in the legislation, a person who refuses to talk at an investigative hearing may end up in jail.

Given that most people, including suspected terrorists, will voluntarily cooperate with the police, it can be expected that the involuntary subjects of investigative hearings will have good reasons for refusing to cooperate. They may be reluctant to help the police because they fear that their words will also help convict them of a broad range of offences relating to facilitating and financing terrorism. If they do talk when faced with an investigative hearing, they will not necessarily be immune from subsequent prosecution. The act provides only that the prosecutor cannot use compelled statements in a subsequent prosecution and that the police must demonstrate they obtained evidence by means independent of the compelled statement. As we will see in chapter 4, the limited immunity provided at investigative hearings accords with Canadian constitutional law, which holds that the rights to silence and against self-incrimination are not absolute.[92] Although the provision for investigative hearings is not likely to be struck down under the Charter, it is a departure from the adversarial traditions of Canadian criminal law and an explicit denial of the subject's traditional right to refuse to speak to police and prosecutors. Even if the extraordinary powers in this section could perhaps be justified to prevent imminent acts of terrorism, investigative hearings can also be used as a shortcut in investigations of past acts of terrorism.

THE DANGERS OF THE WAR AGAINST TERRORISM SPREADING

It will be interesting to see whether the novel powers of investigative hearings and preventive arrests spread beyond the terrorism context to other parts of the *Criminal Code*. So far, there have been no reports that the new powers of preventive arrest or investigative hearings have been used against suspected terrorists since the new law went into force in December 2001. Even if the new provisions are used infrequently, however, they will have a symbolic force and will serve as a precedent in the *Criminal Code* of just how far Parliament can go when it takes a crime seriously. Once the government has authorized departures from traditional principles and shown them to be consistent with the Charter, it may be difficult not to extend the powers to other serious crimes such as organized crime and hate crimes.[93] The exception may become the norm.[94] The experience in other countries, most notably the United Kingdom, has been that incursions on fundamental principles such as the right to silence, introduced even temporarily in response to horrific acts of terrorism, can eventually spread throughout the regular criminal law.[95]

The broad definition of terrorism in the *Anti-terrorism Act* may also encourage the war against terrorism to spread to the war against other crimes. Oxford professor Andrew Ashworth has noted that the "elastic" definition of terrorism in the United Kingdom's *Terrorism Act*, 2000, a definition that is the basis for Canada's new definition of terrorism, creates the danger that "exceptional powers will be extended to other forms of serious crimes."[96] The line between terrorism and organized crime is a fuzzy one, especially when the new financing of terrorism offences are considered. The police are already starting to blur this line by suggesting that terrorist groups, including al-Qaeda, may be attracted to organized crime in order to finance their operations.[97] It is natural for the police to blur the line between terrorism and other crimes because they have responsibility for investigating all crimes.

The laws against terrorism and organized crime may continue to develop in a symbiotic manner. Some of the financing and participation offences in the *Anti-terrorism Act* are borrowed from recent organized crime legislation. In turn, we can expect demands that anti-terrorism powers such as investigative hearings, preventive arrests, and an attorney general's certificate blocking the accused's access to relevant information should be extended to organized crime. Once extraordinary powers are accepted with respect to terrorism and organized crime, it will be easier to expand them to other crimes. The criminal law will grow, just as the Cabinet's list of terrorist groups has expanded.

Even if the new techniques in the *Anti-terrorism Act* do not spread to other crimes, the police may well interpret terrorism in a broad manner. Already, animal rights activists who have committed illegal acts of vandalism, theft, and trespass have apparently been targeted as terrorists by a new National Security Enforcement team of the RCMP and by CSIS. One search by such a team did not find any evidence of terrorism, but discovered evidence of illegal drugs. The BC Civil Liberties Association has complained that such investigations have targeted activity that "would not be the kind of action we would consider terrorism" and that American authorities have used a broad definition of terrorism to influence Canadian law enforcement.[98] Fatal sniper shootings in Washington, DC, are being prosecuted as acts of terrorism. On the basis of limited evidence, a former FBI agent has speculated that the killings of ten people may have been "expressions of extreme anti-American hatred – the same thing that drives Islamic terrorists such as Osama bin Laden." A number of media commentators were quick to add their voices to the idea that the sniper shootings were religiously motivated acts of terrorism.[99] The men accused of the shootings, John Muhammad and Lee Malvo, are being prosecuted under a post-September 11 Virginia anti-terrorism law that applies to crimes committed "with intent to intimidate the civilian population at large." One of its drafters has admitted that, "when we were writing this bill we were thinking about Osama bin Laden and someone flying a plane into the Pentagon. To be honest with you, when we passed this law, I never thought it would be used." US attorney general John Ashcroft allowed Virginia to prosecute the men because the new anti-terrorism law allows the death penalty to be applied without necessarily proving who actually pulled the trigger.[100] Police, prosecutors, and the media may be tempted to define terrorism in a broad manner and to use the politics and religion of suspects as a reason to characterize their crimes as acts of terrorism.

It will also be difficult for the police to use information obtained for anti-terrorism only for such purposes. A spokesperson for then solicitor general Lawrence MacAulay argued that "advance passenger-list information collected since Sept. 11 has already allowed Canadian officials to nab 20 people who appeared on the FBI's most-wanted listed – including six alleged murderers." He added that the information could also be used to capture pedophiles. "The Minister believes strongly that the legislation and the sharing of information is in Canada's best interest, the best interests of children around the world and certainly in the interest of Canada's national security."[101] Although it is difficult to be against the interests of the world's children, there is a danger that measures justified to respond to the threat of mass terrorism will be used for general crime control purposes, compounding the loss of privacy and civil liberties. The *Public Safety Act* introduced at the end of April 2002 proposed to provide the RCMP with access to information to identify any air travellers with an outstanding warrant, not just those who are terrorist suspects. As federal privacy commissioner George Radwanski argued, it was disappointing to see the government invoking "September 11 to justify new police powers that have nothing to do with anti-terrorism."[102]

When the *Public Safety Act* was reintroduced in late October 2002, the government responded to the privacy commissioner's criticisms by allowing only the RCMP to request passenger information for reasons of transportation security. The government added, however, that "if the RCMP incidentally discovered a criminal wanted for a serious crime," it could still use the information to arrest such a passenger and that this was "necessary for public safety."[103] The federal privacy commissioner was not impressed by the changes. He argued that the idea that the RCMP might "incidentally" match a passenger's name with those on its wanted list "insults the intelligence of Canadians." Somewhat melodramatically, he predicted that this concession could lead to general powers to check the identification of those who travel by any means. It may be difficult to expect the police, who have responsibility to enforce all laws, to use information only for limited security purposes.

It is also far from clear that the use of passenger lists for general crime control purposes violates the Charter. In December 2001 the Supreme Court, in a one-paragraph judgment, held that travellers do not have a reasonable expectation of privacy that their customs declaration forms would not be used by the government to catch those who were cheating on their unemployment insurance by going on vacation when they were supposed to be looking for work. The decision was part of a larger retrenchment in the Court's approach to a reasonable expectation of privacy. It signals that information disclosed to the government for one purpose (customs) may be used for another purpose (the detection of unemployment insurance fraud).[104] Although the Court may have intended only to create an exception for the limited purpose of unemployment insurance fraud, it is possible that courts could hold that governments can use airline passengers list for general crime control purposes.[105] The fact that the new provision may be Charter proof rightfully did not deter the privacy commissioner from raising concerns about how the use of travellers' lists for multiple government purposes can harm privacy.

The privacy commissioner was also correct in his defence of the general principle that anti-terrorism powers should not be used for general crime control or other governmental purposes. As he argued: "If the police were able to carry out their regular *Criminal Code* law enforcement duties without this new power before September 11, they should likewise be able to do so now. The events of September 11 were a great tragedy and a great crime; they should not be manipulated into becoming an opportunity ... to expand privacy-invasive police powers for purposes that have nothing to do with anti-terrorism."[106] Unless the government subscribes to this principle, the extraordinary powers introduced after September 11 will spread and be used for other crime control and governmental purposes.

CONCLUSION

The quickly drafted *Anti-terrorism Act* fits into a pattern of new criminal laws being enacted in response to horrific crimes, even though the existing criminal law already applied to the crimes. The narrative and memorial style of such expansions of the criminal law places pressures on general criminal law principles that are not designed with particular horrific crimes in mind. This pressure has resulted in the need for proof of religious or political motive and for new police powers such as investigative hearings and preventive arrests, powers that abrogate traditional principles of the criminal law. It has allowed the Cabinet to usurp judicial powers by deciding whether particular organizations are terrorist groups. The new law also includes a broad definition of terrorism and broad crimes against threats of terrorism, financing of terrorism, and facilitation of terrorism. The new law is, in part, based on provisions designed to fight organized crime, and there are some signs that state powers used to target terrorism may expand and be used with respect to other crimes. In chapter 3 we will examine how many groups in civil society felt threatened by the broad new crimes of terrorism and new police powers in the bill. We will also see how the government defended its new *Anti-terrorist Act* as necessary to prevent another September 11 and as consistent with the Charter and human rights.

3

Criticizing and Defending Bill C-36

Opposition in Parliament and in civil society helped to produce a more robust testing of Bill C-36 than the aptly named American *Patriot Act* faced as it quickly rolled through Congress by votes of 357 to 66 in the House of Representatives and 98 to 1 in the Senate. The ease with which something can be seen as "un-American," while often a source of strength for our southern neighbours, can be a weakness in times of crisis. Conversely, the perennial difficulty of agreeing on what constitutes Canada can have the opposite effect here. Critics of Bill C-36 were generally not made to feel that they were being disloyal or unpatriotic. Canadian nationalists, including George Grant, have long praised the complexity of Canada as "a country of minorities," in which no one vision of national identity or patriotism dominates.[1]

Opposition to Bill C-36 brought together a number of disparate groups in civil society and agencies within government. The traditional constituencies of civil libertarians and legal groups led by criminal defence lawyers spoke out against the bill. These constituencies in themselves would not likely have changed the original definition of terrorism in the bill or achieved sunset provisions for the most controversial police powers. Throughout the 1990s civil liberties groups and defence lawyers had opposed amendments to criminal law to facilitate the prosecution of sexual assault cases, but had lost these battles. They were effectively opposed by feminist groups, who relied not only on legal arguments that equality rights required better protection of female and child complainants in sexual assault prosecutions but also on first-hand testimony from the victims of sexual assault and those in rape crisis centres who worked with such victims. Civil libertarians also found themselves opposed by various minorities, human rights commissions, and many academics on issues such as hate and war crimes and pornography.[2] Alan Borovoy, the head of the Canadian Civil Liberties Association, wrote a book at the end of the decade about the formidable opposition that civil liberties groups were receiving from their traditional allies in the women's movements and the academy and among minorities and government agencies such as human rights commissions.[3] If the usual suspects of civil liberties and defence lawyers alone had expressed their concerns about the anti-terrorism bill, there is a good chance that it, like many other expansions of the criminal law, would have rolled through Parliament with little opposition and few amendments. The lessons of even the partial reform of Bill C-36 are important both for continued democratic engagement with the criminal law and for effective legislative review of the *Anti-terrorism Act*.[4]

The broad coalition of groups that spoke out against Bill C-36 was also necessary to counter the government's powerful claims that the new law not only was necessary to prevent terrorism but that it complied with the Charter and advanced the cause of human rights. The defence of the bill would have intrigued George Grant. The government presented itself as the expert in determining the legal technology that was necessary to prevent another September 11 and to comply with the Charter. In its desire to make Canadians feel more secure, the government made immodest claims about what reform of the criminal law could achieve. It demonstrated little sense that tragedies such as September 11 might be the high price paid for a free and open society. The government's defence of the bill as consistent with human rights confirmed Grant's observation that liberalism "is the only political language that can sound a convincing note in our political realms."[5] Even illiberal definitions of terrorism and strong police powers would now be defended in the name of human and equality rights. The success of such a defence would have established an impenetrable consensus in favour of Bill C-36 and made opposition to Bill C-36 seem almost as "un-Canadian" as opposition to the *Patriot Act* seemed un-American. If the government's arguments had been accepted, they would have established the same "absolutist frame of mind"[6] that prevailed as the *Patriot Act* was implemented. Canada, however, proved to be a more complex and difficult country to govern than the United States even in the immediate aftermath of September 11. Many minorities were not convinced by the government's claims that its bill protected their human rights – and they spoke out.

OPPOSITION TO BILL C-36
AMONG CIVIL SOCIETY GROUPS

What made the opposition to Bill C-36 more vibrant and somewhat more effective than the usual opposition to expansions of the criminal law were the contributions of various groups in civil society which were able to put a human face on those who might be harmed by the broad scope of the proposed law. They included unions and Aboriginal groups which feared that illegal strikes and protests might be considered terrorism; groups representing Arab Canadians and Muslim Canadians which worried they would be targeted and profiled in the wake of September 11; and the refugee community, which worried that a broad definition of terrorism would be used to restrict immigration and to criminalize support for movements in the homelands of immigrants to Canada. This broad array of groups was all able to speak from personal experience about the possible dangers of the law. They countered the new narrative style of using criminal law amendments to memorialize and denounce horrific crimes such as September 11 with stories of their own. In the end, these counter-narratives were not sufficient to stop the law, but they did produce some significant amendments.

A number of groups representing lawyers[7] and civil libertarians testified about their concerns – particularly the bill's consistency with legal principles and its effect on specific groups. Borovoy, as head of Canada's leading national civil liberties organization, was vocal both in the media and before various parliamentary groups. He appealed to legal principle when he argued that the bill should require a judicial warrant before it authorized either the secret recording of Canadians speaking with people in other countries or the declaration of a group or an individual as a terrorist. He argued that new police powers, such as investigative hearings to require people to answer questions, might be justified to stop imminent terrorism but should not be used to help the police in the investigation of terrorism that had already been committed. Borovoy also used concrete examples of people and causes that could be adversely affected by the bill. With reference to support for the African National Congress, Kurds in Iraq, or anti-Castro activities in Cuba, he argued that the prohibition of support for terrorism in foreign lands "makes no distinction between activities that are directed at democracies and activities directed against dictatorships." Domestically, he argued that the overbroad definition of terrorism might be applied to Aboriginal blockades of highways or strikes by nurses, though there was "no earthly reason why the legitimate fight against terrorism requires running that risk."[8] With reference to the history of RCMP illegalities in the name of counter-terrorism, he also argued the Bill C-36 would increase police powers without providing for independent oversight and audit of police activities.[9]

Eric Rice, the president of the Canadian Bar Association, explained that more than two hundred lawyers affiliated with his large group had examined the many provisions of the bill. He raised particular concerns that investigative hearings, broad terrorism offences, and mandatory sentencing provisions would "undermine the operation of the justice system" and adversely affect solicitor/client privilege and the accused's access to relevant information. He argued for a sunset clause for the bill, noting that, in three years "we may decide that some of the provisions are not working ... We may find that they are too much of a burden on our citizens as compared to the benefit they have created. We may find that they have disproportionately impacted certain groups." This latter point was stressed by Andrée Côté, representing the National Association of Women and the Law. Her group feared "that the limitations on the rights and freedoms that are being proposed will have a disproportionate impact on groups of persons belonging to racialized minorities, on immigrants and other historically disadvantaged communities in Canada." She added that even though women are victims of "domestic sexual terrorism," "feminists have never called for the kind of measures we now see in Bill C-36." "It is frustrating to see that abusers always benefit from the presumption of innocence," she explained, "that the guilty are often freed on procedural issues, and that it can be very difficult to obtain legal sanctions that effectively guarantee a woman's security or that validate her experience as a victim," but still she did not support the bill.[10] The opposition to Bill C-36 from feminists and a broad array of other civil society groups was significant. The testimony by many groups about their experiences and fears mirrored the contextual feminist method of law reform that had been so successful in expanding the criminal law in the 1990s.[11]

Grand Chief Matthew Coon Come of the Assembly of First Nations argued that events such as the killing of Dudley George at Ipperwash "demonstrate the risk posed to First Nations by legislation that gives heightened powers to police, narrows the civil rights of those involved in legitimate dissent and protest activities and limits or suspends the civil rights of those perceived by the government to be involved in 'terrorist' activities."[12] He expressed concerns that the Aboriginal movement had already been labelled as terrorist in some quarters and would be vulnerable to such labelling under the new law. Invoking Oka, he was not reassured by the justice minister's statement "that native assertions of aboriginal and treaty rights are not intended to be captured by the broad definition of terrorist activities in the bill ... The actions of governments in the past lead us to fear that the strictest force of law is inevitably applied to First Nations protest and dissent, including – we fear – the misapplication of the anti-terrorism legislation in the future." To ensure that civil disobedience was not defined as terrorism, he stated that "the AFN joins the 37,000 lawyers and judges of the Canadian Bar Association"[13] in calling for the deletion of the disruption of essential services from the definition of terrorism.

A representative of the Canadian Council of Churches and Catholic Bishops expressed concerns about the effects of the bill on charities, "almost one half of which are religious organizations ... The section could catch church groups that in good faith, and after due diligence, provide funds to their overseas partners for humanitarian or development assistance."[14] Mumtaz Akhtar, of Human Concern International, a humanitarian organization offering assistance to Afghanistan but one that had been linked with suspected terrorists in the past, testified before the Joint Committee about his organization having to spend "over $250,000 and too much time defending ourselves" from a determination that it was associated with terrorism. He argued that the funds expended on legal defence would have been better spent on feeding hungry people in Afghanistan. He asked the committee to allow charities an opportunity to respond before they were listed as a terrorist organization.[15] This suggestion was not followed, and judicial review is available only after the Cabinet lists a group as a terrorist organization. Nevertheless, stories from various charities that feared being labelled as supporters of terrorists in foreign lands helped to demonstrate that just as real people were murdered on September 11, so, too, would real people be harmed should charities be disrupted and dismantled under the broad provisions of the *Anti-terrorism Act*.

A representative of the Canadian Union of Public Employees expressed fears that union members who provide essential services and engage in illegal strikes could be deemed as terrorists under the broad definition of terrorism which, at the time, could apply to illegal disruptions of essential public or private services. He also expressed concerns that the bill could prohibit "international solidarity work," such as support for trade unions in South Africa under apartheid. A representative of the Canadian Labour Congress expressed concerns that general strikes against governments might be defined as terrorism. He also noted that his group had actively supported "many groups fighting for democracy in Nicaragua, El Salvador, Guatemala and Chile," but might, under the bill, "be charged with supporting or facilitating terrorism." Representatives of Quebec unions reminded the Justice Committee that almost five hundred Quebecers had been arrested without warrant during the October Crisis of 1970.[16] Many witnesses invoked the excesses of the past, as well as their fears about the future. In all cases, the opponents of the bill attempted to create a counter-narrative to the horrifying story of September 11.

Perhaps indicative of an alarming disengagement from the parliamentary process, no direct representative of the anti-globalization movement appeared before the various parliamentary committees that examined Bill C-36. Nevertheless, a representative of the Canadian Labour Congress allied the labour movement with the anti-globalization movement by expressing concerns that, "given the number of people participating in the extensive civil disobedience and disruptions associated with demonstrations in Seattle, Prague, Washington and Quebec City, police may feel justified in using preventive detention provisions of the bill against protesters."[17] Similarly, a representative of the Canadian Arab Foundation argued that Bill C-36, combined with other legal initiatives, was "an attempt to stifle the current evolution of human rights culture among the general population, as was witnessed at the APEC summit in Vancouver, and the anti-free trade agreements in Quebec City, and elsewhere in the world, including Seattle and Genoa."[18] As we saw in chapter 2, a definition of terrorism which included illegal attempts to disrupt essential public and private services and which defined security to include threats to economic security and attempts to compel corporations to change their behaviour understandably raised alarm bells among some anti-globalization protesters.[19]

Groups representing refugees reflected on their experience under the *Immigration Act* with open-ended definitions of terrorism and provisions that allowed decisions to be made on the basis of information that was not fully disclosed to refugee applicants. They also represented the concerns of refugees and other immigrants that charity and support for political causes in their homelands could be defined as terrorism under the bill. Anu Bose, of the National Organization of Immigrant and Visible Minority Women of Canada, reminded senators that many members of her group had traditions of charity and support for those in their homeland, but they feared that such support could be characterized as terrorism under the bill.[20] The experience of refugee advocates was important because the *Anti-terrorism Act* extended techniques previously confined to immigration law to criminal law.[21] Sharryn Aiken, representing the Canadian Council for Refugees, observed: "We have had long experience with immigrants and refugees in particular being targeted by the terrorism provisions in the *Immigration Act*. Very often, conflicts far from Canada are complex and poorly understood ... The concern we have is that immigrants and refugees will be criminalized under Bill C-36 for activities that are not criminal." Like other witnesses, Aiken reminded the committee of past overreactions. After the October Crisis, the RCMP had "subjected many groups, including the new left, Quebec separatists, unions, the Indian movement, and others to surveillance, infiltration and dirty tricks" in the name of preventing terrorism.[22] She echoed the observation of the 1981 McDonald Commission on RCMP wrongdoing that the fundamental purpose of security must be to protect, not harm, democracy.

A number of Muslim groups appeared before the committee. The Canadian Arab Federation raised concerns about the experience of applying anti-terrorism provisions in the immigration act, the "blacklisting" of groups as terrorists and the erosion of civil liberties. Amina Sherazee, legal counsel for the Canadian Arab Federation, also appealed to history by comparing the broad definition of terrorism in Bill C-36 with the definition of an unlawful association in the infamous section 98, which was added to the *Criminal Code* after the 1919 Winnipeg General Strike. "Section 98 was used to prosecute and imprison those who were seen as enemies of the state, who were inevitably those who challenged the political orthodoxy of the time ... it took 17 years ... to correct it. Let us learn from that history and not doom ourselves to repeating it through the passage of the bill." She argued that this bill would define Louis Riel, Nelson Mandela, and Mahatma Gandhi as terrorists. "It would catch members of the Intifada."[23] She appealed to history and world events to counter the government's argument that the bill would advance the cause of human rights.

The Canadian Arab Federation argued that, since September 11, some Arab Canadians had been "stopped by the police, asked to show identification and interrogated for no apparent reason."[24] These concerns were supported by others, including law professor Joseph Magnet, who observed that some of his Muslim students at the University of

Ottawa had been asked "unpleasant questions" in security clearances, such as "Who are your friends?" and "What do they do?" He argued that similar questions were "likely to be asked in these investigative hearings."[25] In their brief to the Justice Committee, members of the Coalition of Muslim Organizations warned that the effects of Bill C-36 would be disproportionately borne by the 600,000 Muslim Canadians. They gave a human face to traditional concerns about due process by eloquently arguing that "the adverse impacts of this Bill will not be remedied by judicial oversight and *post facto* vindication. Stern judicial sanctions of the State's violation of rights make great case law ... However, case law will not put together ruined families, regain lost livelihoods, or rebuild friendships and trust, which were fractured by the suspicion, innuendo and stigmatization sown by the overly zealous acts of the State."[26] All these arguments placed a human face on the excesses of Bill C-36 and responded to the dominant narrative of fear and victimization that emerged from September 11.

Other narratives were invoked to support the bill. Ed Morgan, representing the Canadian Jewish Congress, argued that "we are the people [bin Laden] is talking about ... We find it hard to do anything but take these kind of threats seriously." As targets of hate crimes, Jewish groups supported the bill's new provision for hate-motivated mischief against places of worship and the ability to delete hate propaganda from the internet. David Matas, representing B'nai B'rith, argued that an anti-discrimination clause should be added to the bill and that the bill, like Canada's provisions for war crimes, should be made retroactive.[27] Although no group representing the victims of September 11 appeared before the committees reviewing the bill, the many powerfully moving stories of the thousands of families whose members never returned home after the morning of September 11 were an important part of the debate about Bill C-36.

The broad alliance of disparate groups that opposed parts of Bill C-36 may be the model for a new type of civil libertarian movement that can effectively counter the new victims' movement. Those who believe in fundamental principles of restraint in the criminal law should work with groups in civil society to demonstrate that such concepts are relevant in the lives of real people. Civil liberties groups can reinvent themselves through engagement with new constituencies, such as anti-poverty, anti-globalization, and Aboriginal groups, or with feminists and gays and lesbians who are opposed to censorship. The experience of the wrongfully convicted is also important in demonstrating that real people can be harmed when the state makes it easier to obtain criminal convictions. Some of the most notorious wrongful convictions – the Guildford Four, the Birmingham Six, and the Maguire Seven in the United Kingdom – arose from prosecutions for terrorist bombings. Provisions designed to make it easier to convict people of terrorism can devastate the lives of innocent people who are wrongly convicted.[28] The organized bar should exercise its independence and talents by reaching out to groups who find their rights threatened. This outreach is especially important when the vulnerable are unpopular minorities.

Opponents of Bill c-36 made practical, narrative, and principled arguments about the harm of overbreadth in the definition of terrorism. By their testimony about personal and historical experience, they demonstrated that real people, not just abstract legal principles, are harmed when the state overreaches. Expertise in the fundamental principles of the law and the often hollow threat of ultimate victory in court are not enough.

OPPOSITION TO BILL C-36 WITHIN GOVERNMENT

Within the government, there was important opposition to some parts of Bill c-36. Independent agencies of the federal government, including the privacy commissioner, the information commissioner, and the Canadian Human Rights Commission, all voiced concerns about the bill. The strongest of these critiques came from George Radwanski, the privacy commissioner, who took strong exception to the preemption of privacy legislation once the attorney general issued a certificate prohibiting access to information to protect national security, national defence, or international relations. In a public letter to the minister of justice, Radwanski argued that it was "simply not acceptable … for provisions that would strip Canadians of all legally assured privacy rights to be rushed through Parliament … there could be no possible excuse for using the cover of anti-terrorism legislation to wipe out privacy protections that have nothing to do with the terrorism issue." Radwanski used his skills as a former journalist to make several well-timed interventions in debates about various anti-terrorism measures so as to ensure maximum media coverage. The government eventually responded to his concerns and won his support for the bill.[29] The agencies of Parliament can play a significant role because of their independence and visibility and because they can challenge the government's expertise in human rights and the law.

There were also some highly unusual glimpses of breaches in Cabinet solidarity in support of the bill. Fisheries Minister Herb Dhaliwal commented that "civil liberties are extremely important to Canadians ... certainly as someone from the ethnic community and a visible minority this is something extremely important to me." He related concerns about the broad scope of the bill to concerns about protecting multiculturalism: "People who come to Canada, come ... because of its freedoms, its openness, the diversity of this society. We have to make sure that these strengths are protected."[30] Dhaliwal expressed particular concern about racial profiling and the provisions for preventive arrest and for denying accused persons access to information. He explained that he had felt the injustice of racial profiling after he was targeted by American and British intelligence during a visit to Bermuda that coincided with a meeting between President Reagan and Prime Minister Thatcher.[31] Unfortunately, it was reported that Prime Minister Chrétien read Dhaliwal "the riot act" for this rare breach of Cabinet solidarity. Chrétien's warnings to Dhaliwal did not stop Hedy Fry, the minister of state for multiculturalism, from continuing to express concern that the bill should be clarified "to be very clear on the civil and political rights of Canadians."[32] Fry, however, soon found herself out of the Cabinet. The representative nature of the Canadian Cabinet can provide an opportunity for members of minority groups to express their concerns about governmental policy. At the same time, however, the tradition of Cabinet solidarity almost always prevents dissenters from going public with their views. In this light, the public comments made by Dhaliwal and Fry were significant and courageous.

Backbenchers have somewhat more freedom than Cabinet members to express reservations about governmental policy. Liberal backbencher and human rights lawyer Irwin Cotler publicly opposed parts of Bill C-36. With skill, candour, and courage, he identified eleven deficiencies in the bill as originally introduced, including overbreadth in its definition of terrorism, the lack of prior notice to a group listed as a terrorist group, concerns about access to information and the right to privacy, the need to sunset provisions for preventive arrests and investigative hearings, the need for charities to have a due diligence defence if their charitable status was revoked, and the need for more oversight mechanisms, such as a parliamentary officer to monitor and supervise the legislation.[33] Although the government did not implement all of Cotler's recommendations, it accepted many of them when it amended Bill C-36 in late November 2001. If Cotler had been in Cabinet, it would have been more difficult for him to make detailed and public recommendations about the deficiencies he saw in the bill. The criticisms of the bill made by ministers and government backbenchers were, unfortunately, all too rare in a parliamentary process that is dominated by the Cabinet and the Prime Minister's Office.[34] They suggest that even in times of perceived crisis, democracy could be improved by loosening party discipline and Cabinet solidarity.

PARLIAMENT AND BILL C-36

Committees in both the House of Commons and the Senate played an important role in recommending amendments to the bill and in providing a public and subsidized forum for various civil society groups to express their concerns about the bill. The Special Senate Committee on Bill C-36 issued an important first report on 1 November 2001. The report was bipartisan, reflecting both the Liberal majority and the Conservative minority in the unelected Senate. It called for extensive changes to Bill C-36, including a five-year sunset on the whole bill, changes to the definition of terrorism, enactment of a non-discrimination clause, appointment of an officer of Parliament to monitor the implementation of the bill, reporting requirements on actions taken under the bill, and judicial review of and time restrictions on security certificates to protect information from disclosure. This unanimous report demonstrated the utility of having committees with a less tight sense of party discipline examine proposed legislation.[35]

The government responded to some but not all of the recommendations made by the Senate Committee. In its late November amendments, the government provided some time limits and judicial review on security certificates, five-year sunsets on investigative hearings and preventive arrests, and required annual reports on the exercise of these powers. It also amended the definition of terrorism so that illegal protests and strikes that disrupted essential services would not generally be defined as terrorism. The government did not, however, follow the Senate Committee's other recommendations, most notably that an officer of Parliament be appointed to monitor activities under the bill, that the whole bill be subject to a sunset, and that an anti-discrimination clause be enacted. The Bill C-36 experience with committees provides a hint of the power that an elected Senate and stronger committees with a less tight sense of party discipline might have in causing the Cabinet to rethink its initial policies.

Unfortunately, debate in Parliament was much less effective than the work of the committees. The government invoked closure, which limited Parliament to two days of debate when the bill was reported back to the House of Commons, and one day of debate after third reading. After this limited time, every question required to dispose of the bill had, in the words of the closure motion, to "be put forthwith and successively without further debate or amendment."[36] Long-time parliamentarian Joe Clark criticized this limit on debate as a "travesty of democracy" and a sign of the decline of Parliament "into deep disrepute." [37] Minister of Justice Anne McLellan defended closure on the basis that "our allies around the world are moving and it would be irresponsible for us, as a government, not to move. A government's primary objective is first and foremost to ensure the safety and security of its people."[38] All the opposition parties – the Canadian Alliance, the Progressive Conservatives, the Bloc Québécois, and the New Democratic Party – agreed on some amendments, such as removing the requirement for proof of religious or political motive, but to no avail. Some government backbenchers argued weakly that they would not be happy voting for the bill, but proceeded to do so in any event. The debate on third reading was particularly lacklustre and not at all reflective of the intense debate about the bill that had occurred in committees and in the media. The leader of the opposition, Stockwell Day, took most of the limited time available after closure, even though his party joined the government in passing the law by a vote of 190 to 47.[39] Party discipline reappeared as the Special Committee of the Senate issued a second report in which the Liberal majority supported the bill as amended, but the Conservative minority dissented on the basis that the government had not implemented many of the committee's unanimous recommendations in its first report.

Although the debate in Parliament on Bill C-36 ended with a whimper rather than a bang, the parliamentary process provided some outlet for criticisms of the bill and some amendments. One experienced parliamentary reporter concluded that the debate over Bill C-36 was "one of the frankest legislative discussions to have taken place in this country in a long time. It has brought out the best in civil society, the opposition parties and the Liberal caucus, if not always the government itself."[40] The committees were certainly important in allowing some academics and a wide variety of civil society groups to voice their concerns about the bill, despite the government's rushed schedule. The first report of the Special Senate Committee, calling for significant revisions to the bill, also demonstrated the potential of committees. Some government backbenchers, senators, and even Cabinet ministers courageously voiced their concerns about the bill, as did the independent agencies of Parliament. All these factors likely contributed to the government's decision to amend the bill. Once these limited amendments were made, however, the government put the lid on firmly and tightly. It limited parliamentary debate and imposed party discipline to ensure quick passage of the amended bill.

The *Anti-terrorism Act* contemplates a continued democratic dialogue about the necessity and wisdom of its many anti-terrorism measures. The law commits a committee of Parliament to conduct "a comprehensive review of the provisions and operation of this act" within three years of the act receiving Royal Assent.[41] Parliament should take the initiative in ensuring that enough evidence has been collected to make the review meaningful and in providing a forum to allow the same broad range of civil society groups which expressed fears about the law to testify about their experiences under the law. Backbenchers and even Cabinet ministers should not hesitate to make their concerns about the law known to the public. Tight party discipline that stifles debate within the government will not serve democracy well in the legislative review of the *Anti-terrorism Act*.

BILL C-36 AND LAW ENFORCEMENT

Much of the debate in the media and in committee focused on legalistic discussions of the definition of terrorist activities, as opposed to questions about how either Bill C-36 or existing laws would be enforced. This concentration played into the government's strategy of suggesting that the legislation itself was Charter proof, while downplaying the possibility that it could be administered in a manner that violated the Charter. Although the Special Senate Committee called for a new officer of Parliament to monitor the enforcement of the legislation, the government rejected this recommendation on federalism grounds. Some reporting requirements were added after second reading to record the "number" of times preventive arrests and investigative hearings were used, but such quantitative data may not be sufficient to judge allegations of abuse, including the possibility of racial, religious, or ideological targeting or profiling.[42] Much greater attention should be devoted to ensuring that oversight bodies can provide efficient inquiries and audits and effective remedies for any abuse of new and existing powers. Bill C-36 is dangerous in this respect because it gives every peace officer in the country increased powers, even though many are not subject to effective external oversight. [43] The *Anti-terrorism Act* is a regressive move back to the pre-McDonald Commission days in the 1970s when the RCMP was the lead agency in security matters and often had trouble distinguishing strong dissent from terrorism.[45]

The comparative lack of attention to law enforcement is also seen in the scant attention given to Bill C-35, a bill that was debated around the same time as Bill C-36. Although it is buried between more mundane provisions concerning tax and liquor exemptions for foreign diplomats, Bill C-35 authorized the RCMP to "take appropriate measures, including controlling, limiting or prohibiting access to any area to the extent and in a manner that is reasonable in the circumstances."[46] This provision could cloak with the legitimacy of specific statutory authorization the 4.5 kilometre fence, 2 metres high, used to keep demonstrators away from the Summit of the Americas conference in Quebec City. The fence had been challenged under the Charter, but the judge held that, in the public interest, it was a justified limit on freedom of expression. Even this Charter review seemed driven by narratives, as the judge remarked on the television coverage presented in evidence of the World Trade Organization demonstrations in Seattle.[47] Although this judgment held that it was not in the public interest to grant an emergency injunction to tear the fence down, it is now being cited by the government as evidence that the new police powers in Bill C-35 are consistent with the Charter, despite continued concerns by civil libertarians that the police may not respect the right of dissent enough when deciding that shutting down public spaces is reasonable in the circumstances.[48] The willingness of courts under section 1 of the Charter to accept reasonable limits on expression may not provide sufficient protection to allow dissent and freedom to thrive. A democratic and contextual approach to law reform would not be limited by the question of whether the way the police responded to anti-globalization protests in Vancouver, Windsor, Quebec City, and Ottawa was Charter proof.

In contrast to Bill C-35, the government's second omnibus anti-terrorism bill, the *Public Safety Act*, originally introduced in November 2001 as Bill C-42, was criticized for the effect it could have on dissenters. Most commentary about the long and complex bill focused on the ability of the minister of defence to designate an area of land, water, or air as a military security zone for reasons of international relations or national defence or security.[49] Concerns were raised that areas around global summits – the frequent site for anti-globalization protests – or even the entire province of Quebec, should sovereignty be declared, could be designated as military security zones to be protected by the armed forces. Opposition member of parliament Val Meredith criticized the bill as the "Kananaskis law," on the basis that it was designed to "keep legitimate protesters" out of the upcoming G8 summit in Alberta.[50] The Bloc Québécois and the Quebec government raised concerns that the army could be sent into Quebec, not as in October 1970 at the request of the Quebec government, but by the unilateral decision of the minister of defence. Minister of Defence Art Eggleton unfortunately played the loyality card by dismissing such concerns as related to the separatist agenda.[51] The *Globe and Mail* took a more Canadian approach by observing: "How wonderfully Canadian to have our civil liberties protected by the separatists."[52] By October 2002 the government decided to scrap the controversial power to declare military security zones when it reintroduced the *Public Safety Act*.

BILL C-36 AND PROFILING

Although there was significant debate about the content of Bill C-36 and, in particular, its definition of terrorism activities, there was not enough discussion about how its enforcement would affect certain groups in our multicultural society.[53] An early Ekos study in late September suggested that 50 per cent of Canadians supported police and customs officials giving special attention to "individuals of Arabic origins." Almost a year later, 48 per cent of respondents still supported this type of profiling, and 37 per cent indicated that September 11 had had a negative effect on their feelings towards Muslims and Arabs.[54] In any event, representatives of the RCMP and CSIS stated that their organizations did not engage in profiling solely on the basis of race and religion. Indeed, such a law enforcement technique would be both discriminatory and inefficient. At the same time, however, September 11 created a danger that people who were perceived to be of the same race, religion, or national origins as the September 11 or other terrorists, or to have similar political beliefs, would be targeted by state or private actors.

In the aftermath of September 11 there were some overreactions, and Arab and Muslim Canadians seemed often to pay the price. Mohamed Attiah was summarily fired on September 20 from his job at a nuclear plant on the basis that he was "a security risk." The main evidence seemed to be that he shared the same name as one of the September 11 terrorists. He commenced a lawsuit and, two months later, was offered his job back.[55] After a high-profile police raid, a Toronto copy shop was widely associated in the media with al-Qaeda. Its owner cooperated with the police, but complained that "people are scared to come to my shop. My wife and children are suffering."[56] Amid much publicity, an Ottawa man, Liban Hussein, who was involved in money transfers to his native Somalia, was listed by the Americans as a terrorist and had his assets frozen, although the Americans eventually dropped his name from the list.[57] A Yugoslavian-born crane operator was fired from his job building a new terminal at Toronto's Pearson Airport when, in reference to US-led bombings of Kosovo, he told a co-worker on September 11 that "the Americans got what they deserved." The Ontario Labour Relations Board later held that the statement amounted to hate speech, but that the firing was a disproportionate response.[58] The Canadian Museum of Civilization decided after September 11 to cancel an Arab Canadian art exhibit, but the decision was reversed when Prime Minister Chrétien intervened.[59] The prime minister also attended an Ottawa mosque after incidents of vandalism against mosques had been reported. Chrétien's principled action subsequently won him praise from the United Nations Committee on the Elimination of Racial Discrimination. However, the committee also warned the government to take steps to ensure that the *Anti-terrorism Act* "does not lead to negative consequences for ethnic and religious groups, migrants, asylum seekers, and refugees as a result of racial profiling."[60]

The legislative debate about the *Anti-terrorism Act* was largely silent on the issue of the possible targeting or profiling of people solely or partially because of their national, racial, or ethnic origins or their religion.[61] This silence is unfortunate, because a sensitivity to the rights of groups and an unwavering commitment to equality and multiculturalism can contribute to a distinctive Canadian democracy.[62] Canada should aspire to non-discrimination in its criminal justice policies so that race and crime do not become as deeply intertwined in Canada as they are in the United States. Before September 11, both the federal government[63] and the courts[64] made important commitments to end the overrepresentation of Aboriginal people in our jails. There is a need to ensure that no group in Canadian society becomes a permanent underclass that is presumptively suspected of crime or of a particular crime such as terrorism.

Given the special significance of multiculturalism and equality in Canada, it is unfortunate that even the American *Patriot Act* expressed a greater concern about the dangers of profiling than the Canadian *Anti-terrorism Act* did. The *Patriot Act* condemned discrimination against Arab Americans, Muslim Americans, and Americans from South Asia and affirmed that "the concept of individual responsibility for wrongdoing is sacrosanct in American society and applies equally to all religious, racial, and ethnic groups."[65] One will read Bill C-36's many pages in vain to find an equivalent statement.

The symbolic statement in the *Patriot Act* did not, of course, prohibit profiling in the United States. Although some police forces refused to cooperate with federal investigations after September 11 because of concerns about profiling, American authorities targeted men from predominantly Muslim countries for immigration and criminal investigations.[66] The Canadian government protested American immigration policies by temporarily issuing travel advisories warning Canadian citizens born in Pakistan and six Middle Eastern countries that they were liable to be photographed and fingerprinted on their entry into the United States. Canadian sensitivity over profiling was increased by the multicultural nature of Canada. Natural Resources Minister Herb Dhaliwal did not pull punches in his criticism of the American policy. He argued that it revealed "the ugly face of America and it is simply unacceptable. All fair-minded Canadians will be very angered by this. And for a country that speaks about human rights and democracy, it's totally outrageous." Liberal member of parliament Sarkis Assadourian pointed out that because he was born in Syria, "I'm the only person in this room who has to be fingerprinted if I go to the United States ... If I'm a second-class citizen I shouldn't give first-class support to the U.S. policy on Iraq."[67] Rohinton Mistry, a Canadian author who has been nominated for the prestigious Booker Prize, cancelled his American book tour. His publisher explained that "as a person of colour he was stopped repeatedly and rudely at each airport along the way – to the point where the humiliation for both him and his wife has become unbearable."[68] The Americans argued that their border policy was not racial profiling because they did not target people solely on the basis of race or ethnicity but in conjunction with other factors.[69] The Canadian government can be praised for at least temporarily coming to the defence of its citizens who might be subject to increased border scrutiny because of their country of birth. It risked the charge of hypocrisy, however, for refusing to commit itself not to use racial or religious profiling in the administration of the *Anti-terrorism Act* and other parts of the *Criminal Code*.

The Canadian government decided not to follow the recommendations of its Senate Special Committee and its own MP Irwin Cotler that a non-discrimination clause, such as that contained in the *Emergencies Act* and in international rights protection instruments, be added to Bill C-36. A non-discrimination clause, like the American condemnation of discrimination, would have been a largely symbolic statement of opposition to discriminatory forms of enforcement in the many new powers provided in the legislation. In itself it would not prevent profiling, or even provide effective oversight or remedies. A more robust approach would have prohibited profiling as a law enforcement technique on the grounds that it is both discriminatory and inefficient. The law could have provided for audits and the collection of statistics to determine whether profiling was occurring.[70] Even the symbolic inclusion of a non-discrimination clause in the *Anti-terrorism Act* would have provided an important statement of principle, one that countered some of the post-September 11 public support for racial and religious profiling.[71]

But the federal government failed to assume leadership or take responsibility on the profiling issue. Minister of Justice Anne McLellan sidestepped the issue by arguing that "this legislation doesn't deal with racial profiling." The fears of communities that believe they would be targeted calls not for a "legislative response," she explained, but for "education" and "basic Canadian values on which the nation is based."[72] This evasion of the issue undermined McLellan's claims that the anti-terrorism law itself, not education or basic Canadian values, would advance human rights. The government was prepared only to punish private human rights abuse and refused to commit itself not to use its new powers in a discriminatory manner. Both Irwin Cotler and the Liberal majority on the Senate Committee eventually backed down and supported Bill C-36 without the inclusion of a non-discrimination clause they had originally advocated. As it stands now, Bill C-36 provides no assurances to those in Canada who may feel they are targeted or suspected simply because they are perceived to be of the same race or religion as the September 11 terrorists. This omission has both symbolic and practical effects. Symbolically, the government has avoided stating that racial or religious profiling is wrong or attempting to justify it as a reasonable limit on equality and non-discrimination rights. Practically, the silence of the law on profiling leaves individual victims of profiling with the difficult task of seeking remedies – remedies that, in most cases, will be expensive and difficult to obtain and will be inadequate and individualistic.[73]

The contextual and narrative approach to law reform that produced Bill c-36 was not accompanied by the same contextual recognition that Canadians will not bear the burdens and risks of the law equally. During its three-year review of the legislation, Parliament should consider whether racial and religious profiling has occurred with respect to anti-terrorism measures. It should revisit its regrettable decision not to include a non-discrimination provision in Bill c-36, and it should seriously consider more robust approaches to prevent discriminatory profiling in the administration of anti-terrorism measures and to provide accessible and meaningful remedies for any profiling that occurs. The head of the RCMP has wisely rejected racial profiling as "clearly unacceptable behaviour, that is contrary to our charter, that is contrary to operational [policy], that is contrary to our values." The head of CSIS has also rejected profiling, which would be both a discriminatory and an inefficient use of scarce law enforcement and security intelligence resources.[74] Unfortunately, the government refused to commit itself in law not to use racial or religious profiling. The government's refusal to take a stand against profiling in Canadian law weakens its defence of the anti-terrorism act as consistent with the Charter and supportive of human rights.

THE GOVERNMENT'S DEFENCE OF BILL C-36

The government's defence of Bill c-36 had three main elements. The first was that the existing criminal law was deficient in preventing terrorism and new laws were necessary to prevent it. The second was that the bill was consistent with the Charter and did not need to be enacted as temporary emergency legislation that might override Charter rights. The third was that the bill advanced the values of the Charter and human rights. All three defences were effective in appealing to a public that wanted to prevent another September 11 and to respect rights.

The Prevention of Terrorism

The government's main defence of Bill C-36 was that existing criminal laws were inadequate to prevent terrorism and that new legislation was necessary to give the police the tools they needed to prevent it. If Canada wanted to avoid its own September 11, new criminal laws were necessary. Indeed, Anne McLellan explained to a reporter that "the graphic shot of the second plane exploding into the World Trade Center became a mental touchstone" that she "kept in mind as she debated with colleagues the measures necessary to ensure that such actions would not happen in Canada and that terrorists would not use this country to launch more attacks on the United States."[75] As we saw in chapter 2, these arguments underestimated the ability of the existing criminal law to punish conspiracies and attempts to commit terrorism, and ignored the fact that September 11 was more a failure of law enforcement than of the law itself. Nevertheless, arguments that new criminal laws were necessary to prevent terrorism appealed to the public. In an opinion poll conducted in late September, the majority of respondents indicated that preventing future attacks was the most important consideration in reacting to September 11.[76] It was difficult for the public to debate with the government its claims that new laws were necessary to prevent terrorism.[77] In chapter 7, I will argue that the preventive vision of Bill C-36 was impoverished because it focused on the investigation and punishment of terrorists, and not on various administrative measures that would limit the weapons terrorists could obtain, increase the security of sites vulnerable to terrorism, and minimize the harms of terrorist attacks.

Compliance with the Charter

A second argument made by the government was that the law respected the Charter. In introducing the bill, the justice minister assured "everyone in the House and all Canadians that we have kept the individual rights and freedoms of Canadians directly in mind in developing these proposals."[78] She reiterated this theme when she told the Justice Committee that the bill "had been subject to a very thorough review on Charter grounds and that its measures have been designed so they will respect the values embodied in the Charter, and, we expect, survive legal challenges."[79] Again, the theme of Charter compliance was politically shrewd, as an opinion poll taken in early October showed that while 58 per cent of Canadians believed that the threat of terrorism outweighed rights and freedoms, 38 per cent of the respondents believed that the Charter should still be respected.[80] Stressing that the law was strong but consistent with the Charter could appeal to both constituencies.

Senior officials who drafted Bill C-36 argued that it should be seen as a source of pride, and not weakness, that the bill was drafted with the restraints of the Charter in mind. Indeed, these officials have a statutory obligation to ensure that the legislation was consistent with the Charter.[81] It is also possible that Bill C-36 could have been even less restrained if the Charter had not figured so prominently in its drafting. For example, it might have criminalized membership, as opposed to participation, in a terrorist organization, and it might have allowed the police to make preventive arrests and conduct investigative hearings without prior judicial authorization. It might have required the accused to prove their innocence and it might have convicted those who did not know, but who ought to have known, that they were facilitating or funding terrorists.

The fact that Justice officials were doing their job of ensuring compliance with the Charter in a difficult situation does not diminish the danger of the government's political decision to stress that Bill C-36 was Charter proof. It is not healthy when criminal justice policy is defined by the minimum standards that citizens can expect courts to impose on their governments. The federal government in particular had both an interest and a history in exploring how far it could push compliance with the Charter. In several high-profile cases in the 1990s, the government had enacted "in your face" legislative replies to unpopular Charter decisions defending the rights of those accused of serious crimes. Even when the government essentially reversed unpopular Charter decisions of the Supreme Court, it argued that it was acting consistently with the Charter. The government's aggressive strategy had been successful, with the Court upholding several of these replies as a reasonable reconciliation of the rights of the accused and the victim and noting that it did not have a monopoly on Charter interpretation.[82] The government had succeeded in reversing Charter decisions it did not like without paying the political price of invoking a temporary parliamentary override of the rights under the Charter's controversial notwithstanding clause. It is against this context that the government's claim that Bill C-36 was consistent with the Charter should be evaluated.

There were other limits to the government's "Charter-proofing" defence. The only issue the government could address was whether the legislation itself would be struck down as an unjustified violation of the Charter, not the more subtle issue of whether the legislation could be applied by the police or trial judges in a manner that violated the Charter rights of particular people. For example, the Charter-proofing defence did not address the danger that some officials might engage in discriminatory profiling or that the investigative hearings could be used in a particular case simply to violate a person's right against self-incrimination. It could also not address whether restrictions on the disclosure of evidence would violate the accused's right to full answer and defence or increase the possibility of a wrongful conviction in a particular case. The government defended the legislation as Charter proof on a global basis, whereas the tough Charter issues would emerge only as the new law was applied in particular cases.

There were other shortcomings of the government's defence of Bill C-36. Consistency with the Charter should be accepted more as a necessity than sold as a virtue. As Ronald Dworkin has argued, there is an important moral difference between celebrating anti-terrorism measures by arguing "that the requirements of fairness are fully satisfied, in the case of suspected terrorists, by laxer standards of criminal justice which run an increased risk of convicting innocent people" and understanding that such standards are unfair, but perhaps regrettably necessary "to protect ourselves from disaster."[83] The government's strategy of arguing that the requirements of fairness and Charter compliance were fully satisfied opened the door both to making the post-September 11 legislation permanent and to the eventual extension of extraordinary powers beyond the context of terrorism. If preventive arrests and investigative hearings fully respected the Charter, there is little reason why they should not be used to combat organized crime as well as terrorism. If they are Charter proof for organized crime, why not for sexual assault or child abuse? Why not for all crimes of violence? Why not for all crimes? One possible consequence of the Charter-proofing defence may be the spread of extraordinary powers to other parts of the criminal law.

The Charter-proofing defence is also vulnerable on democratic grounds.[84] If the debate about anti-terrorism measures is to be accessible to the public, it must go beyond the increasingly complex legal calculus of the Charter. In a democracy it should be open for some groups to conclude that the Charter had not protected their rights in the past and to question the bill, even though it has been carefully vetted by the government's many Charter experts. Democratic debate tends to be concerned whether legislation violates rights, not whether the government can justify the violation of rights as a reasonable limit on rights. The groups in civil society that expressed concerns about Bill c-36 were correct not to be overawed by the idea that the legislation was Charter proof.

Some of the groups that opposed Bill c-36, in particular the Coalition of Muslim Organizations, argued that the government's lawyers were wrong and that many parts of Bill c-36 violated the Charter. Charter-based arguments can be a means for opponents of legislation to get public attention and appeal to fundamental values. A claim that a law violates the Charter can get the media's and the public's attention. Increasingly, it seems as though the only way to get a government to reconsider a policy is to claim that it violates the Charter. For example, the privacy commissioner has opposed government plans for a database on the foreign travels of all Canadians by securing legal opinions from senior and respected lawyers that such a database would violate the Charter. Nevertheless, there are dangers in such a strategy. As we will see in chapter 4, the government had some strong arguments that even the more controversial parts of Bill c-36 would not be struck down by the courts as an unjustified violation of Charter rights. Much popular support for changing or repealing the *Anti-terrorism Act* could evaporate should a court find that it was indeed consistent with the Charter. Those who live by the Charter may also die by the Charter.

Arguments that Bill c-36 did or did not comply with the Charter looked to the courts, as opposed to the agencies of Parliament, as the primary means to hold the state accountable for the exercise of its new anti-terrorism powers. This reliance is unfortunate because the courts generally provide limited after-the-fact remedies, while the agencies of Parliament can provide prospective reform and ongoing audits of the state's powers. As we will discuss in chapter 4, anti-terrorism activities in the immigration context may be reviewed by the courts only on a deferential standard of whether the state has acted in a patently unreasonable fashion. Moreover, in many cases, anti-terrorism investigations will not result in charges, and courts may have little or no role to play in reviewing the propriety of the state's conduct. It is unfortunate that Parliament did not follow the recommendation of the Senate Special Committee on Bill c-36 and establish an independent officer of Parliament to oversee the implementation of the new legislation. It did not even provide additional resources and mandates to existing oversight bodies such as the Security Intelligence Review Committee, which reviews the activities of CSIS, the RCMP Complaints Commission, and the Canadian Human Rights Commission.[85] Such agencies could provide more effective and accessible remedies than the courts for those who may be wrongfully targeted and labelled as terrorists.

Bill C-36 as Supportive of Human Rights

The third theme in the government's defence was that Bill C-36 advanced the cause of human rights. In this vein, the minister of justice argued that "the bill reaffirms the equal right of every citizen of whatever religion, race or ethnic origin to enjoy the security, protections and liberty shared by all Canadians."[86] She cited new provisions allowing the deletion from the internet of material established on a balance of probabilities to be hate propaganda,[87] as well as a new crime of hate-motivated mischief to religious property.[88] New hate crimes and new police powers were presented as advancing equality rights. This approach was consistent with other developments in the 1990s in which the government offered enhanced sentences, new criminal laws, and restrictions on the accused's rights as a means of achieving equality for groups such as women, children, and racial and sexual minorities.[89]

The government's decision to emphasize the new hate crimes in Bill C-36 was politically popular. Although many Canadians did not appear to oppose racial or religious profiling of Arabs and Muslims by state officials shortly after September 11,[90] they were strongly opposed to the commission of hate crimes against such minorities. A strong majority (82 per cent) polled between September 17 and September 20 expressed concern that people of Arab decent or the Muslim religion would become the target of unwarranted racism or personal attacks because of September 11.[91] These fears appear to be warranted, given increases in reported hate crimes since September 11.[92] The new hate crimes in Bill C-36 were one of its strongest selling points.

The fact that the hate-crime provisions were only a small part of Bill C-36 did not stop the government from defending the entire bill as consistent with human rights. Appearing before the Senate Committee, the minister of justice invoked the arguments of international law professor Anne Bayefsky that "terrorism is an extreme violation of human rights. Our responsibility is to defend human rights and to do so by taking the kinds of actions that are in this bill."[93] She also relied on human rights lawyer and law professor Irwin Cotler, who argued that terrorism was an assault on human security and human rights. Terrorism should not be seen simply as a contest between the state and the individual or "national security versus civil liberties," he said, but as a conflict involving the human rights of victims and potential victims of terrorism. It was no less than "the ultimate existential assault on human rights and human dignity and ... the struggle against terrorism, therefore, must be seen as part of the longer struggle for human rights and human dignity."[94] After September 11, Cotler took critics of Bill C-36, such as Alan Borovoy, to task for examining the bill exclusively "from the juridical optic of the domestic criminal law/due process model."[95] His calls for "thinking outside of the box" and a reconceptualization of anti-terrorism as a matter involving not only the state and the accused but also the human rights of victims were influential in the government's defence of Bill C-36. As McLellan explained, the Justice Department used Cotler's ideas to distinguish Bill C-36 from a "law-and-order agenda."[96]

Cotler's arguments follow important developments in both domestic and international law which have proclaimed the rights of crime victims and groups, such as women and some minorities, who are disproportionately vulnerable to certain crimes. In this thinking, rights are violated not only by the state but also by crimes committed by non-state actors. This argument was influential beyond the context of terrorism. It helped to explain a pattern that had developed in the 1990s of justifying criminal laws in relation to sexual assault and hate and war crimes on the basis of concern for the rights of crime victims and the equality rights of groups disproportionately vulnerable to crimes.[97] This approach made overly optimistic assumptions about the ability of criminal law reforms to prevent victimization and to provide security for groups disproportionately harmed by crimes. As we will discuss in chapter 7, the new offences and the new police powers in Bill C-36 are not the most effective means to prevent terrorism and limit its harm to victims.

Another problem was that the new approach invoked the rights of victims without addressing what victims of crimes wanted or needed. Although the government was willing to use claims about the rights of victims of terrorism to justify Bill C-36, the legislation itself did nothing for the twenty-four Canadian victims of September 11. The government somewhat reluctantly agreed to a Canadian Alliance amendment that the proceeds of the forfeited property of terrorists may be used to compensate victims of terrorist activities.[98] In contrast, the American *Patriot Act* included many generous provisions relating to compensation for the families of victims of September 11 and provided temporary tax relief for the victims' families.[99] The families of crime victims, including the families of victims of terrorism,[100] have played a significant role in American law reform, which is generally more populist in nature than law reform in the Cabinet-dominated Canadian parliamentary system. The government's treatment of the Canadian victims of September 11 was not generous. Prime Minister Chrétien refused requests that a memorial to the Canadian victims of September 11 be commissioned. At least one of the Canadian victims of September 11 received a demand letter from Revenue Canada threatening legal action for her husband's back taxes. The widow of Canadian Ken Basnicki, who was killed in the World Trade Center, explained that the 2001 taxes "were due just after I received the news that body parts of my husband were found. Do you know what that does to you? ... . Are Canadian victims less victims than American victims?"[101] Bill C-36 was defended as a means to respond to the massive victimization of September 11, but it did absolutely nothing for the families of the victims.

The human rights justification for Bill C-36 can also be criticized for sugar coating the coercive nature of the criminal law. While Cotler urged civil libertarians to "think outside the box" because "the domestic criminal law/due process model is inadequate" to deal with "transnational super terrorists,"[102] civil libertarians, such as Queen's University criminal law professor Don Stuart, countered with the argument that Bill C-36 was designed to make it easier to place individuals in boxes such as penitentiary cells or detention rooms where they would have to answer questions from the police.[103] There is a danger of thinking that every criminal justice issue should be resolved by balancing the rights of the accused against those of the victim. The accused has a right to fair treatment at the hands of the state, while the victim can claim rights only to non-discrimination and inherently imperfect protection from the state. The idea that the rights of the accused and the victim can be reconciled, although well entrenched in Charter jurisprudence, disguises the hard reality that, in difficult cases, one of the competing rights will be violated.[104] In the anti-terrorism context, it will often be better to ensure fair treatment of the accused than to sacrifice such treatment in the vain hope that unfair treatment may actually prevent terrorism. It is hubris for the state to pretend that a tough and even unfair criminal law will prevent terrorism. At the same time, however, unfair anti-terrorism laws that deem groups and individuals to be terrorists or that withhold information from the accused can produce wrongful convictions, as occurred in several terrorism cases in the United Kingdom.

We do both victims and the criminal law a disservice when we use victims as a reason for not respecting the rights of the accused. Criminal justice must be more than a popularity contest between the accused and the victim, because the victim will win every time. Moreover, there is little evidence that a tougher criminal law will actually deter terrorists. A focus on ratcheting up the criminal law to deal with the real danger of the new "transnational super terrorist" may blind us to the frequent failure of deterrence with ordinary criminals, let alone suicide bombers. It may also blind us to the value of less dramatic forms of administrative regulation that may prevent terrorism more effectively. Perhaps we cannot deter super terrorists, but we can limit their access to weapons, explosives, and even more dangerous biological and nuclear materials. We risk abandoning important principles of criminal law in the face of the incredible suffering of the victims of horrific crimes, while toughened criminal laws do nothing to relieve the suffering of the victims' families. In my view, the two dozen Canadian victims of September 11 would have been better honoured by appropriate memorials, victim compensation, and temporary tax relief than by the rushed amendments that were made to the *Criminal Code*.

We also do the non-discrimination principle a disservice when we use it as a justification for all anti-terrorism measures. To be sure, many acts of terrorism are motivated by hatred on religious and racial grounds, and we must ensure that racism and hatred do not taint the prosecution of such crimes. Victims as well as suspects have a right to claim non-discrimination from the state.[105] Nevertheless, we can affirm the equal value and humanity of every person by applying the regular criminal law in a resolute and non-discriminatory manner to every act of terrorism. Our existing criminal law is based on the proposition that all victims are equal and that hate, like political or religious motives, never excuses crimes. We do not need a special motive-based criminal law to denounce and punish the crimes of terrorism. Murder is always murder.

The thousands who were murdered on September 11 came from many countries and many religions. They were targeted because of the place where they worked. There is little reason to fear that a proper criminal trial of those accused of such crimes, whether in a domestic or an international tribunal, would be derailed by prejudice or discrimination against the victims of September 11. Indeed, the much greater threat of discrimination in this particular context is towards those of Arab origin or the Muslim religion who may be accused, perhaps falsely, of involvement in such heinous crimes.

CONCLUSION

Bill C-36 reflected a new narrative and memorial style of enacting criminal laws in response to horrific crimes. It also demonstrated the eagerness of governments to argue that criminal laws advanced the human rights of crime victims and potential victims of crime. This new approach challenged the traditional conception of criminal law as involving only the state and the accused. Bill C-36 was a particularly dramatic reflection of these developments, but it continued a trend that had been evident in Canadian criminal law throughout the 1990s. We may have misgivings, but it is clear we have entered into a new realm of criminal law reform that will be driven by increased concerns for victims and quick legislative responses to horrific crimes. The question then becomes how those interested in restraint in the use of the criminal law should respond to calls to toughen the criminal law.

One temptation that should be resisted is to conclude that the criminal law has simply become politics and to give up in despair. Such abdication will ensure that traditional principles of restraint will be ignored. There is a need to hold up proposed criminal law reform to principles such as the need for a clearly defined and restrained criminal law, and respect for rights such as freedom of expression, the right to silence, and the presumption of innocence. These principles were not entirely absent from Bill C-36, even as it was first introduced. The Department of Justice deserves credit for not following the British example of requiring those accused of terrorism offences to prove their innocence and in requiring that, in most cases, people would be guilty only if they subjectively intended to facilitate or finance terrorism. Justice lawyers also deserve credit for not making mere membership in a terrorist organization an offence, and in not using the objective standards of fault found in some offences in the American *Patriot Act*. Civil liberties groups and criminal lawyers no longer have the power they once did with respect to criminal law reform, but they still provide an interpretative community that matters. These groups must, as they did in response to Bill C-36, mobilize quickly to place proposed legislation under the microscope, and they should attempt to engage the media and other civil society groups in this process. Promoting respect for basic principles may require making predictions about how the courts will apply the Charter to the proposed legislation, but we should be careful not to make such predictions the only criteria for judging the necessity, wisdom, and even the justice of proposed legislation.

Another temptation that should be resisted is to give up on the legislative process and to wait to challenge new criminal laws in the courts under the Charter. Once the law is enacted, it may be too late. The law will empower the police and provide precedents for other laws.[106] Bill C-36 has been law since December 2001, but we are years away from Charter challenges to it. Even if these challenges are brought, we cannot look to the courts to enforce all the fundamental principles of criminal justice (as we will discuss in chapter 4). We cannot rely on the courts to save us from ourselves. Governments will make strong and often effective arguments that the new law is consistent with Charter rights or that it places reasonable and justified limits on those rights. Government claims that proposed legislation is Charter proof and that it advances human rights should not be allowed to trump debate about the proposed law. The answer to the new narrative and memorial style of toughening the criminal law in response to horrible crimes seems to lie in the type of broad coalition of civil society groups that mobilized to oppose some aspects of Bill C-36. These groups, whether they be unions, refugees, Aboriginal people, charities, or various minorities describing their fears of being singled out, all provided counter-narratives to the government's arguments that new criminal laws were necessary to prevent another September 11 and that these laws represented the true spirit of the Charter and human rights. For the opposition to Bill C-36 to have been even somewhat effective, the legitimate and important concerns of the criminal law bar and civil liberties groups about legal principles had to be supplemented with the human stories of those who could be harmed by the law. Without such opposition, the government's arguments that new laws would both prevent terrorism and respect human rights would have gone unchallenged.

4

The Challenges of Preserving Canadian Law

The government's defence of Bill C-36 as consistent with and even supportive of the Charter begs the question of how the courts will react to cases involving terrorism. History suggests that courts are not immune from pressures to support the legislature and the executive in times of crisis. In rebuffing a challenge to conscription during the First World War, a majority of the Supreme Court declared: "Our legislators were no doubt impressed in the hour of peril with the conviction that the safety of the country is the supreme law against which no other law can prevail." The courts similarly refused to second guess the need for a number of wartime measures, including the deportation of Japanese Canadians after the Second World War.[1] The Quebec Court of Appeal dismissed a constitutional challenge to regulations enacted under the *War Measures Act* during the October Crisis in 1970. One judge rejected an argument by a law professor that the Cabinet's declaration of the FLQ as an illegal organization constituted an executive assumption of judicial power by observing: "There is often a lack of pragmatism and realism distinguishing theoreticians and practitioners."[2] This history raises the question of whether judges, when confronted with challenges to anti-terrorism legislation or executive actions against suspected terrorists, will take a "realistic" and "pragmatic" approach that defers to state power or whether they will preserve Canadian law by insisting on compliance with legal principles of liberty and due process.

The Charter provides judges with more legal tools to insist that legislation and administrative action respect legal principles than they had during the world wars or the October Crisis. The Charter is not, however, a panacea that guarantees respect for fundamental freedoms and legal principles in the new war against terrorism. As we will see, the Charter still leaves judges plenty of room to be realistic and pragmatic in their response to anti-terrorism measures. There is much support for the government's argument that most of the new *Anti-terrorist Act* is Charter proof. The courts have accepted robust limits on Charter rights, particularly when, as is the case with Bill c-36, the government claims that its legislation advances the values of the Charter and human rights, including the rights of victims. Even the strongest powers of the *Anti-terrorism Act* – investigative hearings that require people to talk, preventive arrests on suspicion, and the non-disclosure of relevant evidence to the accused for national security reasons – are probably not unconstitutional. The Supreme Court has frequently distinguished between ideal principles of justice and the minimum requirements of the Charter and stressed that the national security context requires a different balance of competing values. The limits of the Charter in supervising the government's anti-terrorism efforts make the government's argument that its anti-terrorism efforts are Charter proof all the more effective and dangerous.

Although most of the *Anti-terrorism Act* will not be struck down by the courts under the Charter, it would be unwise to assume that the courts will not disrupt some elements of Canada's anti-terrorism efforts. The courts may be more inclined to strike down individual decisions of officials than legislation. Although officials are ultimately accountable to elected majorities, their decisions on security and other matters are not made with the same transparency and public debate as legislation. Before September 11, the Supreme Court refused to allow the minister of justice to approve the extradition of murder suspects to the United States without assurances that they would not face the death penalty. After September 11, the Court held that the minister of immigration could not deport suspected terrorists if there was a substantial risk that they would face torture. The courts, as independent bodies committed to precedent and reason, have an important role to play in reminding us about our deepest and most lofty commitments in times of crisis. They can shed the light of legal principles on security decisions taken by the executive behind closed doors. As Justice Rosalie Abella argued, it is because "the public is likely to be apprehensive and raw for a long time" in the wake of September 11 that judges "will have to be vigilant for a long time ... vigilant in remembering that compliance with public opinion may jeopardize compliance with the public interest"[3] – not to mention fundamental rights and freedoms.

The possibility that the judiciary will place some restraints on anti-terrorism may reignite a Canadian debate about judicial activism. It should not be assumed that anti-majoritarian judicial activism is an "American disease"[4] that Canadian nationalists such as George Grant would oppose.[5] Judicial activism has a long and honorable history in Canada. The Supreme Court opposed populist repression of free speech both in Aberhart's Alberta of the 1930s and in Duplessis's Quebec of the 1950s.[6] During the era of McCarthyism, the Supreme Court – led by Justice Ivan Rand and assisted by F.R. Scott and other lawyers who worked on behalf of unpopular religious and political minorities – shone in its commitment to freedom of speech and freedom of religion, even without the existence of a Charter. Perhaps because of the distance that Ottawa in the 1950s provided from the front lines of the Cold War against communism,[7] our Supreme Court had a much nobler record on issues of dissent during that decade than did the United States Supreme Court.[8] Time will tell whether future historians will be able to say the same about the respective courts' performance in the new war against terrorism. So far, intermediate courts in both the United Kingdom and the United States have been quite deferential to national security claims since September 11,[9] and the post-September 11 record of Canadian courts has been limited and mixed.

Judicial vigilance in the protection of fundamental freedoms, legal rights, and equality rights can be defended as a necessary precondition to a modern and democratic Canadian nationalism that accepts liberal values, while taking special care to preserve a free and open debate that is tolerant of all groups in our diverse and multicultural society. It also befits a Canadian society that accepts the democratic and legal possibility of secession even though separatism is often equated with terrorism in many other parts of the world. Canadian courts can also demonstrate a sensitivity to evolving international law standards that will distinguish their jurisprudence from the insularity of American jurisprudence and contribute to Canada's post-Second World War leadership with respect to the development of international law. Indeed, as we will see in chapter 6, respect for international law and institutions is an important means to preserve Canadian sovereignty in the face of pressure to cooperate with the United States in the new war against terrorism.

WHY THE COURTS WILL NOT STRIKE DOWN THE *ANTI-TERRORISM ACT*

Although the Supreme Court will rarely hear cases involving terrorism, its decisions will set the tone for lower courts. In the last twenty years, the Supreme Court has been the dominant force in interpreting the Charter. At the same time, however, Parliament has frequently and with considerable success designed legislation in response to the Court's Charter decisions or in anticipation of such decisions. The Department of Justice had developed expertise in Charter proofing legislation and in making strategic use of precedents long before it was given the difficult job of quickly drafting anti-terrorism legislation in the weeks after September 11.[10] When Minister of Justice Anne McLellan argued that the *Anti-terrorist Act* was consistent with the Charter, she was largely referring to Supreme Court precedents on a number of Charter rights affected by the legislation. In general, this jurisprudence supports the minister's conclusion that most provisions in the bill will not be struck down by the courts under the Charter.

No Right Is Absolute

One reason that explains the conclusion that Bill C-36 is Charter proof is the structure of the Charter, which not only recognizes various rights but provides under section 1 that limits on every right can be accepted so long as they are prescribed by law, reasonable, and demonstrably justified in a free and democratic society. Indeed, when introducing the bill, the minister of justice, a former law professor, urged people: "Keep in mind that the Charter of Rights and Freedoms does not suggest for a minute that any of the rights therein are absolute."[11] From its long preamble proclaiming terrorism as a substantial threat, through its reiteration of the government's desire to respect both the Charter and its international obligations to combat terrorism, and up to its final provision calling for parliamentary review of the legislation, the *Anti-terrorism Act* has been drafted to make optimal use of the willingness of courts to accept reasonable limits on rights. This flexibility does not, however, take away from the fact that the legislation violates and limits some important rights.

The Presumption of Innocence

There is a plausible argument that the accused's Charter right to be presumed innocent and to require the state to prove guilt beyond a reasonable doubt is violated by the definition of terrorist groups. This definition, as we saw in chapter 2, allows the Cabinet to substitute its decision that a group or even an individual is a terrorist for proof beyond a reasonable doubt in court that the group or individual is a terrorist.

A similar approach was used during the October Crisis, when the Cabinet declared the FLQ to be an unlawful association. The Quebec Court of Appeal, as we saw, dismissed an argument that the Cabinet's declaration usurped a judicial function, with one judge observing that this strong argument lacked "pragmatism" and "realism."[12]

Will the answer be different now that the Charter provides a constitutional guarantee of the presumption of innocence? David Paciocco has argued that defining terrorist groups on the basis of a declaration by the Cabinet converts "assailable propositions of fact" that should be tested in court into "unassailable propositions of law in order to reduce burdens of proof." In his view, "one of the cross-border casualties of September 11 will be the presumption of innocence."[13] Professor Paciocco has a strong legal argument. But Professor Noel Lyon also had a strong argument during the October Crisis that the Cabinet's declaration of the FLQ to be an unlawful association was an unconstitutional usurpation of judicial power.[14] Strong legal arguments, unfortunately, do not always win the day. They are less likely to win the day when they are presented in a national security context and when judges are inclined to be deferential to the government.

A finding that allowing the Cabinet to decide who is a terrorist group violates the presumption of innocence is only half the story under the Charter. The government can still argue under section 1 of the Charter that the violation is a reasonable limit. Despite the traditional and much-venerated nature of the right to be presumed innocent, the Court under the Charter has frequently accepted legislative limitations on the right and has even devised a few of its own. In various cases, it has stressed the importance of making it easier for the state to prosecute drunk driving, pimping, hate propaganda, sexual assault, and other serious crimes of violence.[15] It is difficult to imagine that the courts will not add terrorism to this list. In other words, they will allow the Cabinet's list of terrorist groups to substitute for proof beyond a reasonable doubt before a judge and jury that a listed group is actually a terrorist group. The Court will probably hold that any limit on the presumption of innocence is reasonable and justified in the anti-terrorism context.

Fundamental Freedoms

There is a plausible argument that some parts of the new act, such as the criminal prohibition of threats of terrorism or the display of hate propaganda on the internet, violate freedom of expression. There is also an argument that provisions inviting courts to examine whether a person uses the name or symbol of a terrorist group or frequently associates with terrorists infringes the Charter right of freedom of association. Again, a conclusion that the legislation violates these fundamental freedoms is only half the Charter story. Building on Supreme Court precedents that offences against hate propaganda and pornography are reasonable limits on freedom of expression,[16] the government will have very strong arguments that any limit on free expression or association is a reasonable one. The Supreme Court has been deferential to Parliament's decision to criminalize forms of expression, such as threats of violence, that are far removed from the basic values of individual self-expression and democratic debate.

As is often the case, the section 1 analysis may depend on how the government's objective is defined. It could be argued that criminalizing threats to commit terrorism or association with terrorists will not prevent actual terrorism. The government, however, will likely define the objective of the law more broadly, as responding to the insecurity caused by threats of terrorism or the risk of terrorism. The criminalization of threats of terrorism and association with terrorists are rationally connected with this broader objective. Questions of proportionality, and especially overall balance between chills on free expression and association and gains in security, will, however, still exist. The existence of other offences in the *Criminal Code*[17] may be interpreted as evidence of less drastic means to respond to threats than designating threats of terrorism or participation in a terrorist group to be terrorist activities. Nevertheless, the structure of the Charter suggests that there is plenty of room for courts to take a "pragmatic" and "realistic" approach and to uphold a definition of terrorism that includes threats of terrorism and participation in the activities of a terrorist group.

Privacy

Concerns have been raised that the *Anti-terrorism Act* violates rights of privacy by making it easier to use electronic surveillance for up to a year in terrorist investigations. Although the right against unreasonable search and seizure in section 8 of the Charter has been interpreted to protect reasonable expectations of privacy, the right is not absolute. The state is able to invade a reasonable expectation of privacy once it shows it has reasonable grounds to believe that an offence has been committed and that the recording will reveal evidence of the offence. These standards are satisfied by the wiretap provisions of the *Criminal Code*, even as they are amended by the *Anti-terrorism Act*. In addition, the Supreme Court hinted in one of its first Charter cases that less onerous search and seizure standards may be justified in the national security context.[18] In subsequent years, the Court has stressed the importance of context to Charter analysis.

As we discussed in chapter 2, privacy advocates have protested the use of airline passenger lists compiled for security reasons to facilitate police investigations and arrests of people wanted for other crimes. The federal privacy commissioner has raised the spectre that the use of such lists and the compiling of travel databases are only a short step from requiring all travellers to show authorities their identity papers. Whatever the validity of these privacy concerns, the government's construction of lists of airline passengers for transportation security and the use of such lists for other governmental purposes may well be consistent with the Charter. The government will rely on an important but neglected judgment released by the Supreme Court a few months after September 11. The case involved a customs declaration form that was used by unemployment insurance officials to detect that a passenger was receiving unemployment insurance while out of the country on a holiday and unavailable for work. Given the importance of the issue of possible violation of the right against unreasonable search and seizure, the Supreme Court's one-paragraph judgment was surprisingly brief. Nevertheless, it was a unanimous "by the Court" judgment signed by all nine Justices. It stated: "There was no violation of s.8 of the Canadian Charter of Rights and Freedoms on the facts of this case. We concluded that the appellant cannot be said to have held a reasonable expectation of privacy in relation to the disclosed portion of the E-311 Customs information which outweighed the Canada Unemployment Insurance Commission's interest in ensuring compliance with self-reporting obligations of the Unemployment Insurance benefit program."[19]

This decision follows a pattern of the Court taking a less generous approach to the definition of what is a reasonable expectation of privacy. It built on a 1993 case in which the Court held there was no reasonable expectation of privacy in records of electricity consumption which the police used to determine whether people were growing marijuana in their basements. In subsequent cases, the Court held that a man did not have a reasonable expectation of privacy in his girl-friend's apartment; that passengers did not have a reasonable expecta-tion of privacy in cars; and that high school students did not have reasonable expectations of privacy with respect to searches by school officials.[20] The Court's reasoning in its post-September 11 customs declaration case suggests that people may not have a reasonable expec-tation of privacy that information revealed to the government for one reason will not be used for other reasons. The Court's reasoning also reflects its penchant for stressing that all difficult Charter issues must be resolved by balancing the interests of the state against the interests of the individual. One danger of balancing in the privacy context is that the privacy of innocent people may be balanced against the inter-ests of the government in detecting the guilty.[21]

The government has announced plans to use some amendments to customs legislation after September 11 to keep a database on the foreign travels of Canadians for a six-year period. The privacy com-missioner has strongly opposed this "big brother" travel database. He commissioned retired Supreme Court Justice Gérard La Forest to provide a legal opinion. La Forest concluded that even under the more restrictive approach to privacy taken by the Court in recent years, the database would violate the privacy rights of millions of Canadians. He argued that the travel information was more detailed and personal than information about electricity consumption. He also pointed out that the government would have access to the information in the travel database for a much broader range of purposes than detecting fraud against the unemployment insurance scheme. In addition, governmen-tal agencies could access travel records without either individualized suspicion or prior judicial authorization. La Forest may be correct that the Supreme Court will distinguish its prior restrictive privacy cases and find that the proposed travel database violates the Charter. The government has shown some willingness to respond to the legal opin-ion of La Forest and other respected lawyers because "it is committed to making this legislation work within the Canadian Charter of Rights of Freedoms."[22] There is a chance, however, that the Court could hold that the travel database is no more offensive under the Charter than gaining access to electricity records or customs forms. Such a judicial finding that the database was Charter proof should not take away from the fact that it would still invade the privacy of millions of Canadians who are not suspected terrorists.

Equality

Concerns have been raised that powers under either the *Anti-terrorism Act* or other laws could be used in a manner that involves racial, ethnic, or religious profiling. Profiling would occur, for example, if travellers were subject to secondary inspections at customs because they had Arabic names, wore certain religious clothing, or were born in certain countries. Information on the race, colour, and ethnic origin of travellers detained for secondary inspection is now being collected by Canadian customs as a result of a settlement of a human rights complaint. The complainant has expressed hopes that remedial measures will occur "if the majority of people who are being referred to secondary searches are racial minorities, whether they are black or whether they are Arabs now that there is all the terrorism concerns."[23]

Section 15 of the Charter guarantees the equal benefit of the law without discrimination on various grounds, including race, national or ethnic origin, religion, or lack of Canadian citizenship. As my colleague Sujit Choudhry argued, profiling would seem to be a paradigmatic example of an equality rights violation.[24] A person would be singled out and denied liberty because of a stereotype that associates people with terrorism because of an immutable personal characteristic such as skin colour. Nevertheless, some problems could emerge in establishing that profiling constitutes a Charter violation. In a customs case, the Supreme Court has suggested that targeting homosexual erotica might be permissible if it was based on evidence that such erotica "is proportionately more likely to be obscene than heterosexual erotica."[25] In another case, the Court indicated that distinctions based on age may not be discriminatory if they are based on sound statistical generalizations about the merits.[26] As Professor Choudhry argues, however, such "statistical generalizations cut against the grain of ... equality itself – that is, that individuals not be judged on the basis of presumed group characteristics, but rather on the basis of their individual traits."[27] Courts will also have to resist the temptation to minimize the indignity of limited intrusions on a person's liberty because of race, religion, or ethnic or national origins. There will be a temptation to say that a few minutes spent in a secondary inspection does not offend human dignity. The government may defend profiling practices on the basis that they are preferable to greater intrusions on the liberty of all travellers. These arguments should not prevail. Profiling is discriminatory and degrading. It is also an inefficient law enforcement technique.

Nevertheless, claims that profiling violates the Charter will not be easy to establish.

Neither the *Anti-terrorism Act* nor any other security legislation authorizes Canadian officials to engage in racial or religious profiling. As we discussed in chapter 3, the law-makers have ducked the profiling issue by neither authorizing nor prohibiting it. Legislative silence on profiling limits the remedies available for those who might successfully challenge profiling practices.[28] Only affected individuals will be able to obtain remedies for profiling. In many cases, a legal challenge will result in more grief than gold. Damage awards for Charter violations have generally been quite modest, with some cases awarding only nominal sums such as $500. Canadian courts have also been reluctant to order institutions to change profiling practices. One gay and lesbian bookstore went all the way to the Supreme Court, only to obtain a simple statement or declaration by the Court that customs had violated their equality rights. The small bookstore has had to start new and expensive litigation alleging that customs has again engaged in discrim-inatory profiling of the books they import.[29] A statutory prohibition on profiling would likely be more effective than Charter litigation.

Silence and Self-Incrimination

Compelling a person at an investigative hearing to reveal information about terrorists that he or she may have assisted violates the person's right to silence and against self-incrimination. It also offends traditions of adversarial justice which date back to the abolition of the Star Chamber in 1641 and the case of John Lilburne, who was imprisoned for two years because he would not testify under oath to the Star Chamber about whether religious books he shipped from England to Holland were seditious. As Lilburne argued, "I was condemned because I would not accuse myself."[30] Those who refuse to testify under oath and incriminate themselves at an investigative hearing may end up in jail, condemned for not accusing themselves. Surely such modern-day star chambers violate the Charter.

The government has, however, carefully constructed investigative hearings with an eye to minimize the likelihood that the courts will invalidate them under the Charter. There are procedural safeguards, such as prior judicial authorization and access to counsel during the hearings. But these procedural protections are fairly weak. There is not much point in having lawyers if all they can do is tell their clients they can be punished if they do not talk. The more substantive reason why investigative hearings are Charter proof is that they build on a number of Supreme Court cases which hold that the right against self-incrimination, like all Charter rights, is not absolute. In general, people can be forced to incriminate themselves so long as the state cannot use their statements, or statements derived from them, in subsequent investigations and proceedings against them.[31] The *Anti-terrorism Act* provides those subject to investigative hearings to such "use and derivative use immunity" protections. Investigative hearings were defended as a Canadian version of the American grand jury, in which people can be threatened with punishment for not talking. An important difference, however, is that the Americans have to grant people who "take the Fifth" a broader form of immunity against prosecution for any offence they may reveal to the grand jury.[32] Even the less generous Canadian immunity protections may not apply if the subject of the investigative hearing ends up before a court in another country.[33] Although the investigative hearings are the boldest departure from legal principles in the *Anti-terrorism Act*, they will not likely be struck down under the Charter because of the court's willingness to accept limits on the right against self-incrimination. The courts may devise remedies for individual cases of abuse, but they are not likely to strike down the new procedure of investigative hearings.[34]

Fundamental Justice and Fairness

Another potential Charter challenge is for an accused to argue that the new crimes of terrorism are substantively unfair and, as such, violate the principles of fundamental justice under section 7 of the Charter. The state could be required to prove that the accused subjectively knew he was assisting terrorists because of the high penalties and stigma attached to a conviction of a terrorism offence. The Court has used similar reasoning to require full subjective fault for murder, attempted murder, and war crimes. It would not be a stretch to add terrorism to this short list.[35] Perhaps for this reason, the new offences generally require the state to prove that the accused knowingly facilitated or financed terrorism. There are some departures from the general principles of subjective fault, and the courts may hold that they violate the Charter. In recent years, however, courts have been reluctant to extend such Charter protections and more willing to defer to legislative definitions of crime which place greater emphasis on the harm caused by the accused as opposed to the accused's fault or knowledge of that harm.[36] In any event, a court that found that parts of the new crime of terrorism were substantively unfair because they did not require full subjective fault would probably not strike the entire offence down. Under recent more deferential remedial doctrines that have been used to save the overbroad offence of possession of child pornography, courts would likely save the offence by reading such restrictions into the law.[37] Courts are unlikely to strike any of the multiple new terrorism offences from the *Criminal Code*.

Another possible Charter challenge would be to argue that some new offences are fundamentally unjust because they are unnecessary to stop terrorism. Making it an offence to provide legal, medical, or other services for the benefit of a terrorist group could be unnecessary for the legitimate objective of stopping terrorism. Those who make such an argument rely on a controversial 1994 Supreme Court decision that it was overbroad to the legitimate objective of protecting children from sexual offences to prohibit all convicted sex offenders from loitering in all public places, including public places where children could not reasonably be expected to be present.[38] The argument would be that criminalizing all dealings with terrorist property and the provision of all services to terrorists, regardless of the lack of connection to any act of terrorism, is not necessary to prevent terrorism.[39]

Such arguments, however, will likely fail. One reason is that most of the new offences require that the accused intends to facilitate terrorism. As in the law of attempts, acts that would not otherwise be criminal can be punished primarily because of the accused's guilty intent. Second, the government would argue that its purpose was not simply preventing terrorism, but the broader objective of protecting people from the fear or risk of terrorism. The government would hold that there is a rational connection between renting property or providing medical services to a terrorist and facilitating acts of terrorism. The Supreme Court has already accepted the legitimacy of using the criminal law to prohibit pornography and hate propaganda, even though the connection between such forms of expression and violence cannot be proven with certainty.[40] Finally, the recent record of the courts in supervising the substantive content of criminal law under the Charter has been one of restraint. The vast majority of criminal laws challenged as excessively vague, overbroad, or substantively unfair have been upheld.[41] Given these deferential trends, the courts will not likely erase the many new terrorism offences that Parliament created in the immediate aftermath of September 11.

Fair Trial and Disclosure

The attorney general has a power under the *Anti-terrorism Act* to issue a certificate prohibiting court-ordered disclosure to an accused of information obtained in confidence from a foreign entity or information that, if disclosed, might harm national security.[42] Such national security certificates could violate the right to disclosure of the state's case and the right to a fair trial. Nevertheless, the government's defence of the *Anti-terrorism Act* as protective of human rights may help to save this power from invalidation under the Charter. The Court has already upheld under the Charter broad legislative restrictions on the accused's ability to obtain disclosure of the therapeutic records of complainants in sexual assault cases. It stressed that the accused's rights should be defined (and in reality limited) by the competing privacy and equality rights of the complainant; by the need to defer to the balance Parliament struck between those competing rights; and by the social interest in encouraging the reporting of sexual offences.[43] In a post-September 11 case, the Supreme Court upheld the constitutionality of allowing the government, when national security or foreign confidences were at stake, to make its case to a court with the other side not being present and without even allowing the judge to edit and summarize the government's case for the affected individual. The Court was influenced by the federal government's pragmatic arguments that any less restrictive approach would compromise the ability of Canada to receive intelligence from foreign sources. The government stressed that Canada relied on American, British, and French intelligence and was vulnerable to be cut off from much important intelligence if there was any perception that information would be even inadvertently disclosed.[44] This decision arose in the context of lawyer Clayton Ruby's request to see his CSIS files, and not in a criminal case or a decision to list a group or an individual as a terrorist. Nevertheless, it suggests that the Supreme Court may be receptive to the national security and foreign confidence limitations that the *Anti-terrorism Act* places on an individual's ability to know and test the government's case.

The courts may apply a more deferential approach in the terrorism context if they accept the government's argument that terrorism is itself an assault on the human rights of vulnerable groups or that the state has a heightened interest in national security and maintaining the confidence of foreign intelligence services. Such arguments may tilt the balance in the government's favour, even though the accused's rights would still be violated and the risks of a wrongful conviction or a wrongful listing as a terrorist would be increased by the failure to disclose the state's case to the accused for adversarial challenge. A more activist Supreme Court recognized in the early 1990s that a failure to make full disclosure of the state's case contributed to wrongful convictions, including wrongful convictions in Irish Republican Army terrorism cases in the United Kingdom.[45] Even if the provisions in the *Anti-terrorism Act* providing for the use of evidence never disclosed to the accused are found to violate the Charter, the courts are encouraged by the act to order remedies that are designed to ensure a fair trial in particular cases, as opposed to invalidating the entire provision. Any future Charter victory is likely to be minimal.

A Charter-Proofed Law?

The above analysis suggests that the minister of justice accurately reflected deferential trends in Charter jurisprudence when she told Canadians that the *Anti-terrorism Act* was consistent with the Charter. The bill was drafted to take advantage of the willingness of courts to accept limits on all Charter rights, including basic rights such as the right against self-incrimination, the presumption of innocence, the right to full answer and defence, and the right to disclosure of the state's case. The case for holding that the act's limits on rights are reasonable, however, should not obscure the hard reality that the new law violates some important rights of the accused. The government has traded the hope of deterring and convicting terrorists in the future against the certainty of limiting the rights of those listed or accused of terrorism. The idea that the new law is Charter proof has obscured the fact that it still violates the rights of suspected terrorists.

My earlier conclusions that the *Anti-terrorism Act* was Charter proof have been contentious.[46] Some argue that I have underestimated the ability of the courts to protect fundamental rights[47] and even defamed the Charter.[48] I will be happy to be proven wrong on this point because I believe that courts should be active in enforcing the rights of minorities and in preserving legal principles that legislators and administrators may be inclined to ignore and finesse.[49] Nevertheless, we must also be candid about the limits of Charter adjudication and avoid taking an overly romantic or simplistic view of the Charter. Although many in the public may think that compliance with the Charter guarantees justice, it is not that simple. It is often difficult and expensive to make Charter claims. Most accused take the path of least resistance and plead guilty. Most innocent people who are hassled by the police seek no remedies. Even when a case gets to court, the government wins most Charter cases. The Charter is an ambiguous document that allows rights to be both protected and limited. The meaning of the Charter changes with the times and the composition of the Supreme Court. Some recent trends suggest that the courts are becoming more deferential to governments than they were in the early years of the Charter.[50] The tendency towards deference may only increase when the issue is seen as one of national security, foreign relations, or the exigencies of a new war against international terrorism. Courts may be reluctant to strike down large parts of a law that the government has argued is necessary to prevent another September 11 and that has been so carefully vetted by the government's Charter experts.

Others have argued that I have suggested that there was something "insidious" about the government's laudable goal to ensure compliance with the Charter.[51] My point has not been that the government should design legislation that violates the Charter, although I do think that the attorney general has an obligation to insist that the override be used when the government clearly violates the Charter, as interpreted by the Supreme Court.[52] Rather, my intent is to illustrate the political flaws when the government sells its legislation as Charter proof. Such a strategy may deceive a public who thinks that consistency with the Charter means that rights are not infringed. In truth, consistency with the Charter is nothing more than a prediction that the courts will not strike the legislation down. Legislation that violates important rights and traditions can be presented by the government as consistent with the Charter so long as the government is confident that the limits on those rights are reasonable. Selling legislation as Charter proof is objectionable because it suggests that the government can do, in the words of Edmund Burke, "whatever a lawyer tells me I may do," as opposed to "what humanity, reason and justice tell me I ought to do."[53] Constitutionalism in Canada before the Charter was built on the notion that those in power should not exercise their legal powers to the fullest extent possible even in times of perceived crisis. It was fundamental to British constitutionalism that what was legal might nevertheless be improper and even unconstitutional. I fear that we are losing sight of this older sense that power must be restrained by decency, prudence, and tradition, not just the legal limits that lawyers and courts impose on us.[54] A lawyer's conclusion that an investigative hearing that forces people to talk will not be struck down by the courts under the Charter does not mean that such an innovation should be enacted. Charter proof or not, investigative hearings still violate centuries of respect for the right to silence and are not likely to be effective in preventing terrorism.

THE SUPREME COURT

Although much of the *Anti-terrorism Act* is likely safe from direct Charter challenge, it would be premature to conclude that the independent courts will not place some fetters on the anti-terrorism strategies of governments. The most important role of the judiciary will be to bring light and legal principles to bear on the decisions that the executive takes in the name of national security. Two of the Supreme Court's recent decisions place important and valuable restraints on the manner in which terrorists may be treated. They are *United States v. Burns and Rafay*[55] and *Suresh v. Canada (Minister of Citizenship and Immigration)*,[56] which hold, respectively, that extradition to face the death penalty and deportation to face torture will violate the principles of fundamental justice in section 7 of the Charter. In both cases, the Court performed its anti-majoritarian role admirably by examining the fundamental principles of Canadian and international law to reach unpopular conclusions. In *Burns and Rafay*, the Court took note of the reality of wrongful convictions, including those of suspected terrorists in the United Kingdom.[57] In *Suresh*, the Court concluded that torture violates fundamental norms of Canadian and international law.[58] In both cases, the Court refused to be blinded by the serious nature of the charges against the Charter applicant and resisted the temptation to minimize Canadian responsibility for what would happen once the accused was removed from our shores. Burns and Rafay were charged with the gruesome and bloody murder of Rafay's parents and sister, while Suresh was alleged to be an important member of the Tamil Tigers, a group that has committed many acts of violent terrorism in Sri Lanka, including suicide bombings. Despite the seriousness of these allegations, the Court reminded Canadians of values they were inclined to forget in the understandable urge to expel dangerous persons from their midst.

The public and its elected representatives may well be inclined to send notorious murderers or terrorists to face the death penalty or torture, and it is not surprising that the Supreme Court received considerable criticism for its anti-majoritarian efforts in these cases. *Burns and Rafay* was greeted with angry op-eds in both the *Globe and Mail* and the *National Post* accusing the Court of judicial activism and the "imperial arrogance" of imposing the justices' "personal beliefs" on Canadian and foreign governments.[59] The Canadian Alliance's criticisms of the case were revived in the wake of September 11 when the then leader, Stockwell Day, criticized the government for failing to undo "the damage of the Burns and Rafay decision which allows criminals to flee the consequences of their actions if they can make it to Canada and hide behind our soft laws."[60] The Alliance also demanded that the minister of justice reopen argument in the *Suresh* case to stress to the Court that the issues had changed since September 11. The *National Post* criticized *Suresh* as a similar "piece of judicial activism" to *Burns and Rafay*, but even worse because it was decided against the backdrop of a deadly threat to Canada and other nations. It editorialized:

Torture is always wrong. Yet it is inevitable that torture may sometimes occur in nations whose commitment to human rights has been understandably vitiated by regular encounters with suicide bombers. Whether we deport terror suspects to such nations is a difficult and often agonizing decision that must be made on a case-by-case basis. It is a decision that should be made by government officials, not judges.[61]

Conservative critics of judicial activism may be quick to exploit the scary and emotive context of terrorism after September 11 to advance their arguments that judicial review is the undemocratic and dangerous imposition of the worldview of judicial elites.[62]

As is the case with other Charter decisions, however, *Suresh* and *Burns and Rafay* both recognize rights and contemplate limitations on them. Although the Court has articulated a broad principle against Canadian participation in the death penalty or torture, it has in both cases deliberately and explicitly left open the possibility of exceptions. It did so without providing any indication of what might constitute an exceptional case. This void raises the pressing question of when, exactly, will the Supreme Court allow a suspected terrorist to be removed from Canada to face death or torture?

Alan Dershowitz has argued that torture should be judicially approved and controlled in cases in which a suspected terrorist withholds information that could prevent another September 11. He even suggests that judicial warrants authorizing torture would be consistent with the American Bill of Rights.[63] His advocacy of torture is both morally and practically suspect. The examples he uses, such as a ticking nuclear bomb, are classic cases of emergency or exigent circumstances in which the police generally do not have time to obtain warrants. Many experienced interrogators also believe that "torture just makes the person tell you what they think you want to know so you'll stop hurting them."[64] Even more troubling is Dershowitz's idea that torture may in some cases be morally right and constitutional. Although it is possible to imagine a circumstance in which an official could be excused from engaging in torture to save many lives, this exception would be a far cry from saying that torture is legally justified or constitutional. Torture is always legally, morally, and constitutionally wrong. At most, it might be excused after the fact. Unfortunately, the Supreme Court did not recognize this truth in *Suresh*. It left open the disturbing possibility that deportation of a terrorist to face torture may in some cases be constitutional and judicially approved.

It is difficult to know why the Supreme Court was reluctant to say that deportation to face torture is always unconstitutional. There can be only speculation about what the Court meant by its undefined reference to exceptional cases. One possibility is that the Supreme Court may have believed that deportation to face torture could be constitutionally acceptable in Dershowitz's ticking nuclear bomb case. Dershowitz suggests that authorities in the Philippines successfully used torture to thwart a terrorist plan to assassinate the Pope and crash eleven airliners into the Pacific Ocean.[65] But it is not clear that the lengthy process of deportation to face torture is the appropriate response in an emergency ticking nuclear bomb case. Another alternative is that the Court might be prepared to accept deportation to face torture if the only alternative was to release a dangerous terrorist on Canadian soil. Similar concerns led the British government after September 11 to enact very controversial legislation that allows for the indefinite detention of foreign terrorists or their supporters who cannot be deported. The British legislation was enacted in part because Britain is bound by judicial decisions that are similar to *Suresh* in preventing deportation to face torture, but which are absolute and do not contemplate any exceptions.[66] The chance of terrorists going free because they cannot be deported to face torture has probably been overestimated both in the United Kingdom and in Canada. In many cases such a dangerous international terrorist could be prosecuted domestically for a variety of offences relating to terrorism. In both Britain and Canada, a terrorist can be prosecuted for funding, facilitating, or committing acts of terrorism in foreign lands. The terrorist could also be extradited (albeit with assurances that the death penalty not be applied) to another country to face trial for terrorism committed in that country. In the highly unlikely event that these alternatives are unavailable, however, Canadian courts may well be asked to make an exception to the rule against deportation to face torture in order to stop the release of a dangerous terrorist on Canadian soil. *Suresh* allows Canadian courts to make such an exception.

There are reasons to prefer the British approach of always refusing to deport terrorists to face torture, even at the cost, if necessary, of enacting extraordinary legislation to authorize their detention. The British approach recognizes that torture is always morally and legally wrong, while the Canadian approach raises the disquieting possibility of our Supreme Court actually approving of deportation to face torture. An article in *The Economist* recently stated that "no court in any democratic country, including the United States, would agree to send a defendant to another country if it were known that he would be tortured there." Nevertheless, it was precisely this disturbing possibility that the Supreme Court of Canada left open in *Suresh*.[67] In reply, it could be argued that the new British legislation authorizing indefinite detention of foreign terrorists is also morally suspect. That is true, but indefinite detention is less morally repugnant than participation in torture. Moreover, the British approach was the result of democratically enacted legislation that included a temporary override or derogation from the fair trial rights of the European Convention for Human Rights. The British people had an opportunity to decide if they wanted to take such a step, and they will have another opportunity to reconsider the matter when the derogation expires and its possible renewal is debated. The British made temporary exceptions for terrorists, but they did not place their courts in a position of upholding the legality or constitutionality of deporting a terrorist to face torture.[68] In contrast, *Burns and Rafay* and *Suresh* invite the federal government to ask courts to find that some notorious and dangerous terrorist constitutes an exceptional case for extradition or deportation to face death or torture. They run the risk of allowing courts to participate and approve of state processes resulting in the execution or torture of terrorists.

How Canadian courts will determine exceptions is not known. They may approve of deportation or extradition to face death or torture by deferring to a minister's judgment that it would be constitutional to make an exception from the general legal rule. This approach ignores the fact that ministers are not independent courts: they act in their own cause. They do not want to be the person thought responsible for releasing a deadly terrorist. A court may also approve of an exception from the general legal rule because it is the pragmatic and realistic thing to do, given the public outrage and fear that may follow a judicial decision allowing a dangerous terrorist to go free. In my view, courts should not defer to a minister's interpretation of what constitutes an "exceptional case" under the Charter and they should not hold themselves accountable to the public outrage that would greet an unpopular decision that even a notorious terrorist cannot legally be deported to face torture or death. If exceptions to legal rules have to be made in extreme cases, the exceptions should be made the way the British have made them since September 11. The legislature should be prepared to take democratic responsibility for temporarily overriding the law.[69] The courts should never approve of torture. They are the only institution that can be relied upon to uphold legal principles and protect unpopular minorities in times of public alarm and agitation.

The *Suresh* decision sends out even more ambivalent signals than *Burns and Rafay* about the Court's relation with government. Consistent with the new trend towards saving possibly unconstitutional law through interpretation, the Court upholds the government's power to deport people because of legislatively undefined acts of "terrorism." With reference to the events of September 11, the Court also interpreted threats to the security of Canada in a broad fashion that can include "distant events that indirectly have a real possibility of harming Canadian security."[70] Perhaps most important, the Court indicated that the minister of immigration's discretion to deport and to decide whether a refugee faces a substantial risk of torture should be reversed only if it was exercised in a patently unreasonable manner. Indeed, in the companion case of *Ahani*, the Court provided no relief because it concluded that the minister of immigration had not acted in a patently unreasonable manner in deciding that a refugee from Iran was a security risk to Canada and that this person would face a minimal risk of harm if returned to Iran. Because of the minister's findings, Ahani was not even entitled to procedural protections.[71] The courts subsequently approved his removal, even though the United Nations Human Rights Committee had asked that Ahani be allowed to remain in Canada until it considered his case. Noting that Ahani had already been in jail for nine years on the basis of the minister's certificate designating him a security risk, only one judge in dissent would have kept Ahani in Canada until the United Nations considered his case. The dissenting judge warned: "The courts in their commendable efforts to support the government's defence of this and other countries from terrorism must bear in mind that 'the history of liberty has largely been the history of observance of procedural safeguards.'"[72]

Suresh is a Janus-faced decision. Its willingness to defer to executive actions that are not patently unreasonable and its willingness to contemplate that deportation to face torture might be constitutional in an exceptional case stand in tension with its bolder and anti-majoritarian declaration under the Charter that it is, as a general rule, unacceptable to deport people to face torture. The willingness of the Court in *Suresh* to defer to the executive in the war against terrorism is underlined by its decision to endorse a decision in the immediate aftermath of September 11 by an English Law Lord. In his postscript, Lord Hoffman recognized not only the special information and expertise that the executive has in security matters but the more troubling idea that security decisions "require a legitimacy which can be conferred only by entrusting them to persons responsible to the community through the democratic process. If the people are to accept the consequences of such decisions, they must be made by persons whom the people have elected and whom they can remove."[73] Lord Hoffman's remarks ignore the fact that elected officials have an incentive to err on the side of security, especially if the people who are detained and deported are unpopular minorities with no political clout. His implicit idea of the democratic illegitimacy of judicial action seems strange in the Canadian context, in which the judiciary is clearly given an important democratic role in our Constitution. His statement also suggests that the Court may, sometime in the future, defer to ministers who insist that they have an exceptional case in which it would be dangerous not to extradite or deport a terrorist to face death or torture. Rather than endorse Lord Hoffman's troubling dicta deferring to the executive as more democratically legitimate than the judiciary, the Supreme Court would have been better to endorse the approach taken by Chief Justice Roy McMurtry, who, as an elected attorney general, had helped create the Charter. McMurtry cheerfully admitted at the 2002 opening of the Ontario courts that "courts are not necessarily democratic institutions as they are not bound by the majority of public opinion," but then argued that it is "not democracy ... when the majority takes away the rights of a minority."[74] McMurtry appreciated the new anti-majoritarian role of the courts much better than Lord Hoffman.[75]

The anti-majoritarian role of the courts is more necessary than ever after September 11. This is especially true in a security context, where certain minorities may be subject to stereotyped assumptions of danger and both the legislature and the executive are prepared to sacrifice rights in the hope of increased security. Unfortunately, it is unclear whether the deference to the executive that characterized the administrative law parts of *Suresh* will not in some cases also influence the Court's approach to *Charter* review and, in particular, its willingness to find exceptions to the general constitutional principle that Canada should not send terrorists to face torture or the death penalty. To be sure, the Court deserves credit for not allowing the emotive aspects of either *Burns and Rafay* or *Suresh* to sway its judgments and for insisting in those cases that suspected murderers and terrorists not be sent away to face death and torture. The Court stood up for important values that were ignored in the executive and legislative process. Nevertheless, the Court's permanent invitation to governments to attempt to persuade it to make exceptions from its principled legal rules will present a continued challenge for judges. After September 11, even the independent judiciary will have to make special efforts to avoid the temptation of being more deferential towards the government and taking a realistic and pragmatic approach to claims of injustice whenever the government claims it is acting in the name of national security.

THE FEDERAL COURT

The Supreme Court will eventually find itself in the hot seat again in the anti-terrorism context, but it is the Federal Court that is now in the front lines. Even before Bill c-36, the Federal Court, as a court created to resolve disputes involving federal laws and agencies, exercised jurisdiction over security-related immigration matters and the disclosure of sensitive information in court proceedings. Under the new *Anti-terrorism Act*, it is vested with extensive and at times exclusive duties of judicial review with respect to decisions such as the federal Cabinet's listing of an organization as a terrorist group, the deprivation of its charitable status, the forfeiture of its property, and the review of the federal attorney general's power to prohibit the disclosure of information in court proceedings. The Federal Court is primarily an administrative law court and it may well approach its new duties through the lens of the deferential standard of patent unreasonableness used in *Suresh* and other cases. The federal government is a formidable repeat player that is almost always a party to litigation in the Federal Court. Bill c-36 recognizes the increased responsibilities of the Federal Court by providing for the appointment of more judges to it.[76] The prospect of more post-September 11 appointments to the Federal Court raises the difficult issues of the lack of transparency in the federal judicial appointment process[77] and even "the possibility of court-packing."[78] The ultimate guarantee will be the personal integrity of each judge, but the institutional position of the Federal Court cannot be ignored.

Some provisions in Bill c-36 place the judges of the Federal Court in a difficult position. For example, the solicitor general is empowered to make *ex parte* motions (motions with only the government and not its opponent present) to require the judge in a private hearing to consider information "obtained in confidence from a government, an institution or an agency of a foreign state" or from organizations of foreign states. The judge can use information obtained, for instance, from the Central Intelligence Agency in determining the reasonableness of the Cabinet's decision to list a group as terrorist, but only if the judge decides not even to summarize the information for the listed entity.[79] If the judge declines the invitation to make the hearing something of a Kaflkaesque charade, however, and insists that the information must at least be summarized for the listed entity, the solicitor general can simply pull the information, with the judge being instructed by the act not to consider it. This procedure could result in a decision to uphold the listing of a group as terrorist without the disclosure of even a summary of the evidence to the listed entity. Secret communications between the federal government and the Federal Court without the other side being present are antithetical to the role of the independent courts. Indeed, the Supreme Court in *Tobiass v. Canada* held that such off-the-record and secret communications between the government and the Federal Court about delays in rendering judgment on the deportation of a suspected war criminal violated judicial independence:

First, as a general rule of conduct, counsel for one party should not discuss a particular case with a judge except with the knowledge and preferably with the participation of counsel for the other parties to the case. ...

Second, and again as a general rule, a judge should not accede to the demands of one party without giving counsel for the other parties a chance to present their views.[80]

In the interests of assuring that intelligence gathered by other nations can both remain secret and also influence a judge's decision to uphold the listing of an entity as a terrorist group, the *Anti-terrorism Act* transgresses these principles of judicial independence. It requires judges of the very Court that was rightly criticized for entertaining *ex parte* communications from the federal government in the past to consider similar communications again from the federal government. The only difference is that the communications are specifically authorized in the new anti-terrorism law, and the Federal Court has no choice but to consider the government's secret pleas.

The Federal Court does not appear to be happy with its enhanced role under the *Anti-terrorism Act*. One of its longest-serving and most respected judges, James Hugessen, gave an extraordinary speech on the subject at a conference examining the effects of September 11 on Canadian law and democracy. He indicated that the judges of the court had discussed the matter and he would not issue the usual disclaimer that he was only speaking for himself. He expressed the judges' concerns about their role under national security legislation in the strongest of terms: "We hate hearing only one party. We hate having to decide what, if any, sensitive material can or should be conveyed to the other party." Without the benefits of an adversary system in which both sides were represented, he stressed that judges have great difficulty doing their jobs. "We do not like this process of ... having to try for ourselves to see how the witnesses that appear before us ought to be cross-examined ... If you have a case that is only being presented on one side, you are not going to get a good case." He suggested that a system be created that enabled lawyers with appropriate security clearances to have full access to the sensitive information and to challenge the federal government's case. Without such a system, Judge Hugessen candidly confessed, "I sometimes feel a little bit like a fig leaf."[81] Something is quite wrong with the state of the law when a judge feels compelled to make such statements. Nevertheless, the Supreme Court has recently indicated that, in the context of information that could harm national security or the confidence of foreign governments, Charter requirements of procedural fairness can still be satisfied by the Federal Court hearing the government's case without the other side being present.[82]

The *Anti-terrorism Act* also forces the Federal Court, an administrative law court, into the criminal trial process. The attorney general of Canada is given the power effectively to override a trial judge's decision to require the disclosure of information to the accused on the basis that the information was obtained in confidence from a foreign government or service or for the purpose of protecting national defence or national security.[83] This provision has aptly been described as "a mini-notwithstanding clause,"[84] except that a certificate lasts fifteen years, not the five years of an explicit legislative override of Charter rights, and there is no requirement of the transparency of legislation. The party adversely affected by the attorney general's certificate has a right to appeal the attorney general's decision – not to the trial judge who knows about the case, but to a single judge of the Federal Court of Appeal. This appeal provision was added only after lawyers and the privacy and information commissioners loudly complained that their jobs would be made impossible by unreviewable security certificates. Nevertheless, the appeal provision added to the act is extremely weak. The reviewing judge of the Federal Court is able to overturn the attorney general's decision only if the information blocked from the accused is not information from foreign sources or information about national defence or security. This is a superficial form of judicial review. The reviewing judge is not allowed to balance the need for disclosure to ensure a fair trial against the harm of disclosure to international relations or national defence or security, as recommended by the special Senate Committee.[85] The reviewing judge also cannot edit the information so that suspected terrorists can have access to information helpful to their defence, but not information helpful to their terrorist activities. Finally, the Supreme Court is deprived of a say on this matter because the act specifically precludes a further appeal from the single Federal Court judge.

In most cases, the single judge of the Federal Court will uphold the attorney general's certificate because of the very limited grounds of review. But that decision does not end this tortuous dialogue. The matter may find itself back before the trial judge who originally ordered disclosure. That judge then has the power under the law to "make any order that he or she considers appropriate in the circumstances to protect the right of the accused to a fair trial."[86] The trial judge cannot go behind the security certificate, so the range of remedies available to protect the accused will be limited. If a fair trial is impossible without access to the information covered by the attorney's general certificate, this remedy should be a stay of proceedings. This drastic remedy will end the case against the accused terrorist and allow that person to go free.[87] In recent years, however, the courts have been very cautious about granting such drastic remedies. For example, they refused to stay proceedings against Tobiass because the improper communications between the federal government and the Federal Court, without the other side being present, did not make a fair trial impossible. The trial judge may well conclude that the case can still go forward and rely on the idea that the accused can still have a fair trial, albeit not the fairest possible trial.

The dialogue promoted by the *Anti-terrorism Act* between the courts and the attorney general over access to sensitive information is a dangerous game of constitutional chicken. Trial judges can assert the last word, but only if they are prepared to end the case and allow an accused terrorist to walk.[88] Parliament could have provided for a better and more direct dialogue to occur, without the Federal Court having to hear appeals from disclosure orders of trial judges. The attorney general could have been required to justify the case for non-disclosure directly to the court that had ordered disclosure. The trial court would be in the best position to strike the appropriate balance between the need for security and the need for disclosure, and to this end could have devised less drastic remedies that involve editing or summarizing the information for the applicant, closing the court, or even appointing a lawyer with appropriate security clearances to challenge the government's case. As matters stand, there is now a right to appeal to the Federal Court that is so limited as to be meaningless. The government has acted as if it does not trust trial judges to strike the appropriate balance between fair trial rights and national security.

TRIAL COURTS

The *Anti-terrorism Act* places trial judges in a difficult position by vesting them with responsibility for administering the new concepts of preventive arrests and investigative hearings. In both cases, the trial judges will know that the attorney general has already consented to the use of these extraordinary powers. Provincial court judges are required to determine whether there are reasonable grounds to suspect that an arrest or a recognizance with conditions is necessary to prevent the carrying out of any activity that falls within the broad definition of terrorism. The judge is also given the discretion to adjourn hearings for up to forty-eight hours, thus possibly extending the period of preventive arrest on suspicion to a maximum of seventy-two hours.[89] The new law unfortunately provides no guidance for this crucial discretionary decision. It is also not clear whether the suspect will be detained in a detention centre or a police lock-up, where the police may have continual access to the suspect.[90] Trial judges will have to make discretionary decisions about how long suspected terrorists will be subject to preventive arrests.

If satisfied that the police officer has reasonable grounds to suspect that the arrestee will engage in terrorism, the judge will have to decide whether to impose a recognizance. A decision to impose such a "peace bond for terrorists" will likely be widely publicized and will stigmatize a person as a suspected terrorist.[91] A person subject to such a peace bond may well be shunned by financial institutions, landlords, and other service providers who legitimately fear prosecutions for financing or facilitating terrorism. The judge will also have to decide what conditions to impose as part of the peace bond. Some conditions, such as prohibitions on the possession of firearms and explosives, may be uncontroversial, but others may affect the political, economic, or religious life of a person who, at the end of the day, has been established only as a reasonable suspect to engage in terrorist activities. Finally, if the arrestee does not cooperate and refuses to enter into the peace bond or breaches its conditions, the judge may jail the terrorist suspect. The suspected terrorist will be jailed for defying state authority rather than for a terrorist crime. It will be the provincial judiciary that has to administer the new concepts of preventive arrests on suspicion.

Under the investigative hearing provisions, provincial or superior court judges have to decide whether to order a person to disclose information about a terrorism offence. The judge is empowered to decide objections on the grounds of laws relating to non-disclosure of information or privilege, but otherwise must allow the attorney general to question a person and require the production of things, even though the person objects on grounds of self-incrimination. If the person refuses to talk or cooperate at the investigative hearing, the judge must decide what to do. Again, the new law provides no guidance for this crucial discretionary decision. Options include the immediate use of contempt powers or subsequent prosecutions for disobeying a court order. Judges presiding at investigative hearings may find themselves echoing the words of Supreme Court Justice Robert Taschereau, who, at the 1946 royal commission into the Gouzenko spy affair, warned reluctant witnesses (who correctly feared they would subsequently face spying charges) that "we have the power to compel you to speak ... we have the power to punish you if you do not answer."[92]

David Paciocco has made an interesting argument that the new investigative hearing provisions offend written and unwritten principles of judicial independence because they place judges in the "unflattering" and "ill-suited" role of having their judicial powers "conscripted by the government for coercive purposes."[93] Given that the government will argue that most targets of investigative hearings are only witnesses, not the accused, and that the judge retains a discretion to decide whether and how to order the accused to talk, I am not confident about the success of a Charter challenge to the investigative hearings provision. Nevertheless, I fully agree with Professor Paciocco that the image of criminal trial judges presiding at modern-day star chambers in which people are required to incriminate themselves is not a happy one.

The provisions in the *Anti-terrorism Act* for mandatory consecutive sentencing in terrorist offences and for deeming the commission of terrorist activities as an aggravating factor in sentencing follow recent trends in imposing more mandatory terms and statutory direction for judges at sentencing. These developments are based on a mistrust of the judiciary and on a desire to score political points by proclaiming as aggravating factors those the courts already consider as reasons to increase an offender's sentence.

There was no evidence that, without legislative direction, trial judges would have been lenient with convicted terrorists. In the past, the courts have stressed the need to deter and denounce terrorist crimes with stiff penalties. For example, the leader of the "Direct Action" group that bombed Litton Systems in Toronto in 1982 received a sentence of life imprisonment. In the same case, however, the court also recognized that factors such as the youth of the accused, whether they were a leader or a follower, and whether they had remorse should still be considered as mitigating factors. It reduced the sentence of the youngest and most remorseful member of the group to fifteen years' imprisonment.[94] The new provision for mandatory consecutive sentences for terrorism offences could fetter such uses of sentencing discretion, especially if combined with existing mandatory sentences for firearms-related offences. Mandatory consecutive sentences violate general Canadian sentencing principles and could produce terms exceeding the expected life span of the accused. Such American-style super sentences may seem unobjectionable if applied against sophisticated international "super-terrorists" intent on producing the death and destruction seen in New York on September 11, 2001, or in Bali on October 12, 2002. Nevertheless, mandatory consecutive sentences could result in excessive punishment if applied to misguided and now remorseful young people who did not recognize the full implications of their actions when they committed multiple crimes of facilitating, financing, or committing acts of terrorism.

CONCLUSION

Judges from the Supreme Court to the provincial court will feel the impact of the new anti-terrorism measures, along with governmental and public expectations that the balance between security and freedom has shifted since September 11. The role of the independent judiciary becomes both more important and more unpopular in times of perceived crisis. The new responsibilities of administering and determining the constitutionality of the *Anti-terrorism Act* come at a time when Canadian courts are becoming more concerned with issues of judicial independence. All judges should take special care to demonstrate their independence from the governments that will approve the use of the many new anti-terrorism powers and offences. Unfortunately, some of the provisions of the new law strain judicial independence by allowing governments to attempt to influence the court without the other side being present. The new law also requires judges to make difficult decisions about how to compel answers from reluctant people at investigative hearings and whether to extend periods of preventive arrests.

The challenges of September 11 come on the heels of growing criticisms in some quarters that our courts are soft on crime and on refugee applicants, captured by minority interests, and too eager to make decisions best left to the elected branches of government.[95] Challenges to new anti-terrorism measures could engage all elements of these critiques of judicial activism. Judges will have to defend the rights of persons accused of terrorism who may also be members of unpopular minorities. They should do so with confidence that they have a legitimate and important role in Canadian democracy. They need not blindly defer to what the legislature and the executive believe is necessary for security. Even the boldest of judicial rulings under the

Charter need not necessarily be the last word if the legislature is prepared to justify its decision to limit or even override rights as interpreted by the Court. The challenges of September 11 for the judiciary are great, but similar to those faced in the immediate past.

In cases such as *Burns and Rafay* and *Suresh*, the Supreme Court has demonstrated that the independent courts can play an important role in reminding us of our best standards of decency and evolving standards of international law, precisely when we are most likely to ignore or finesse them. The Court has also reminded us of the sobering reality that people can be wrongly convicted of terrorism. The independent courts can play a valuable role in reminding us about the rights of the unpopular and the despised, but we must not assume that the courts alone will ensure just and tolerant anti-terrorism policies. Even cases such as *Burns and Rafay* and *Suresh* confirm the pattern of the Charter in simultaneously affirming and limiting rights. They leave open the possibility that the courts may not upset some ministerial decisions to send notorious terrorists to other countries to face torture or the death penalty. In undefined "exceptional" cases, Canadian courts could even accept Dershowitz's argument that torture, or least deportation to face torture in another country, might be constitutional. The British, to their credit, have accepted judicial decisions that deportation to face torture is always wrong and illegal. The courts in Britain have not, however, had the last word, as legislation has been enacted that overrides fair trial rights and allows terrorists who cannot be deported to be indefinitely detained. The British people will have an opportunity to reconsider whether they are prepared to derogate from fair trial rights to achieve this result. Should Canadian courts accept that, in an exceptional case, deportation or extradition to face torture or death is consistent with the Charter, the Canadian people will not be able to reconsider such a decision. Constitutional justice in Canada will have been permanently tarnished.

The ambiguous structure of the Charter, as well as recent more deferential trends in Charter jurisprudence, makes it unlikely that the courts will strike down major parts of the *Anti-terrorism Act*. Even investigative hearings, preventive arrests, and secret government evidence not revealed to the other side are likely Charter proof. These objectionable features of the *Anti-terrorism Act* are probably more likely to be scrapped at the three-year parliamentary review of the act than by a Charter decision. Whether this cancellation occurs will depend in part on the strength of Canadian democracy – a topic to which we now turn.

5

The Challenges of Preserving Canadian Democracy

George Grant worried that the collapse of a distinctive Canada would produce a homogenous public debate dominated by a narrow range of American voices.[1] The concentrated ownership of Canada's media and the collective shock at the terrible events that had occurred so close to Canada on September 11 created some danger that the Canadian media would speak as one and not reflect a full and vigorous debate about the causes of terrorism and Canada's appropriate response. Yet the debate in Canada in the months following September 11 seemed both indigenous to Canada and more spirited and diverse than the comparable American debate. This difference was certainly true with respect to the *Patriot Act*, which was wrapped in American nationalism and enacted more quickly and with much less opposition in the legislature and in civil society than Bill c-36. As Ronald Dworkin observed, the American "government's dubious laws, practices, and proposals have provoked surprisingly little protest in America. Even some groups that traditionally champion civil rights have, with surprisingly few reservations, supported the government's hard line ... [I]t is politically difficult for elected officials to criticize or oppose hugely popular government policies. John Ashcroft [the attorney general of the United States] has already told us that those who oppose his policies provide aid and comfort to the terrorists."[2]

The reaction in Canada was quite different. As we saw in chapter 3, opposition parties, independent officers of Parliament, and even some governmental backbenchers and Cabinet ministers all voiced concerns about some aspects of Bill c-36. The presence of conservative and socialist strands in Canada's political culture meant that there were a number of parties in Parliament that were prepared to contest the government's claims that Bill C-36 was necessary to prevent terrorism and that it respected human rights. The opposition parties also protested the government's use of closure and party discipline to enact the law. The presence of an elected party committed to the peaceful and democratic separation of Quebec from Canada also meant that the government's anti-terrorism policies were debated with an awareness of the danger of conflating terrorism with democratic self-determination – an awareness that is, unfortunately, not present in many other parts of the world.

Parliamentary committees listened to dissenting academics and civil society groups that would have had great trouble being heard in the American media, let alone in its legislative committees. Other than a few cases that are noteworthy because they are exceptions, Canadians who voiced concerns about the government's anti-terrorism efforts were not criticized as disloyal or unpatriotic. The issue of whether Canadians were anti-American became a hot political topic, but the sense of difference that many Canadians feel in relation to Americans also provided some perspective in which to place September 11 into a larger context. September 11 stimulated a robust debate in Canada about the causes and consequences of September 11 and Canada's relation with the United States.

THE PRESS

The day after September 11, the *Globe and Mail* published a long article by Thomas Homer-Dixon warning that the greatest danger was overreacting to the attacks. It was necessary to address the "roots of this madness," including the underlying disparities of wealth in the world. He also argued that "because the 'enemy' in this case is so diffuse and indeterminate, it would be easy to turn against groups and people within our societies – against anybody who looks different, who expresses opinions that vary from the norm, or who has been associated, at one time or another, with suspect people or causes."[3] NDP leader Alexa McDonough argued for a "commitment to pursuing peaceful solutions to the tensions and hostilities that breed such mindless violence." Her remarks won her "the uncontested award for the dumbest statement of a tragic day" from *Globe and Mail* columnist Jeffrey Simpson.[4] McDonough, however, continued to oppose Canadian participation in the war in Afghanistan on the basis that she had "grave reservations about a coalition of countries being the judge, jury and executioner."[5] This stand cost her politically both nationally and in her home riding, which contained a large military base, but the Canadian multi-party system and the tory and socialist touches in Canadian political culture that Grant celebrated allowed such concerns to be voiced. It would be difficult to imagine either of the two national parties in the United States taking such an internationalist and pacifist stance.

Soon after September 11, the *Globe and Mail* also published a column by anti-globalization activist Naomi Klein posing the question: "Did US foreign policy create the condition" for "a war not so much on US imperialism, but on perceived US imperviousness."[6] To be sure, these comments were rebutted on the pages of the *Globe* by others who argued that the "root cause" approach effectively excused terrorism.[7] Still, it was healthy for democracy that Canada's self-proclaimed national newspaper featured a wide range of debate about the causes and consequences of September 11, even in the immediate aftermath of the tragedy. A little more than a week after the attacks, Haroon Siddiqui wrote in the *Toronto Star* that the terrorist attacks were in part related to "American complicity in injustice, lethal and measurable on several fronts," including the Middle East, Afghanistan, and Iraq. He argued that "a broad spectrum of the Canadian middle class, including academics, professionals and business people, is coming to the view that what America needs, beyond any tactical strikes or smart bombs it might deploy, is a more humane and even-handed approach to the world."[8] As we will see, the arguments made by Homer-Dixon, Klein, and Siddiqui were criticized by others as both anti-American and naïve. Nevertheless, in the days after September 11, the Canadian press[9] presented a fairly broad range of perspectives. There were no reports of Canadians in the media losing their jobs for criticisms of the war against terrorism, as there were in the United States.[10] The Canadian media, unlike the American media, were not measured on whether they were patriotic in their coverage, and they seemed to avoid some of the self-imposed restrictions that the American media placed on themselves.[11]

THE UNIVERSITIES

Canadian academics did not hesitate to criticize the federal government's proposed *Anti-terrorism Act*. A book entitled *The Security of Freedom: Essays on Canada's Anti-terrorism Bill*[12] was published in November 2001 after a conference at the University of Toronto's

Faculty of Law that featured many critics of Bill c-36 and some defenders, including senior officials from the Department of Justice. It is difficult to believe that senior American justice officials in the midst of defending the *Patriot Act* would have taken the time to listen to so many professors complain about their bill. Most of the essays in the book were highly critical of Bill c-36, especially its potential to define some illegal strikes and protests as terrorism and its introduction as permanent, not emergency, legislation. The tone of much of the book is unapologetically critical of the anti-terrorism bill as it was originally introduced. It is useful to compare this Canadian book to a special issue of the *Harvard Journal on Law and Public Policy*, which also featured essays by academics on legal responses to September 11. Even though it was published in 2002 when some of the emotional impact of September 11 had dissipated, the Harvard volume has a strikingly different tone from the University of Toronto volume. The collection starts with the text of President Bush's remarks at the National Cathedral on September 14, 2002, and his address to Congress six days later. Most of the essays express support for American anti-terrorism efforts, including the use of military tribunals to try those captured in Afghanistan. It features arguments by prominent law professors about the importance of patriotism, and a suggestion by Cass Sunstein, a renowned liberal academic from the University of Chicago, that a good strategy to prevent terrorism "is to prevent the rise of enclaves of like-minded people."[13] Only a minority of the essays are critical of the government's anti-terrorism efforts.[14]

The reactions of American academics were monitored after September 11 by the American Council of Trustees and Alumni. It published a report of 115 instances in which academics were, in their view, "distinctly equivocal and often blaming American itself" for September 11. The council included Lynn Cheney, wife of the American vice president. It listed with specific attributions statements that would have seemed mild or innocuous in the Canadian context. The presumptively unpatriotic statements by American academics included a statement by a Princeton dean to think about the treatment of Japanese-Americans during the Second World War and a statement at Harvard Law School that there should be an attempt to "build bridges and relationships, not simply bombs and walls."[15] Canadian academics made much more critical statements without fear of their patriotism being questioned or being listed by a self-appointed censorious group of university trustees and alumnae. One Canadian academic, however, did feel adverse consequences for criticizing American policy in the wake of September 11.

The Thobani Affair

University of British Columbia professor Sunera Thobani made headlines by arguing at a conference that "from Chile to El Salvador to Nicarugua to Iraq, the path of U.S. foreign policy is soaked in blood ... And other countries of the West, including shamefully Canada, cannot line up fast enough behind it. All want to sign up now as Americans and I think it is the responsibility of the women's movement in this country to stop that, to fight against it ... Pursuing American corporate interest should not be Canada's national interest." She added: "The American nation that Bush is invoking is a people which is bloodthirsty, vengeful and calling for blood."[16] Thobani's criticisms went beyond those that Haroon Siddiqui had published in the *Toronto Star* in their use of the oft-quoted rhetoric that American policy was "bloodthirsty" and "soaked in blood." The phrases may have been extreme and distasteful, especially so soon after September 11, but freedom of expression is most needed to protect those who may be widely perceived as going over the line.

Many people concluded that Thobani had gone way over the line. The premier of British Columbia, Gordon Campbell, denounced her comments as "hateful." Prime Minister Chrétien told Parliament that she had made "a terrible speech that we condemn 100 per cent."[17] The official opposition nevertheless argued that the government was complicit in Thobani's actions because of federal funding of the conference and the presence of Hedy Fry, secretary of state for the status of women and multiculturalism, on the same panel. The police revealed that they were investigating whether Thobani should be charged with wilfully promoting hatred against Americans. An RCMP hate crime unit officer offered the unusual explanation that "we have a complaint against someone who is obviously from a visible minority, whom the complainant feels is promoting hate. Normally, people think it's a white supremacist or Caucasians, promoting hate against visible minorities ... We want to get ... the message out that its wrong."[18] These police comments about an ongoing police investigation were improper and unfair to Thobani. They also reflected the public obsession with Thobani's colour and demonstrated little awareness of the law, which restricted hate propaganda to statements made about a group distinguished "by colour, race, religion or ethnic origin."[19] A police investigation of an academic for hate propaganda because of harsh criticisms of American foreign policy was a direct chill on freedom of expression.

In an open democracy, it was only to be expected that Thobani's provocative comments would be greeted with strongly worded disagreement. Her comments and rebuttals of her comments contributed to an important debate about the causes of September 11 and American foreign policy. Nevertheless, a good deal of the criticism was unfairly personal, because it focused on Thobani's status as an immigrant to Canada. The *Vancouver Sun* asked: "Why is she here, in the West she apparently loathes?" and the *Victoria Times Colonist* commented: "Canada welcomed her into this country, then gave her a stage and money. In return, she has repeatedly criticized our way of life and directed sheer hate at our friends."[20] Others in the media argued that Thobani's speech was a symptom of Canada's undue tolerance of dissent and multiculturalism. For *National Post* columnist Christie Blatchford, the conference at which Thobani spoke was "as much a product of the federal Liberal Party as multiculturalism." The analogy was not meant as praise. Blatchford criticized Chrétien for devoting "about as much time in recent speeches to harshly condemning the handful of racist incidents that have occurred here since September 11 as to ruing the original sin" of the terrorist attacks.[21]

Despite the comments of the police, the premier, and the prime minister, Thobani's employer, the University of British Columbia, supported her right to make controversial comments. Its academic vice president told a news conference that freedom of speech was the "cornerstone of university culture. This is the stuff of democracy, a core value that our society seeks to protect in its struggle against terrorism." The university's strong support of freedom of speech in the face of criticisms from its provincial funder and corporate donors can be contrasted with the failure of some American universities to respect freedom of speech in the aftermath of September 11. The University of California at Los Angeles, for example, suspended librarian Jonnis Hargis for five days because of an email he sent, noting with respect to civilian deaths in the American bombing of Iraq: "We call it 'collateral damage' except when it happens to us. So who are the real terrorists anyway?" UCLA officials concluded that these comments "demonstrated a lack of sensitivity that went beyond incivility and constituted harassment."[22] Canadian universities took a more robust approach to academic freedom.

Although most mainstream media comments were highly critical of Thobani's speech, she also had her defenders. Both the conference organizers and the National Action Committee criticized the media's reaction to her speech. The *Ottawa Citizen* wrote an editorial criticizing the hate crime investigation. "Ms. Thobani has been criticized for her views; for her part, she provoked her intellectual foes into trying to articulate their values. All this is healthy. We believe her to be mistaken, but we are grateful that, mostly, Canada does not smother such opinions."[23] Thobani's lengthy response to the controversy was reported and posted on numerous web sites. Judy Rebick wrote in *Canadian Dimension* magazine that the reaction to Thobani's speech was "meant to put a chill on a growing anti-war movement" at a time when "public opinion in Canada is much more divided than in the United States."[24]

There was support for Rebick's claims that the public, like Thobani, saw a connection between American foreign policy and the September 11 attacks. A poll conducted in late September 2001, shortly before Thobani spoke, indicated that while 50 per cent of respondents believed that fanaticism and hatred against the United States were the most important causes of September 11, 33 per cent believed that US foreign policy was the most important cause. This belief was highest among younger people, with 43 per cent of those under twenty-five years of age and 37 per cent of those under sixty-five years of age believing that the most important cause of September 11 was the US foreign policy that Thobani had criticized.[25] Others made the point that those like Thobani who related September 11 to American foreign policy could not explain the fact that many of the terrorists were wealthy Saudis, and that the women who she claimed were the victims of "the West" were not treated better in non-Western regimes.[26] My point is not to argue whether "blowback" theories that relate September 11 to American foreign policy and "the West" are justified, but only to illustrate that they were a sometimes controversial part of the democratic debate in Canada about September 11.

THE CHRÉTIEN AFFAIR

Although he was critical of Thobani's speech, Prime Minister Chrétien received a taste of similar criticism for his remarks broadcast on the first year anniversary of the tragedy. He commented that September 11 made him think that "the Western world is getting too rich in relations to the poor world ... we're looked upon as being arrogant, self-satisfied, greedy and with no limits ... you cannot exercise your powers to the point of humiliation of the others."[27] Chrétien's remarks were made during the summer of 2002, while he was working on African development, but broadcast on the emotional one-year anniversary of September 11. They set off almost as much controversy as Thobani's comments in the immediate aftermath of September 11.

The leader of the official Opposition, Stephen Harper of the Canadian Alliance, argued that Chrétien should apologize both to the Americans and to the victims of September 11 for his "shameful" remarks. Former prime minister Brian Mulroney denounced Chrétien's words as "false, shocking, morally specious ... essentially the case the terrorists have tried to make." The *National Post* editorialized that "the accusation that the West is a colonial aggressor humiliating the Muslim world is an old theory – Osama bin Laden has advanced it many times in his various declarations of war. That Mr. Chrétien should draw lessons from September 11 that echo bin Laden's accusations in oblique terms is a disgrace." A daughter of one of the Canadian victims of the World Trade Center attack commented: "Both my Mom and I are appalled because basically he's saying that America deserved what happened on September 11 and that's not true – nobody deserved it – and I'm appalled that the prime minister said that ... I feel like writing a letter apologizing to the United States for what he said."[28]

The remarks of the Canadian prime minister did not go unnoticed in the United States. Bill O'Reilly, a commentator on the Fox network, stated that "Chrétien is a socialist who believes the West owes something to radical Muslims and to the rest of the world." An American Naval War College instructor writing an article in the *National Post* argued that Chrétien was "the hands-down winner of the race to see which Western leaders can say the most shameful and ludicrous things about 9/11." In his view, "Chrétien's attempt at neo-appeasement" reflected "Anti-Americanism" and marked "another stage in Canada's slide in international influence." A Canadian writing in the *Wall Street Journal* commented that "Mr. Chrétien could not resist an opportunity to vent his frustration about the U.S. and his alleged concern for the poor provided the perfect foil for his anti-Americanism. That he has chosen the plight of the poor is commendable. That he has linked them to terrorism is insulting and wrong." She added that Chrétien, like many Canadians, "like to portray themselves as more civilized and caring than Americans, yet they cannot imagine living without American capital markets, technology, investment and entertainment." Canadian columnist Robert Fulford raised similar concerns, noting that "Chrétien put it as only a Canadian could: [The Americans] lack niceness." With reference to the rebuilding of Germany and Japan after the Second World War, Fulford argued that "niceness has been a specialty of the Americans much more than the Canadians."[29] This incident was not the first time since September 11 that Fulford had raised concerns that Canadians were being anti-American.

As was the case with Thobani, not all the reactions to Chrétien's remarks were negative. Former prime minister Joe Clark commented that he had "read carefully the transcript of what [Chrétien] said with regard to the relations of poverty, extremism and terror. And I think it is beyond question that there is a direct relation between those phenomena and I think it was appropriate for the Prime Minister to say so."[30] Clark went on to criticize Chrétien for decreasing spending on foreign aid. As with Thobani's remarks, there was also some public support for the connections that Chrétien made between September 11 and the West's treatment of the developing world. A public opinion poll taken shortly before Chrétien made his comments revealed that 69 per cent of Canadian respondents thought that the United States bore "some responsibility" for September 11. These attitudes were in turn subject to criticisms for "blaming the victim," but they were not out of line with European opinion polls on responsibility for September 11.[31] My point again is not to argue that "blowback" or "poverty" explanations of terrorism are justified, but to point out that a large number of Canadians subscribed to them, only to find that a professor and then a prime minister were criticized for being anti-American when they voiced these views.

The criticisms of Chrétien's remarks as anti-American or as offering an excuse for terrorism were unfair. Whatever his problems with syntax, the prime minister chose his words carefully. As the Prime Minister's Press Office noted in a press release, "it was wrongly reported" that Chrétien "singled out the United States for responsibility for the terrorist attacks of September 11, 2001" when he pointed "to the need for all Western developed countries to reflect on the long-term consequences of the growing divide between rich and poor nations."[32] Chrétien's approach left his own government open to the criticisms that it had not done enough for the developing world, criticisms made by Joe Clark. Chrétien wisely did not comment on the motives of the September 11 terrorists or attempt to excuse their crimes. Rather, he tried to place the crimes committed on September 11 in a broader context, and he ended up being unfairly criticized as anti-American for doing so.

Chrétien's perceptions of how the West is perceived in other parts of the world is accurate. Moderate religious leaders in Indonesia, the world's largest Muslim country, echoed Chrétien's remarks a few days later when they raised concerns that "the war on terrorism will not be successful and will even spark new terrorism, if the U.S. and other Western states continue with their arrogant power." A month later these moderates would denounce the terrorist bombings in Bali, but, like Chrétien, they argued that "the core of the problem, namely global injustice," needs to be addressed as part of the war against terrorism.[33] It would be unfortunate if Canadians became oblivious to such non-Western perceptions for fear that anyone who expresses them is being anti-American. It would also be unfortunate if the political costs of placing terrorism in a larger political, social, and economic context became so great that all politicians could do was denounce the evil of terrorism and defend tougher criminal laws to catch and punish terrorists.

CANADIAN NATIONALISM
AND ANTI-AMERICANISM

A number of commentators cited both Thobani's and Chrétien's controversial comments as examples of anti-Americanism in Canadian nationalism. Robert Fulford argued that while "usually our anti-Americanism is less direct, more subtle" than in Thobani's speech, it was tied to larger and unhealthy currents of Canadian nationalism. He argued that "CBC radio has run earnest little pieces, written by assistant professors, who urge the Americans to restrain themselves and express the pious hope that this crisis will somehow enlighten our impetuous neighbours to the south and make them more mature. The reigning ethic of these commentaries is moral equivalence: Yes, terrorists are bad but we should remember the flaws of the Americans, too." He worried that while "the idea of dealing even-handedly with both sides holds a particular appeal for Canadians," it may make us unable to distinguish "friends from enemies."[34] He also voiced anger at Canada for "taking its place on the sidelines" in "the struggle between civilization and chaos."[35] At the same time, the Canadian penchant for being even handed did not look so bad when compared with President Bush's blunt demands that countries must be either for or against the United States in its war against terrorism and evil. The dichotomy of "friends" and "enemies" that Fulford found lacking in Canada would have prevented Canadians from appreciating the grievances that many in the world have against the United States and other wealthy nations.[36]

Before Thobani's remarks, Fulford had argued that "anti-Amercanism is not the game we have so often considered it. America is the most vital and progressive country in the world, the most significant source of democratic impulses, our best friend by far, and the place where much of our culture originates." American influence was "infinitely more beneficial" than harmful, and Canadians had to ask themselves: "Can we afford to share anything with those who base their politics on hating America?"[37] In follow-up columns, he wrote that his mail indicated there were many Americans living in Canada "who feel they are objects of contempt" but "believe they should not disclose their feelings, as if to do so would mark them as ungrateful immigrants."[38] The idea of Americans in Canada as the victims of Canadian chauvinism seemed a bit strained, especially given the demonstrations of sympathy and affection that so many Canadians displayed towards their American neighbours in the days following September 11. The people who were most at risk after September 11 of being labelled as ungrateful immigrants were those, such as Thobani, who harshly criticized the United States and those who were perceived to be of the same race or religion as the September 11 terrorists.

Nevertheless, Fulford had a point that Canadian nationalism must be based on something more constructive than anti-Americanism. Writing shortly after the events, Peter Gzowski took a lighter approach to the issue by reaffirming his commitment to be "as Canadian as possible under the circumstances." He still thought that "we've been bullied on everything from PEI potatoes to softwood lumber" by the United States, but he also recognized that he was an "American with a difference to be sure, but an American still," who shared not only the pain of the United States but many of its values.[39] Gzowski and Fulford both urged Canadians to build their identity on something more positive than anti-Americanism, and Gzowski in particular believed that Canadians were up to the task.

Others were not so optimistic and believed that September 11 would hasten an on-going process of continental integration. In a series of long articles published in the *National Post*, Professor Michael Bliss focused not only on the importance of keeping the border open but on the prospect of Canada adopting the American dollar and US tax, tariff, security, defence, and immigration policies.[40] A significant part of Bliss's argument was rooted in a sense that Canada had become an increasingly mediocre "northern suburb" of the United States.[41] J.L. Granatstein, another senior and respected historian, also made arguments that Canada had no realistic and sensible choice but to follow American interests on matters of foreign and military policy.[42] After September 11, Canada had to follow the Americans in order to avoid the economic disaster that would result from a closed border. In chapter 6, we will examine this idea that the economic imperative to keep the border open must be linked with other components of Canadian sovereignty.

There were also robust defences of Canadian nationalism and Canadian differences from American immigration, foreign, and military policy. Soon after September 11, former foreign affairs minister Lloyd Axworthy called for the jurisdiction of the International Criminal Court to be expanded to include terrorism against civilians.[43] He wrote other articles warning that Canada was risking sovereignty on a number of fronts by increased cooperation with the United States. He warned that Canadian participation in American military operations in Afghanistan damaged Canada's international reputation by "being complicit with Washington's flouting of the Geneva Conventions."[44] He criticized increased American opposition to the International Criminal Court, observing that the "disdain of the Americans is palpable; they'll resort to crude means to wreck any form of international architecture with which they disagree."[45] Axworthy urged Canada to follow its traditions of having a "distinctive voice," such as "the Pearson stand against the Vietnam war, the Trudeau mission on nuclear arms, the Turner campaign on free trade and the Chrétien opening to Cuba."[46] Canada's new foreign affairs minister, Bill Graham, made some efforts to pursue the type of agenda that Axworthy had observed was lacking in the immediate aftermath of September 11. Graham defended the International Criminal Court from American objections, voiced opposition to American plans for missile defence, refused to duplicate American lists of terrorist organizations, stressed the need for the United States to act through the United Nations on Iraq, protested American treatment of Canadians suspected of association with terrorists, and issued a travel advisory to protest American immigration policies that targeted Canadian citizens who had been born in Pakistan and Middle Eastern countries.

Later in 2002, however, Graham retreated on most fronts. The travel advisory was withdrawn, there was a new willingness to discuss missile defence with the Americans, Hezbollah was listed as a terrorist group, and there was even a suggestion that Canada could join the United States in a war against Iraq without UN approval.[47] It was not easy for those in power to be Canadian nationalists in the wake of September 11.

There was also significant support for the United States in Canada. Marcus Gee of the *Globe and Mail* wrote that "the United States has gone out of its way since the events of September 11 to seek the cooperation of other nations in the struggle against terrorism." He argued that Canadian fixation on American opposition to the International Criminal Court, the Koyoto Accord, and the ban on landmines ignored the fact that the United States had signed "scores of treaties on matters ranging from the protection of endangered species to the control of chemical weapons and the regulation of international trade."[48] Another *Globe* columnist followed with an argument that the American empire was a benign one, motivated by "an American desire to help people and to protect people ... there is no nation on earth better suited, for everyone's sake, to being the sole superpower."[49] David Frum of the *National Post* stated that Graham's protests against American policy would result only in "suspicion and disregard ... because in Washington attention and respect are earned." He predicted that Canada would not be allowed to sit with the United Kingdom and Australia "at the alliance's adult table, where the decisions are made," but "at the children's table where the noises won't disturb the grownups."[50]

The debate over the proper nature and continued viability of Canadian nationalism after September 11 was healthy and important. Those such as Michael Bliss who argued that continental integration was inevitable mirrored the arguments that George Grant had made in the wake of the Cuban Missile Crisis. Bliss's prediction of the death of Canadian nationalism and autonomy might possibly provoke a new Canadian nationalism, just as Grant's *Lament for a Nation* provoked a new wave of Canadian nationalism in the late 1960s. Many Canadians may find the idea that Canada must inevitably follow the Americans because of September 11 to be both unappealing and untenable. There is an obligation, however, to build a new nationalism on something more constructive than simply anti-Americanism. The new nationalists that Grant inspired in the 1960s built on his analysis to argue that Canada was different from the United States because of tory and socialist strains in our political culture, not because they did not like Americans. Although a new nationalism should be built on more than reflexive anti-Americanism, it will also have to be based on a confident sense that Canada is a better alternative to the United States. One danger, however, is that Canadian pride about our differences with the United States will be criticized in the post-September 11 environment as unacceptable anti-Americanism.

THE IMPORTANCE OF HISTORY
TO CANADIAN IDENTITY

To George Grant, the impossibility of Canada in the modern age was linked to the impossibility of true conservatism, by which he meant not the laissez-faire liberalism that passed as conservatism in the United States (and now in Canada), but a grown-up appreciation of tradition, history, and the fallibility of man. He argued: "As Canadians we attempted a ridiculous task of trying to build a conservative nation in the age of progress, on a continent we share with the most dynamic nation on earth. The current of modern history was against us."[51] Grant was right about the ahistorical nature of the American polity. Apart from the frequent and inaccurate analogy to the attack on Pearl Harbor, the American response to September 11 was stunningly present-minded. As we have seen, an unfortunate dean at Princeton was publicly chastised for asking Americans to remember the internment of Japanese-Americans during the Second World War. The group that listed this man and one hundred other professors as being soft on terrorism seemed oblivious to the similarities between their lists and those compiled during the McCarthy era.[52] The United States seems to be a nation that does not want to be reminded of its history. American amnesia about recent history prevented people from remembering that a toughening of criminal and immigration laws in the wake of the Oklahoma City bombing or the use of seventy-five cruise missiles to retaliate for the bombings of American embassies in East Africa did not prevent September 11, or that the United States had funded and armed bin Laden and his followers when they fought a Soviet invasion of Afghanistan and Saddam Hussein's Iraq in its war against Iran.

One possible sign of a continued conservative strain in Canadian politics was a willingness to situate the events of September 11 in the context of other historical events. The Canadian debate about September 11 was often thick with historical analogies, and Canadians debated recent anti-terrorism measures with a mature awareness of past failures. These blemishes included the inquisitorial royal commission into the Gouzenko spying affair, in which judges required spy suspects to incriminate themselves;[53] the wartime internment and deportation of Japanese Canadians after Pearl Harbor;[54] the refusal to accept Jewish refugees from Nazi Germany;[55] the invocation of the *War Measures Act* during the October Crisis;[56] and the illegal activities committed by the Royal Canadian Mounted Police in the name of national security after the murder of Pierre Laporte and the kidnapping of James Cross in October 1970.[57] Some supporters of the government's anti-terrorism policies were offended by the analogies because, as they accurately pointed out, current policies do not contain provisions that authorize equivalent actions. Nevertheless, it is important that we be conscious of past overreactions in times of crisis. Historical analogies can help to provide a sense of perspective in times of crisis and a counter-narrative to the powerful narrative of victimization and fear that resulted from September 11.

One of the distinguishing features between Canada and the United States may be a greater Canadian willingness to confront injustices of the past. A conservative country would remember its past, both its triumphs and its mistakes, and not view September 11 as an inexplicable blip in the march of progress. A conservative country in a progressive age would also be inclined to feel a little guilty about its past. Canada seems to be such a country, while the United States is most definitely not such a country. A concern about not repeating these injustices could be a sign of the mature and confident conservatism that Canadian nationalists such as George Grant hoped would help distinguish Canada from the United States.

DEMOCRACY AT HOME AND ABROAD

After the October Crisis of 1970, there was little terrorism in the name of a sovereign Quebec. The democratic movement for sovereignty continued and led to the election of the separatist Parti Québécois in 1976 and to two peaceful referendums on whether the people of Quebec wanted to separate from the rest of Canada. After Direct Action's bombing of the Litton Systems plant in Toronto in the early 1980s, those opposed to nuclear arms did not engage in continued terrorism. The peace movement engaged in more democratic means to stop Canada's involvement with nuclear arms, such as the unsuccessful Charter challenge to the testing of cruise missiles in Canada.[58] In both these cases, terrorist acts of violence resulting in death and injury were widely stigmatized and the perpetrators were punished on the basis that political motives do not excuse crimes. Nevertheless, those who shared the political beliefs of the terrorists were able to advance their cause in a peaceful manner. They were not stereotyped or stigmatized as terrorists. A free and open democracy cannot guarantee that terrorism will never occur, but it does allow those with strong political or religious beliefs an outlet to make their criticisms and advance their causes. A well-functioning democracy makes it easier for the criminal law to be applied robustly and for stigma to be attached to those who would resort to terrorist violence.

Canadian support for democracy abroad may also help prevent terrorism. Canada could have a special role to play in questioning American alliances with countries such as Pakistan and Saudi Arabia which do not respect democracy. Without the weight of the responsibility of global leadership and its consequent *realpolitik*, Canada is in a good position to question whether American support for repressive regimes may, in the long run, backfire. Without the weight of being the prime target of international terrorists, Canada can also counterbalance perceptions in Southeast Asia and elsewhere that the new war against terrorism means that countries will be judged in North America "not by the integrity of their elections or the justice of their courts, but by the vigor with which their army and police combat Al Qaeda."[59] Canada also has a unique experience to offer the world in the peaceful discussion of separatism, and it can provide important lessons for emerging democracies such as Sri Lanka and Indonesia in resisting the temptation of conflating terrorism with the legitimate cause of democratic self-determination.[60] Even in the wake of the Bali bombings, Canada and other countries should offer assistance for policing and judicial reforms in Indonesia. These reforms may enable Indonesia to resist reversion to internal security laws that allowed prolonged detention without trial and that have been used against potential terrorists in Singapore and Malaysia.[61] Although often supportive of the US government and sceptical of root-cause theories of terrorism, Marcus Gee has persuasively argued that, "in the war against terrorism, democracy is the best weapon ... [O]ne of the reasons that extremism thrives in some Islamic countries is that autocracies ... leave no outlet for peaceful dissent. With no way to express themselves democratically, frustrated people often turn to violence."[62] The building of democracies cannot guarantee that terrorism will not occur, but it creates both peaceful alternatives to terrorism and the moral legitimacy necessary to punish terrorism as an inexcusable crime.

CONCLUSION

The fact that opposition to various anti-terrorism measures has not been seen as "un-Canadian" or as an act of support for terrorism is a sign of strength, perspective, and maturity in Canadian democracy. Those in power must continue to set a democratic tone that does not tar critics with the deadly brush of disloyalty or sympathy for terrorists. They should avoid telling critics they must be "for us or against us" or appealing to a warlike solidarity, as President Bush has frequently done in the aftermath of September 11. Canadian openness to full debate and to seeing different sides of an issue, including non-Western perspectives, should not be dismissed as anti-American or as refusing to stand on the right side in a clash of civilizations. Rather, it should be celebrated as part of a free, democratic, and multicultural democracy that, almost alone in the world, has gone from separatist violence to democratic debate in legislatures, courtrooms, and referendums about the real possibility of peaceful separation. Those who urge greater integration of Canada into the United States may see Canada as a mediocre and powerless player that sits at the children's table of the world's economic and military powers, but many others continue to see Canada as a model for the world of a free, democratic, bilingual, and multicultural society. It is a matter of some irony that one of the few things that can be seen as un-Canadian is the idea of a loyalty oath or the notion that dissent from a national mission is unpatriotic.

One regrettable exception to a civil and open debate about terrorism occurred when Prime Minister Chrétien, in response to a question from Bloc Québécois leader Gilles Duceppe inquiring into the Canadian handover of prisoners without assurances of compliance with the Geneva Conventions, responded: "It was not imprudent for the government, as part of the war on terrorism, to side with the people who were attacked, and not to become defenders of terrorists, like the Bloc Québécois."[63] Chretien's atypical statement was widely criticized. Bill Blaikie of the NDP called it "a form of parliamentary McCarthyism," and others likened Chrétien's remarks to those made by American attorney general John Ashcroft, who suggested that those who raise "phantoms of lost liberty ... only aid terrorists ... [and] give ammunition to America's enemies."[64] Fortunately, Chrétien's remarks did not deter others, including some from the Liberal backbench, from questioning Canada's handover of the prisoners to American authorities. The Canadian multi-party system may facilitate a broader and more open debate about the causes and consequences of terrorism than has occurred in the United States. Significantly, however, Chrétien's heavy-handed attempts to portray an opposition party as defenders of terrorists played much better south of a border. In concluding an article entitled "Canada alters security policies to ease concerns of US," the *New York Times* reported that the prime minister "shot back" that the Bloc Québécois had "become defenders of terrorists for not backing the government 100 percent in a time of war."[65] A reaction that was interpreted in the United States as a sign of strength and patriotism was seen in Canada as a warning of a dangerous descent into McCarthyism and jingoistic nationalism.

It was healthy that September 11 prompted a full and open debate in the Canadian media about the causes and consequences of the terrorist attacks. This debate included those who related September 11 to American foreign policy and those who defended American policies. It was also appropriate that September 11 prompted a re-evaluation of the place of anti-Americanism in Canadian nationalism. Canada shares much with the United States, and Canadian nationalism should be built more on what Canadians consider to be good about Canada than what they consider to be bad about the United States. Nevertheless, comparisons, even invidious comparisons, with the United States are inevitable. It costs to be Canadian – and Canadians should not have to apologize for explaining why they still do not want to live in the United States. There is a danger that charges of anti-Americanism (or for that matter pro-Americanism) may be thrown around as a substitute for more productive debate on the merits of various immigration, military, and foreign policies that may be considered as a response to September 11. Despite the danger of the anti- or pro-Americanism labels being used as a substitute for thought, the debate about Canada's relation to the United States since September 11 has been vigorous, with prominent commentators arguing the case for continental integration and others arguing the case for continued Canadian nationalism. It is to the challenges of preserving Canadian sovereignty after September 11 that we now turn.

6

The Challenges of Preserving Canadian Sovereignty

Useful comparisons can be drawn between September 11 and the Cuban Missile Crisis of October 1962. Both events discredited a Canadian nationalism that appeared to be anti-American and led to a shift in Canadian policy towards closer cooperation with the Americans. Canada's acceptance of nuclear missiles after the missile crisis led George Grant to declare Canadian sovereignty and nationalism to be dead. Grant's pessimistic conclusion, penned thirty-eight years ago, makes interesting reading today:

Canada has ceased to be a nation, but its formal political existence will not end quickly. Our social and economic blending into empire will continue apace, but political union will probably be delayed. Some international catastrophe or great shift of power might speed up this process ... The dominant forces in the Republic do not need to incorporate us. A branch-plant satellite, which has shown in the past that it will not insist on any difficulties in foreign or defence policy, is a pleasant arrangement for one's northern frontier.[1]

The pleasant arrangement of even formal Canadian autonomy contemplated by Grant was not so pleasant after September 11. The television version of the *West Wing* worried about terrorists crossing into the United States from Canada, while the real West Wing authorized in the *Patriot Act* the tripling of its personnel on the "northern border."[2] If the Americans had made good on such a dramatic fortification of the northern perimeter of the American fortress, the Canadian economy could have been devastated.

The increase in economic integration since Grant's time placed enormous pressure on the Canadian government to cooperate with the

Americans in the aftermath of September 11. Americans were aware of Canadian economic vulnerability, with the *New York Times* reporting that Canada had coordinated its security policies with American policies because of "the economic shock that Canada suffered late last year when long border and port delays throttled Canadian exports to the United States, by far its largest customer."[3] Ironically, much of the Canadian cooperation had been directed not at the economic imperative of keeping the border open and secure but at more controversial issues of immigration, foreign, and military policy.

Polls taken after September 11 revealed that large numbers of Canadians were prepared to trade sovereignty for security. One poll suggested that 85 per cent of respondents wanted a joint North American security perimeter. The public also did not seem to distinguish between keeping the border open and secure and preserving a sovereign immigration policy, as 87 per cent of the sample said they wanted to eliminate "major differences between how the countries treat undocumented travellers, refugee claimants and illegal immigrants."[4] So soon after September 11, however, Canadians could not realize the full implications of adopting American immigration rules, which had yet to be tightened in response to September 11. Other polls suggested more support for Canadian sovereignty, with about half of the respondents believing that September 11 would have no adverse effect on Canadian independence. Indeed, a quarter of all respondents in this poll believed that September 11 would actually boost Canadian independence.[5] This last group had a point, as September 11 could further differentiate American and Canadian approaches to immigration, international law, and the use of force. As we will see, however, these people were overly optimistic about Canada's actual short-term performance on these matters.

KEEPING THE BORDER OPEN FOR BUSINESS

As waits at the border crossings spanned hours after September 11, many people expressed concern about the effects of these delays on the Canadian economy. Some lamented that the Americans might no longer be open to an association modelled on the European Union, as former prime minister Brian Mulroney had been recommending. Others, including Mulroney, argued that North American free trade now required Canada, the United States, and Mexico to agree to a new joint security perimeter.[6] Some corporate leaders were blunt about the tradeoffs they believed would have to be made between sovereignty and the economy. Four days after September 11, the chief executive officer of Canadian Pacific bluntly declared: "Canada will have to adopt U.S-style immigration policies if it doesn't want the border between the two countries to become almost impossible to cross ... We have to make North America secure from the outside. We're going to lose increasingly our sovereignty, but necessarily so."[7] The fact that these comments were made from the head of a company that was the first to link Canada together by rail from the Atlantic to the Pacific only underlined the threat of September 11 to Canadian sovereignty.

Despite public and corporate support for a joint security perimeter in which Canada would adopt American immigration standards, the Canadian government responded cautiously in the weeks following September 11. A week after the attack, Prime Minister Chrétien told the Liberal caucus that "the laws of Canada will be passed by the Parliament of Canada."[8] Foreign Affairs Minister John Manley echoed this sentiment, commenting that Canadians are not "prepared to say that Washington can dictate our policies for who comes into Canada." Tightening the borders "may do absolutely nothing to make America safer from terrorists, but it could throw a wrench into our economy, not to mention theirs."[9] In a speech in early November, Manley noted that "business people on both sides of the border are justifiably concerned about continued delays" at a border over "which some 200 million people cross each year, and some US$1.3 billion in commerce crosses each and every day. An enormous 87 percent of Canada's merchandise exports cross that border; 25 percent of all U.S. exports are sent north ... These are essential inputs to both our economies." Of course, the Canadian economy was much more vulnerable than the American economy to a fortress-type border.[10]

Canadian caution on matters affecting the border did not stop the Americans from acting unilaterally. The *Patriot Act* enacted in October 2001 provided for a tripling of border personnel on "the northern border." The United States was prepared to do whatever was required to protect its citizens. The implications of such actions for Canada, given its heavy reliance on trade with the United States, were obvious and frightening. Although the United States would seriously wound itself economically by closing or slowing down the border, such measures could kill the Canadian economy. Much of the almost C$2 billion that crossed the border every day was moved by trucks. Post-September 11 border delays disrupted "just in time" production schedules designed to increase efficiency. For example, 47,000 fewer cars were produced in September and October of 2001.[11] The year 2001 saw a modest decline in Canadian exports of goods and services to the United States compared with the year 2000, a decrease that can be attributed to the American economic slowdown as well as to September 11.

Fortunately for the Canadian economy, the tripling of American customs officials authorized by the *Patriot Act* did not materialize and the free flow of goods and people between Canada and the United States largely resumed. After an initial slump, the Canadian economy, including exports to the United States, rebounded. American border policy continues to favour Canada over Mexico, with twenty-six times the number of border patrol agents working the shorter southern border than the northern border. This proportion translates to one American border guard every 350 metres on the Mexican border, and one to every 25 kilometres on the Canadian border.[12] Nevertheless, the border remains vulnerable, and the Canadian economy could be seriously damaged should the Americans devote the same type of resources to their border with Canada as they do with Mexico.

A JOINT SECURITY PERIMETER AND VISA CONVERGENCE?

Framework agreements on border matters were not announced until December 2001. The first, a Canada-US Statement on Common Security Priorities, was announced in Windsor with US Attorney General John Ashcroft on December 3, 2001. It contemplated special joint border security patrols, more border guards, coordinated visa policies, and increased overseas immigration officers. Solicitor General Laurence MacAulay explained that "anything that helps U.S. security helps Canada," while Immigration Minister Elinor Caplan explained that the agreement would stop "queue-jumpers, criminals, those who pose security risks, or terrorists ... before they even get to Canada and the U.S."[13]

British Columbia premier Gordon Campbell praised the agreement for attempting to speed up cross-border trade, but Maude Barlow of the Council of Canadians criticized it on the basis that the Americans were asking Canada to "give over its visa, refugee and foreign policy independence." The most controversial part of this announcement was the proposed "safe third country" agreement that could drastically reduce refugee claims, but it was largely ignored in the media. Instead, the news cycle was stolen by Ashcroft's statement that 600 National

Guard troops would temporarily be used to augment the strength of American customs and immigration officials. Ashcroft explained that the National Guard would not function "as troops at all," but Stockwell Day, the leader of the opposition, complained that "Canadians now watch with dismay as the longest undefended border in modern history, a source of pride for over a century to Canadians, is being defended by hundreds of US troops."[14] Ironically, there were complaints on both sides of the border when the eventual withdrawal of the National Guard troops threatened to increase border delays. The economic imperative of keeping the border open should not be underestimated.

A day after the border agreement was announced, Caplan stated that Canada would require visas for eight more countries, including Zimbabwe and Grenada. She had told Ashcroft of the new requirements during their Windsor meeting, but stated that Ashcroft had not demanded them. She added: "I've talked before about visa convergence, but Canadian policy will be made in Canada." In December 2001, a majority of a parliamentary committee recommended full visa convergence to address any impact felt at the border because of different visa requirements. The NDP dissented on the basis that the recommendation failed "to acknowledge the significant differences in the historical development of Canada and the United States. Canada, for example, has close historic ties with Commonwealth and Francophone nations that differ from the American experience. Our relationship with specific countries may differ at times – Cuba is an obvious example. These relationships are reflected in our foreign policies and manifested in our visa requirements."[15] The border agreements did not require visa convergence, but only consultation on visa requirements.[16] Canada subsequently imposed visa requirements for visitors from Saudi Arabia and Malaysia. The Malaysian high commissioner argued that Canada was following the United States and adding to a "general anti-Muslim hysteria that is out there." Malaysia, like Canada, is a member of the Commonwealth, but also a country that some of the September 11 terrorists had visited. Still, new Canadian visa requirements fell short of full visa convergence with the United States. Unlike the United States, Canada did not impose restrictions on visas to men aged sixteen to forty-five years who come from twenty-six Muslim countries.

There were other border irritants between the two countries. Canada expressed concern about a Canadian, Michel Jalbert, who was detained in the United States for five weeks after he crossed the border to buy gas without going through customs.[17] It also protested the deportation to Syria of Maher Arar, a Syria-born man travelling on a Canadian passport, who had stopped in the United States on his way home to Canada.[18] Canada's immigration minister, Denis Coderre, called without success on New York senator Hillary Clinton to apologize for her comments about lax border policies. Coderre protested that "it's so easy to say that it's Canada's fault" and argued that Clinton's comments fed a "myth" of Canada as a safe haven for terrorists. Clinton's comments were made during a nationwide manhunt ordered by President Bush for five men of Middle Eastern or Pakistani origin who were thought to have illegally entered the United States from Canada, perhaps to commit acts of terrorism late in 2002. The manhunt was eventually abandoned amid reports that a man in Canadian custody, who had later been extradited to the United States, had lied to authorities.[19]

The biggest border controversy was over a new American system that authorized the fingerprinting, photographing, and registration of visitors and directed the attention of American customs officials to people born in Iran, Iraq, Libya, Sudan, Syria, Pakistan, Saudi Arabia, or Yemen, regardless of their citizenship.[20] Foreign Affairs Minister Bill Graham criticized this American policy as discriminatory to Canadian citizens born in those countries. Canada went so far as to issue a travel advisory that Canadian citizens born in those predominantly Muslim countries could "attract special attention from American immigration and security authorities" and should carefully consider whether they "should attempt to enter the United States for any reason, including transit to or from third countries."[21] By November 2002, 1400 Canadians had already been fingerprinted and photographed under the American national security entry-exit registration system. Some of them reported they had been intimidated by American officials who argued that "only people who have something to hide don't want to be fingerprinted." Others were denied entry into the United States for a time and complained they "were extremely humiliated, embarrassed and stripped of ... rights and freedom ... as a human being and also as a Canadian citizen."[22] Three Canadian computer scientists born in Iran and Iraq and working in California were jailed for five days after they reported for registration. One of them stated: "I couldn't have imagined that in the United States anybody would be treated like this ... Would I have walked in if I were a terrorist?" An American official explained the detention on the basis that "the INS came under very harsh criticism in the wake of 9/11."[23] Some Canadians born in Arab and Muslim countries became fearful of entering the United States. A high school from Toronto, one of the world's most multicultural cities, cancelled a field trip to a Buffalo, New York, art gallery after American officials could not assure school officials that some of the students would not be subjected to special scrutiny.[24]

The Canadian complaints about how their citizens were treated in the United States were not well received by all Americans. Former presidential candidate and talk-show host Pat Buchanan responded that the complaints were "juvenile whining" from a "free loading" country – "Soviet Canuckistan" – which was a "safe haven for terrorists."[25] Ashcroft was more diplomatic, but still vigorously defended the requirments for photographs, fingerprints, and registration. He argued that the new American system was not based simply on a person's country of birth and that it did not amount to racial or religious profiling. Canada withdrew its travel advisory on the same day that Ashcroft went to Niagara Falls, New York, to defend the American policy and to argue that "no country is exempt in the war against terrorism."[26] The Americans retained their registration system and extended it to those born in most Muslim countries, including Indonesia, Egypt, Jordan, and Kuwait. Ashcroft was again unapologetic and explained: "We recognize after September 11 that we must have a better understanding of who is entering and exiting our country."[27]

By late 2002, many Canadians were becoming uncomfortable with the implications of a strategy that would tie Canada's visa and border policies to American policies in a joint security perimeter. Canadian officials responded negatively to American plans to require visas for visitors, including Canadian permanent residents who were citizens of India, Pakistan, and Sri Lanka, which, together, send Canada nearly 50,000 landed immigrants a year. Coderre expressed concerns that American visa requirements might amount to "racial profiling ... A Muslim is a potential terrorist? What's that? That's clearly not the Canadian way and I have to look for answers here." Graham acknowledged the right of the Americans to craft their own visa policy, but stated that he would explain to the Americans the steps Canada had taken to grant permanent resident status, including the post-September 11 issuance of photo identification cards. Prime Minister Chrétien, however, seemed less concerned, observing that if people did not have a Canadian passport "it's no longer my problem. It's their problem."[28]

Even if Canada could not change American visa policies, it was clear that Canada would not adopt all the American policies. Full visa convergence with the United States would sacrifice Canadian sovereignty. It would also have a harmful effect on multiculturalism in Canada by adversely affecting many new Canadians and their families. At the same time, full visa convergence would be no guarantee that another September 11 would not occur. Most of the September 11 terrorists were able to obtain visas under American requirements that, even before September 11, were more restrictive than Canadian requirements. Visas can be processed in a perfunctory manner. Extraordinary steps such as fingerprinting and photographing visitors may assist more in apprehending people after they have committed crimes than in preventing crimes. Even if visas and other border restrictions could in some cases help deny entry to terrorists or assist in their apprehension, their value would still have to be weighed against their over-inclusive nature in targeting people, based in part at least on citizenship or place of birth.

An interesting poll of Americans and Canadians conducted in early May 2002 confirmed that the public in both countries had widespread suspicions about the oft-noted porous border. Of the American respondents, 77 per cent believed that potential terrorists had slipped into the United States through Canada, while 81 per cent of the Canadians held the same belief. What is most interesting, however, is the different perceptions about the appropriate remedy. Over 70 per cent of Americans placed the blame not on Canada, but on their own immigration and border security. In contrast, 42 per cent of Canadians blamed the Canadian immigration and refugee system, with an additional 20 per cent blaming both the Canadian and American systems. Canadians are more inclined than Americans to blame Canada for allowing terrorists into the United States.[29] The approach preferred by the Americans – tightening their own policies – has consequences for Canadians, but at least it allows Canada the freedom to maintain more generous and welcoming policies, ones more befitting Canadian immigration and multiculturalism policies.

The risks of terrorists crossing the border are obvious, but we should not assume that any system of border security – especially one that accommodates the free flow of goods, services, and people that is part of our modern economy – will eliminate the possibility that Canada might be a "staging ground" for a terrorist attack on the United States. No one is advocating a new Berlin Wall along the world's longest undefended border. Nevertheless, a number of prominent Canadian military analysts have argued that Canada must make good on its longstanding promise that the United States will not be attacked through Canada.[30] The analogy ignores the fact that Prime Minister Mackenzie King made this promise with respect to the Japanese and German armies, not terrorists of various nationalities and citizenships operating alone or in small cells. Canadians should not be too quick to make promises that terrorists will not cross the border or to accept blame when they do. They should also not be too quick to accept the idea that improving border security requires convergence with increasingly restrictive and discriminatory American visa and registration policies. Needless to say, the Americans are completely free to restrict their own policies. Canada, however, does not have to follow suit. Indeed, Canada's reputation in the world and the multicultural identity of Canada could benefit by retention of its more generous policies. At the same time, Canada's prosperity may be jeopardized should the United States decide that Canada's visa, refugee, immigration, and border policies present unacceptable risks to American security.

THE SMART BORDER AGREEMENT

The "smart border" framework agreement was announced in Ottawa by Foreign Affairs Minister John Manley and American Homeland Security Director Tom Ridge in December 2001. Prime Minister Chrétien and President Bush subsequently met in Detroit in September 2002 to report on steps taken in its implementation. This agreement focused on steps to allow low-risk people and goods to cross the border more efficiently, as well as on better use of technology and information sharing to ease border flows. The idea of the "smart border" incorporated modern techniques of risk assessment, information sharing, licensing, pre-clearance, and the use of technology rather than the older idea found in the *Patriot Act* of simply adding guards or troops at the border. In a joint press release at their Detroit meeting, Chrétien and Bush noted that "a secure and efficient border is key to our economic security."[31] Canadian business groups were understandably enthusiastic about smart border reforms that would allow containers, trucks, and people to enter into licensing and screening arrangements that would classify them as low risk and enable them to cross the border more efficiently. As we will see in chapter 7, such administrative reforms, and the use of technology to screen all people, have the potential to provide better security while respecting liberty, equality, and privacy.

The smart border approach was not, however, without hitches. There were concerns whether American customs officials who were pre-clearing containers in Canada could bring their guns, and whether joint travel databases could result in violations of privacy. Business leaders argued that smart border technologies should be used not only by corporations but by individuals, despite concerns that identity cards based on fingerprints or optical scans might adversely affect privacy.[32] After two days of meetings with Ridge in December 2002, Manley expressed frustration with American plans to require all non-Americans entering their country to register. Manley pointed out that such a system "would turn Detroit into a parking lot. There are truck drivers who make four crossings a day on the (Windsor-Detroit) Ambassador Bridge ... we've got 200 million crossings now on the land border. How can that possibly function if you really want to record the names of every person going in and coming out." Less than a month later, the Americans announced a plan that would require Canadians entering the country to provide not only their names but their date of birth, citizenship, passport number, place of issuance, and residence in the United States. The plan will apply to air and boat travellers. There was no mention of the land crossings, which were the source of Manley's justifiable fears about turning border cities into "parking lots."[33] If the Americans extend such time-consuming registration requirements to land crossings, Canada may be required to apply smart border technologies to all individuals regardless of concerns about their costs and effects on privacy.

REFUGEES AND THE SAFE THIRD-COUNTRY AGREEMENT

The most controversial part of the smart border agreement had little to do with the important goal of ensuring that traffic could move over the border in a secure and efficient manner. The smart border agreement contemplated the negotiation of a safe third-country agreement, which was initialed by both countries at the end of June 2002 and signed later that year. The agreement would prevent people over eighteen years of age or without close relatives in Canada from making a refugee claim to Canada if, as they fled their home country, they had first reached the safe country of the United States. It would also preclude refugee applicants who originally landed in Canada from applying for refugee status in the United States. The nature of transportation and border flows, however, means that the main effect of the agreement will be to stop refugee applicants who first landed in the United States from seeking status under the more generous Canadian refugee system. The smart Canada-US border that was open for business would be closed for almost all refugee applicants.

In 2000–1 over 11,000 refugee claimants to Canada, constituting 37 per cent of that year's refugee claims, embarked from the United States.[34] Unless Canada dramatically increases its acceptance of refugees from other countries, the safe third-country agreement may substantially reduce the number of refugees Canada will accept. The agreement responded to American perceptions that Canada's "liberal" refugee policies constituted a threat to American security. It also provided a means for Canada to make its refugee policy less generous under the cover of a security agreement with the Americans. The refugee agreement was linked with further progress on facilitating border flows, including fast lanes for pre-cleared trucks. Deputy Prime Minister John Manley announced: "We're well on our way to creating a smart border for the 21st century, one's that open for business, but closed for terrorists." [35] But the border was being closed not so much to terrorists as to refugee applicants.

Manley defended the safe third-country agreement by arguing that it was not designed to stop refugee claims, but to deal with them "in a more effective way" by requiring people to seek "asylum in the first safe country they entered," whether that be Canada or the United States. This argument ignored the fact that over a third of all refugee applicants to Canada land first in the United States from the country they are fleeing. The new safe third-country agreement would prohibit most of these people from applying for refugee status in Canada and require them to make their claims under the less generous and more punitive American refugee system. Indeed, in a November 2001 speech in New York City, Manley had recognized that many refugees come to Canada by way of the United States. He fought back at American perceptions of Canada as a terrorist haven by arguing: "We Canadians have our own share of security worries at the border: last year 50 percent more criminals were stopped trying to get into Canada from the United States than the other way around. Almost half of our refugee claimants enter from the United States; most of the guns used in crimes in Canada are imported illegally from the United States."[36] Leaving aside the unfair grouping of refugees with crimes and guns, Manley's recognition that Canada accepts many of its refugee claimants from the United States belies his subsequent statements that the safe third-country agreement is not designed to stop refugee claims. All the responsibility for this agreement cannot be placed on the Americans. Canada may have used post-September 11 border concerns as an excuse to adopt a more restrictive refugee policy. There appears to be some support in Canada for tightening immigration and refugee policies. In November 2001, 49 per cent of Canadians in one poll supported restricting "the number of immigrants that come to Canada from Muslim countries. The poll was repeated in November 2002, and 44 per cent of the sample still supported such restrictions and 42 per cent opposed them.[37] The safe third-country agreement does not specifically target refugee applicants from Muslim countries; it applies to all refugee applicants who land in the United States before Canada.

Canada had previously initiated plans in the mid-1990s to implement a safe third-county agreement between Canada and the United States. A leading immigration law scholar and an official with Amnesty International had criticized that proposed agreement as a possible violation of the Charter because it would deny refugee applicants a hearing as required under the Supreme Court's controversial Charter decision of *Singh v. Canada*.[38] James Hathaway and Alex Neve argued: "It is simply wrong to apply the force of Canadian law to anyone without simultaneously granting the benefit of protections we believe necessary to achieve fairness. Second, Canadians remain committed as a matter of national conscience to the protection of genuine refugees who manage to reach us. Deflection runs afoul of both these principles by mechanistically and summarily excluding asylum seekers without any inquiry into their need for protection."[39] They expressed special concern about deflecting refugee applicants back to the United States on the basis that "the United States has regularly proved unwilling to honour the most basic of all internationally mandated refugee rights, namely the entitlement of refugees not to be returned to the risk of persecution."[40] They also noted: "The American asylum system is problematic in terms of its reliance on internationally condemned detention practices and its denial to claimants of either a meaningful right to counsel or competent interpreters at asylum hearings. Perhaps the most draconian step was the adoption in 1996 of a summary exclusion procedure."[41] A refugee applicant turned backed by Canada at the US border will not enjoy the same international and constitutional law safeguards as those who are able to come straight to Canada.

Immigration lawyers expressed similar concerns about the 2002 safe third-country agreement, noting that the American treatment of refugee applicants would become even tougher under post-September 11 plans to place immigration under the authority of the Department of Homeland Security.[42] Refugee applicants in the United States had to deal with more restrictions on work and social assistance, and they were not able to make claims if they had been in the country for a year.[43] The United States has not entered into as many international agreements affecting refugee applicants as Canada. The United Nations high commissioner for refugees noted differences between the American and the Canadian standards and argued: "You have to try to go for the better [Canadian] standard, not the lower standard." The effect of the agreement would, however, be that many refugee applicants who might otherwise come to Canada would have their refugee status determined under the stricter American system.

The United Nations commissioner also made the important point that none of the September 11 terrorists were refugee applicants. Indeed, a study of forty-eight Islamic terrorists who entered the United States between 1993 and 2001 revealed that only three were refugee applicants. In contrast, a third of the terrorists, including most of the September 11 terrorists, were on temporary visas issued by the United States, and another third were permanent residents or naturalized American citizens. Refugee applicants are subject to more intense scrutiny than many other visitors. Terrorists such as Ahmed Ressam were denied refugee status, though they were not deported.[44] "Global terrorists have not exploited the refugee determination system to gain access to Canada, though several tried. Entering Canada via the refugee stream exposes a refugee claimant to authorities, to a security clearance, to divulging information in filling out a refugee claim form. Any sophisticated terrorist would reasonably be expected to avoid such an exposure. Further, there are far easier options for gaining entry into either Canada or the United States."[45] Despite the fact that the vast majority of terrorists entered the United States under American laws,[46] the American media still regularly featured stories that "Canada's liberal refugee and immigration policies" made it a "safe haven for terrorists."[47]

The Canadian Council for Refugees criticized the safe third-country agreement as the "none is too many" agreement, in reference to the policy used by Canada to deny entry to Jewish refugees from Nazi Germany before the Second World War. They argued that, "by signing the agreement, Canada joins a sorry group of countries that take the

'Not in my backyard' approach to refugees. Canada receives less than one half of one percent of the world's refugees. Why should we reduce our share even further?"[48] Analogies to the "none is too many" policy may be excessive, but the agreement will make Canadian refugee policy less generous, something that many of its defenders seem to accept and applaud.[49] The placement of the agreement in a security document, however, allows the Canadian government to escape some of the responsibility for taking fewer refugees. At the same time, the security value of the safe third-country agreement is doubtful. At most, a few terrorists might be stopped at the border. Terrorists, however, will have an incentive to avoid the scrutiny inherent in a refugee application. Moreover, many, many more innocent refugees will be prevented from applying for refugee status. They may also be forced to go underground and live illegally in either the United States or Canada. Those who do so will not be subject to any security screening.

The initialling of the safe third-country agreement was announced on the same day that Bill c-11, the new *Immigration Act*, took effect and limited refugee applicants to one application. The night before the announcement, there were 121 refugee applicants camped out at just one border crossing, hoping to get into Canada before the changes went into effect. They included a Pakistani man who had been living in New York City, but who had been visited by FBI agents asking to see his papers, and an eleven-year-old Peruvian girl, who was clutching a teddy bear decorated with Canadian flag pins.[50] As fears about the toughening of American immigration policies and the implementation of the safe third- country agreement mounted, unusually high numbers of refugee applicants came to Canada from the United States. A Pakistani man who had overstayed his student visa in the United States explained his decision to apply for refugee status in Canada: "It's too dangerous to stay; I'm too frightened by the mood in the U.S. ... America is so full of hatred and vengeance toward Muslims. So I come to Canada, a more humanitarian place."[51] Such a person would be most likely precluded from applying for refugee status in Canada once the safe third-country agreement comes into effect. Innocent and desperate people will be hurt by the broad scope of the safe third-country agreement that was negotiated as part of the smart border agreement. The narratives of these people did not seem to influence Canadian policy-makers, who have allowed refugee policy to be linked and driven by anti-terrorism policy. Canada has been too quick to respond to perceptions both at home and in the United States that Canada's refugee policy makes it a haven for terrorists.[52]

FREE TRADE?

Canadian anxieties about cooperating in the American war on terrorism seem driven by economic concerns about keeping the border open for free trade between the two countries. A detailed examination of Canadian-American trade is beyond the scope of this work, but the smart border and safe third-country agreements, as well as Canadian military participation in Afghanistan, do not seem to be guaranteeing the free flow of goods and services over the border. In 2002 the United States imposed prohibitive tariffs on softwood lumber imports from Canada and provided American farmers with massive subsidies. Canadian officials opposed these measures vehemently. Some representatives of Canada attempted to link Canadian cooperation in the war against terrorism with the case for free trade. In an article in an American newspaper opposing the 29 per cent tariff on Canadian softwood, Ron Irwin, Canadian counsel general to New England, stressed that "Canadians welcomed without hesitation the opportunity to assist their American brothers and sisters in defeating terrorism. Canada has committed just under 3,000 military personnel to Operation Enduring Freedom, the most sent abroad since the Korean War. A third of Canada's navy fleet has been deployed." Irwin went on to assert that "Canadians do these things not because we expect a quid pro quo,"[53] though he himself had linked a free trade issue with Canada's military role in Afghanistan. Linking free trade issues with Canadian cooperation with American anti-terrorism and military efforts is a dangerous game. It runs serious risks of eroding Canadian sovereignty on matters of military and foreign policy. It also does not appear to work in ensuring free trade.

Irwin's unsuccessful plea for freer trade reveals the dilemma in Canada's understandable anxieties about keeping the border open after September 11. Attempts to cooperate in the war against terrorism, even those that sacrifice some Canadian autonomy, may be neither a necessary nor a sufficient condition for ensuring free trade. Canada may be making changes to its criminal justice, foreign, military, and immigration policies in an attempt to keep the border open, only to find that the Americans will, for other reasons such as protecting their struggling lumber and agricultural sectors, still impose trade restrictions that may be devastating for Canada. A safer and more sovereign strategy would be to challenge American protectionism through existing treaties and trade agreements.[54] We should not assume that full Canadian cooperation in the war against terrorism will keep the border open for business. Conversely, we should not assume that policy differences with the Americans on such matters will result in American trade retaliation.

CANADA GOES TO WAR IN AFGHANISTAN

Canada quickly signed up for the war against the Taliban regime and al-Qaeda in Afghanistan. Prime Minister Chrétien explained that "some soldiers and some civilians might be affected, but sometimes that is the price we pay to have peace and destroy the evil of terrorism."[55] Foreign Affairs Minister John Manley echoed these sentiments and added: "Canada has a good reputation, we trade on that reputation in the world, but let's make no mistake about it: Canada does not have a history as a pacifist or a neutralist country."[56] In the weeks after September II, there was a surge of interest in the Canadian military, which required a second basic training centre to be opened.[57] Once hostilities started in Afghanistan, Canadian warships and elite Canadian special force ground troops were dispatched, followed by 750 ground soldiers. The Canadians entered the war in Afghanistan not as peacekeepers in a United Nations contingent but as combat soldiers acting in concert with American forces.

Because of resource constraints and other peacekeeping commitments, Canada's ground troops remained in Afghanistan for only a six-month tour of duty. Four of the Canadian soldiers – Sergeant Marc Léger, aged 29; Corporal Ainsworth Dyer, aged 24; Private Richard Green, aged 21; and Private Nathan Smith, aged 27 – did not come home because they were killed by "friendly fire" from a US aircraft. There was national outpouring of sympathy for the soldiers and their families, but there was also considerable anger. "On radio call-in shows, in coffee shops and on news Web sites, the message was the same: What was the U.S. fighter pilot thinking when he dropped a laser-guided bomb onto a training ground outside Kandahar? ... [M]any Canadians were in no mood to give the United States the benefit of the doubt. There was bitterness that U.S. President George W. Bush had sent no direct message to the Canadian public even though he had expressed his condolences to Prime Minister Chrétien."[58] The anger only increased when an American Board of Inquiry found that the pilot, Major Harry Schmidt, a former instructor in the navy's "Top Gun" school (who was nicknamed "Psycho" because of his aggressiveness, but was described by his commanding officer as a "world class tactician, patriot and born warrior leader"), had failed to exercise appropriate flight discipline and had engaged in inappropriate use of lethal force. After observing ground fire from the Canadian training exercise, Schmidt had asked for permission to fire, was told to hold fire, but then declared he was under attack, dropped from 23,000 to 10,000 feet, and released the laser-guided bomb on the Canadian soldiers. Thirty-two seconds later the American pilot was told by the air controllers that he had fired on "friendlies." No aircraft had been shot down from the ground in Afghanistan and the bomb was dropped on an area that the pilot ought to have known was occupied by friendly forces.

Canadians could not complain that American authorities did not take the incident seriously. The Americans responded more quickly and more harshly to this incident than they did to other similar incidents that had resulted in the deaths of a significant number of civilians in Afghanistan. Schmidt and another pilot – his wingman, who had warned him about the possibilities of "friendlies" – were charged with involuntary manslaughter, aggravated assault, and dereliction of duty in the deaths of the Canadian soldiers. If convicted, they both face a maximum of sixty-four years in prison.[59] The Americans responded to errors in the use of military force with the force of criminal sanction. This use of the criminal law in aid of military discipline provoked widespread support for the pilots in the United States. The governor of Illinois, the state in which the pilots were based, held a fundraiser for their legal defence. He argued: "They didn't do this on purpose. They're solid, sound citizens. They're not cowboys." The Illinois Senate passed a resolution in support of the pilots. A representative of a veterans' organization made the point that the pilots were not "hunting Canadians." The use of the criminal sanction risked making the pilots martyrs without necessarily examining systemic failings that led to a significant number of friendly fire incidents in Afghanistan, inadequate briefing of the pilots, and the regular use of amphetamines, or "go pills," by US pilots on long flight missions. It was also not clear how Canada or the families of the dead soldiers would benefit from the prosecutions. As a representative of one of the families observed, sending the pilots "to prison, that's not going to bring the boys back." Some Canadians began to feel uneasy about the substantial domestic support the American pilots have received and the vigorous defence they mounted.[60]

The American pilot who killed the four Canadian soldiers never saw them. With some ground combat exceptions, the American-led war in Afghanistan was another example of what Michael Ignatieff has described as a high-tech "virtual war." The war in Afghanistan was defended as part of a war against terrorism and as a liberation of the people, and especially the women, of Afghanistan from the repressive Taliban regime. Although Ignatieff accepts that some wars may be justified, he cautions about virtual wars that result in minimal casualties for the aggressor and that are fought in the name of abstract values such as human rights. He warns: "The language of human rights provides a powerful new rhetoric of abstract justification" that runs the risk of luring countries "into wars that end up abusing the very rights they were supposed to defend ... What is to prevent moral abstractions like human rights from inducing an absolutist frame of mind which, in defining all human rights violators as barbarians, legitimizes barbarism?"[61] Just as the coercive realities of the criminal sanction have been disguised by defending it as necessary to protect human rights, so the brutal realities of wars have been sugar-coated through the same rhetoric of human rights.

Post-September 11 rhetoric about fighting wars against the evil of terrorism are, if anything, even more slippery than the rhetoric of fighting wars in the name of human rights. Prime Minister Chrétien mirrored President Bush's rhetoric when he defended the war as necessary to "destroy the evil of terrorism." [62] As Stephen Toope has argued, however, there is a danger in such labels. "In the battle of good against evil, there is no room to ask whether or not it is just possible that the evil may have some valid grievances against the good ... Part of our security lies in our understanding of the threat we face, a threat that we have sometimes fed through the heaping on of bitter grievance."[63] In part because it is not in the frontlines and because it is such a multicultural country, Canada should be in a better position than the United States to understand such grievances. As a weak military power, Canada should be less attracted to high-tech wars fought in the name of abstract values. Canada has important experience in the multilateral diplomacy that may avoid such wars, and in the difficult tasks of keeping the peace and building democracies after the bombings have stopped. Canada is in a good position to recognize the limited efficacy of military force in improving human security, preventing terrorism, and building lasting solutions based on human rights and democracy.

Nevertheless, Canada added its small military contingent to the American effort in Afghanistan and, as we will see, participated in American violations of international law in the treatment of captives.

Although many in Canada and the United States saw Canada's military contributions in Afghanistan as too small, Canada paid a price. Four Canadian soldiers were killed and eight others were wounded. Canada's reputation as an international peacekeeper that respected international law was harmed. It is also not clear whether the war in Afghanistan achieved all its objectives. The Taliban were removed, but al-Qaeda and its leader, Osama bin Laden, apparently survived the war. In a tape released in November 2002, a voice that was identified as bin Laden's cited Canada, along with Great Britain, France, Italy, Germany, and Australia, as a country that would pay for its support of the American attacks. He stated: "Remember our people killed among the children of Palestine, in Iraq. Remember our dead in Afghanistan ... as you bomb so will you likewise be."[64] Canada should not be deterred by such threats, but it should have more cautiously deliberated the costs and the benefits of joining the American-led war in Afghanistan.

MILITARY SPENDING

Canadian military participation in the war in Afghanistan focused the public's attention on the budget cuts sustained by the Canadian military throughout the 1990s. In 1990, 8.7 per cent of the federal budget was spent on the military, but by 2002 the total represented only 1.2 per cent.[65] The war in Afghanistan demonstrated in graphic terms the consequences of such cuts. Canadian soldiers did not even have desert camouflage, and they relied on aging Sea King helicopters. Resource constraints made only one six-month tour of duty feasible for the ground troops. The American ambassador publicly and repeatedly prodded Canada to spend more on the military.[66] Canadian defence minister John McCallum eventually complained about the American interventions: "I would not urge the president of the United States or the U.S. ambassador to Canada to do my job to ask for more defence spending, I think that is a Canadian matter ... It is a made-in-Canada decision, so while Mr. Bush may be asking for what I am asking, I am not asking for his help."[67] Even before the counterproductive American interventions, there was significant support in Canada for increased military expenditures. There was less of a consensus, however, about how the military will best serve Canadian interests, with some arguing that more money was needed to enable the Canadian military to fight with the Americans and others suggesting that such "interoperability" should not be a priority, given Canadian needs and traditions with respect to peacekeeping.

The federal budget in December 2001 was presented as a "security budget" and it allocated an additional $500 million over five years to the military. This amount was criticized as woefully insufficient if Canadian forces were to be able to integrate with technologically sophisticated American forces. Problems in linking aging Canadian equipment with state-of-the-art American war technology were experienced both during the UN-authorized Gulf War in 1990–1 and during the Kosovo air campaign. The Canadian military has placed the ability to operate with American forces high on its list of priorities, but this cooperation raises some important policy questions. Will Canadians support massive increases on military spending? Should the goal be to have the technology, training, lift, and communications necessary to fight alongside the Americans? Is it realistic to expect Canada, or other countries, to keep up with the American military? The United States spends 40 per cent of all the money the world spends on defence. "This gap in resources translates into a technology gap, as Europeans have found in Afghanistan. No wonder Lord Robertson, NATO's secretary-general, worries aloud about European 'pygmies.'"[68]

Even if the necessary billions were available to ensure that all Canada's armed forces could operate seamlessly with American forces, how would this ability affect Canadian foreign policy? Danford Middlemiss and Denis Stairs have raised concerns that Canada risks being seen as "so fully integrated with the United States ... that it can no longer be regarded as a useful interlocutor, much less an independent player." They also question whether a focus on interoperability between American and Canadian armed forces may leave Canada "with little choice but to go when – and only when – the Americans go," and then in a manner that compromises the autonomy of Canadian command.[69]

One alternative to the expensive goal of full combat interoperability with American forces is to build on Canada's traditional strength in international peacekeeping, even at the price of having a military that might be best suited to filling such a niche. "Instead of duplicating high-tech naval, air and army capabilities that the U.S. already has in abundance, Canada may actually acquire more influence for its investment" by augmenting its peacemaking role.[70] To be sure, credible and sustained peacekeeping will require increased military spending, as Canada now ranks a lowly thirty-first in its support for UN peacekeeping.

Nevertheless, a focus on the United Nations and peacekeeping has the potential to "act as a counterweight to the political and economic influence of the United States as well as a more general expression of Canada's claim to be acting as an independent, sovereign political entity."[71] Peacekeeping cannot be done on the cheap, but it may require less investment in the high-tech hardware needed to fight in combat with the Americans.

Peacekeeping is a complex subject. Some, including Ignatieff, have argued that contemporary peacekeeping requires combat skills and equipment, while others, including retired Major-General Lewis McKenzie, suggest that a difference remains.[72] The commander of Canadian ground troops in Afghanistan was reported as saying that Canadian participation in combat "established our credibility in the coalition. Canada has been tainted with an image of being blue-hatted peacekeepers, and I think ... the aggressiveness and tenacity that the troops showed ... dispelled the myth ... We were like a pack of rabid pit bulls in satisfying the coalition's end state."[73] These comments – made not by an over-eager private but by the experienced commander of our troops in Afghanistan – raise questions about whether military participation in Afghanistan may harm the ability of Canadian forces to act as peacekeepers.

Peacekeeping and related efforts at building democracy may help to prevent terrorism. There are strong arguments that Canada could have made a better and more distinctive contribution to the campaign in Afghanistan not by sending combat troops but by waiting and sending peacekeepers and others to help build a democracy after the Taliban was disposed. Former foreign affairs minister Lloyd Axworthy commented that when he visited Afghanistan in November 2001, "there was a heartfelt cry for help, not for more combat soldiers, but for builders and peacekeepers. There was a chance for Canada to have taken a lead in helping to define the nature and role of an international presence, to use our scarce resources not as fungible for US military capacity, of which there is more than enough, but to be there as a major player in the post-war reconstruction in a country which is today verging on anarchy." Janice Stein has similarly warned that "without soft power," at which Canada can excel, "Afghanistan will again regress to civil war, Al Qaeda will take root in the chaos and the military victory will be Pyrrhic."[74]

Canada's credibility as a peacekeeper is fragile. Its reputation was harmed by the torture and killing by military personnel of a defenceless young Somali in 1993. Canada's reputation depends not only on a well-trained and adequately financed military but also on a foreign policy presence that is perceived by others in the world as different and autonomous from that of the United States. Unfortunately, there are perceptions in many parts of the world that Canada is increasingly integrated with the United States.[75] For example, the prestigious British newspaper, *The Guardian*, has already argued that Canada is increasingly being seen as "joined at the hip to the U.S. yet with a diminishing ability to influence the increasingly volatile colossus as their side."[76] Focusing on ensuring that our troops have all the technology necessary to fight along with the Americans may actually decrease the contributions that Canada, including its military, can make on the international stage. A Canada that is perceived by the world to be the fifty-first state will not have much impact, even if our tax dollars are significantly reallocated to ensure that Canadian troops can fight side by side with the Americans.

THE DEFENCE OF NORTH AMERICA AND AMERICA'S NEW NORTHERN COMMAND

Canada has been a partner in the North American Aerospace Defence Command (NORAD) since its creation in 1958. This partnership recognized the reality of common North American vulnerability to nuclear attack from the former Soviet Union. Canada was literally caught between the Soviet Union and the United States during times of nuclear crisis such as the Cuban Missile Crisis. Participation in NORAD had some strategic benefits for Canada and allowed the Canadian military to participate in the NORAD command structure. A Canadian officer was on command in NORAD on September 11 and ordered both American and Canadian fighter pilots into the air. Nevertheless, "almost from its inception, NORAD also raised concerns among some Canadians over loss of autonomy in decision-making," such as when the Canadian parts of NORAD were automatically placed on alert during the Cuban crisis.[77]

NORAD was quietly renewed for another five-year term shortly before September 11, but there are serious questions whether its place in the defence of North America will be eclipsed by the creation of a new Northern Command. The American government has mandated this new organization with the defence by air, land, and sea of all of North America, including responsibility for working with civil authorities in the event of another September 11.[78] US Defence Secretary Donald Rumsfeld described Northern Command as "the most significant reform structure of our nation's military command structure" in over fifty years. It began operation in October 2002 under the same commander and in the same facilities as NORAD. Unlike NORAD, however, the Canadian military will not be part of Northern Command.

Defence minister McCallum has rejected the idea of Canada joining Northern Command on the basis that Canadian sovereignty would be threatened. At the same time, however, Canada did agree to a joint planning group that will establish guidelines for cross-border military operations in the event of a terrorist attack or a natural disaster. The group will be composed of fifteen senior Canadian military officers and fifteen senior American officials, headed by the Canadian who serves as deputy commander of NORAD. The defence minister correctly pointed out that "neither terrorists nor biological agents have any respect whatsoever for the 49th parallel; so it is only prudent, only common sense, for Canadians and Americans to plan together to protect the lives of our citizens." He also argued that Canadian sovereignty would be preserved because American troops would operate in Canada only under Canadian military command.[79]

There is a division of opinion about whether Canada should participate in the Northern Command. The Canadian Alliance military critic has argued that without formal Canadian participation, "it's almost like Canada is a protectorate, that we're depending on the United States." The American ambassador to Canada has also argued that closer military coordination would not infringe Canadian sovereignty "even one iota" because "if the U.S. engages in an operation under the rubric of homeland security that Canada does not think is in its national interest, then Canada can simply decide not to participate by not providing forces."[80] Others opposed the idea that Canada might join Northern Command on the basis that it could require much more military spending, result in Canadian soldiers being ordered to violate Canadian or international law, affect Canada's peacekeeping commitments, and make more people see Canada as an adjunct of the United States.[81]

The question of whether Canada should participate in Northern Command is a difficult one and it is a positive, yet somewhat confusing, sign that all sides in the debate argue that their positions are the most consistent with Canadian sovereignty. The Canadian government has pursued a cautious policy that amounts to cooperation with the

American military if necessary, but not necessarily cooperation. There is much to be said for a pragmatic case-by-case approach to military cooperation in the defence of North America. As McCallum argued: "If we disagree with the U.S. over, for example, softwood lumber or Iraq, just to take two examples, that does not mean that either side does not want to plan together" to deal with terrorism scenarios.[82] Important work is ongoing to allow better Canadian and American coordination in the protection of North American seaports from the import of materials, including nuclear and chemical weapons, which could be used in terrorism. The joint American-Canadian planning group to deal with both terrorism and natural disasters will work out of the Colorado Springs headquarters of both the American Northern Command and NORAD, while not being officially part of either body.[83] As we will see in chapter 7, the use of the military to respond to both catastrophic terrorism and other disasters can be part of a broad human security strategy, and coordination and cooperation between the military of the two countries may well be required. There are many ways that the Canadian and American military can work together to defend the security of North America, and not all of them demand that Canada join Northern Command or drastically increase its military spending to enable the Canadian Forces to join their American counterparts in high-tech combat.

MISSILE DEFENCE

September 11, as well the revelations about nuclear weapons in North Korea, strengthened the United States's resolve to take itself out of the anti-ballistic missile treaty and to deploy anti-missile batteries in Alaska in 2005.[84] At first it appeared as though Canada would oppose American plans for a missile defence system in a vigorous manner. Canada was one of 118 countries, but the only member of NATO, to support a draft UN resolution that indicated that the development of missile defence would be a setback to nuclear disarmament and lead to a new arms race.[85] Subsequent to these events, however, Canada softened its stance on missile defence. It indicated that it was prepared to discuss Canadian involvement and that it would send a high-ranking political and military team to Washington for that purpose. The American ambassador to Canada had again placed public pressure on Canada to cooperate with his country. He argued, "We obviously want Canada to participate and we're making the case," as he distinguished

a missile defence system from the "weaponization of space" which Bill
Graham, the Canadian foreign affairs minister, had rejected as "immoral,
illegal and a bad mistake." Former foreign affairs minister Lloyd
Axworthy, however, argued that Canada was changing its traditional
opposition to missile defence "without any public debate, without
parliamentary approval."[86] It remains to be seen whether the United
States will be able to develop a successful system and whether Canada
will participate in it. Canada's softened stance may reflect a recognition
that missile defence will occur with or without Canadian participation.
Indeed, many argue that Canada had best recognize that American
policies will prevail. They suggest that early cooperation, rather than
protest, is in Canada's interests.

A QUESTION OF CHOICE?

The debate about whether Canada should join the Northern Command
or missile defence or whether it should participate in American-led wars
presumes that Canada has a choice. Some knowledgeable commentators think that Canada does not have the luxury of choice after September 11. Jack Granatstein has argued that Canadians should accept
the American commitment to missile defence and a war against Iraq
as both inevitable and in Canada's interest. He fears that, without such
cooperation, the Americans will simply do what they feel they must to
defend North America without either consultation with or participation
by Canadians.[87] Professor Granatstein is not alone in this view. Professor Douglas Bland has made the extraordinary prediction that "it seems
likely that the U.S. will blockade its northern border, undertake covert
operations in Canada and act unilaterally to defend itself by deploying
its armed forces in Canada wherever the President deems it necessary."[88] Granatstein has also warned of severe economic costs to
Canada if cooperation on key and controversial elements of American
foreign policy is not forthcoming. With respect to a war against Iraq,
for example, he observed: "If Canada hangs back, re-enforcing the
perception that Canadian anti-Americanism and 'high falutin' morality
too often verge on the unbearable, the costs to Ottawa might be very
high indeed."[89] In his view, Canada really has no choice but to follow
the Americans. Although he is critical of "anti-Americanism," the
image of the United States that emerges from Granatstein's arguments
is one of America as a bully prepared to resort to economic blackmail
to ensure that Canada joins its fights. Proponents of the no-choice

school stress that initial Canadian reluctance to join American efforts only squanders what little influence Canada may have over joint operations with the United States. If Canadian cooperation is inevitable, it is best to try and get in on the ground floor.

Canada's willingness to join the United States in combat in Afghanistan raises many questions about the extent to which Canada can maintain a military and foreign policy that is independent from the United States. Stephen Clarkson has observed that, by placing Canadian troops under American command in Afghanistan, "Ottawa chose deliberately not to exploit its strength in peace-building, which focuses on reconstructing a civil society from the devastation of war." He argued that "integrating its troops in the U.S. military machine gave the message to the White House that Canada is fully on side ... An acid test for their autonomy in the field will be whether Canadian troops observe the Geneva convention on prisoners of war, which Washington has decided to ignore by refusing to regard the captives it has taken as legitimate soldiers."[90] As we will see, Canada failed that acid test of both autonomy and respect for international law.

CANADIAN COMPLICITY IN AMERICAN VIOLATIONS OF INTERNATIONAL LAW

Both the Canadian Special Forces (JTF2) and the Canadian Navy were involved in the capture of combatants in and around Afghanistan and their subsequent delivery to United States forces. Indeed, the elite JTF2 forces were reported to have "worked directly with the FBI agents who decided which of the Taliban and al-Qaeda prisoners would be released and which would be held for further interrogation or sent to the U.S. base in Guantanamo Bay, Cuba." [91] Although it can be argued that members of al-Qaeda captured in Afghanistan do not qualify for prisoner-of-war status under the Geneva Conventions because they do not wear identifiable insignia,[92] this argument is much weaker with respect to the Taliban and others who took up arms in Afghanistan against the American invasion. In any event, the *Geneva Convention on Prisoners of War*, consistent with the rule of law, contemplates that all captives should be accorded prisoner-of-war status until a competent tribunal has made its decision.[93] As international law professor Michael Byers has argued: "Anyone detained in the course of an armed conflict is presumed to be a PoW until a competent court or tribunal determines otherwise."[94] This understanding means that American interrogation of the captives from Afghanistan in the absence of a determination that they were not prisoners of war violated international law. Even in the unlikely event that none of the detainees qualify for prisoner-of-war status, the American approach to those captured in Afghanistan may violate other international laws, including the fair trial obligations of the *International Covenant on Civil and Political Rights*.[95] Concerns have also been raised about the American treatment of the captives, which included chaining, hooding, shaving their beards, and sometimes sedating them before they were flown twenty-seven hours to the US naval base in Guantanamo Bay, where they were initially housed in constantly illuminated chain-link cages partly open to the elements. Nearly 10 per cent of the detainees were shipped to Cuba, even though they were deemed to be of no intelligence value after repeated interrogations in Afghanistan.[96] By August 2002 there were almost 600 detainees from forty-three nations in the camp. None had been charged, but several had attempted to commit suicide.[97]

American treatment of detainees taken from Afghanistan raises the disturbing prospect that prisoners in the new war against terrorism will enjoy neither the protections afforded prisoners of war nor the protections afforded suspects of crime. Those who argue that the fight against terrorism requires a new paradigm that transcends traditional distinctions between crime and war[98] should take note that the detainees in the war against terrorism at Guantanamo Bay have slipped through the cracks of the existing laws of war and of crime. The captives do not benefit from either the rights of prisoners of war or the criminally accused. They languish in a legal vacuum of indefinite detention in which neither the law of war nor the law of crime applies. American military power and interests, as opposed to either American or international law, rule.

Canada cannot distance itself from American violations of the Geneva Conventions and other international laws in the detention and interrogation of captives taken from Afghanistan. Canadian troops handed some of the captives over to the Americans – not once, but at least twice. Canadian troops who handed captives to the Americans may have violated the Canadian Charter, which has been held to apply to Canadian police officers on foreign soil.[99] If, as we discussed in chapter 4, extradition or deportation can trigger Charter review, than handing captives over to the Americans for indefinite detention and interrogation at Guantanamo Bay in violation of international law may also violate the Charter. There are death penalty issues as well. The captives, if ever tried before an American military tribunal, could receive the death penalty. The Canadian law discussed in chapter 4 suggests that it is generally unconstitutional for Canadian officials to hand people over to foreign states without assurances that they will not be executed or tortured.[100]

There are also fair trial issues. President Bush's military order declares "that an extraordinary emergency exists for national defense purposes" that makes it "not practicable to apply in military commissions under this order the principles of law and the rules of evidence generally recognized in the trial of criminal cases in the United States district courts."[101] Bush's order has a chilling clause that purports to vest the commissions with "exclusive jurisdiction with respect to offenses by the individual." It asserts that detainees subject to it "shall not be privileged to seek any remedy or maintain any proceeding ... or to have any such remedy or proceeding sought on the individual's behalf in i) any court of the United States, or any State thereof, ii) any court of any foreign nation, or iii) any international tribunal."[102] The above clause purporting to oust the jurisdiction of American and international courts is offensive to the rule of law. It was protested by a large number of American law professors, who noted that convictions of terrorists had in the past been secured in American courts.[103] Guantanamo Bay was chosen in part because the United States Supreme Court decided, in a 1993 case involving Haitian refugees held there, that American law does not apply.[104]

The ouster of the jurisdiction of international tribunals in the Bush military order should have been particularly embarrassing for Canada, given its role as an influential supporter and proponent of the International Criminal Court. President Bush's military order follows American opposition to the ICC. The Bush administration has renounced President Clinton's signature on the treaty creating the court and has lobbied that its troops should have immunity from prosecution there. Donald Rumsfeld argued: "We ought to be exempt from that so there isn't that kind of political harassment that can take place unfairly, particularly when you know you're fighting the global war on terror."[105] Bill Graham warned the Americans: "It can't be a world where it is always just their justice and their way of applying the rules. It has to be truly globally accepted rules of justice."[106] When the United States eventually convinced the UN Security Council to give all peacekeeping operations a one-year grace period from prosecutions in the ICC, Canada's ambassador to the UN declared it "a sad day for the

United Nations."[107] Canada can be praised for not backing down in its support for the ICC, but it can be criticized for hypocrisy in allowing its troops in Afghanistan on at least two occasions to deliver captives to American troops who may detain and try the captives under an American military order that ousts the jurisdiction of all international courts.[108]

The role of Canadian troops in handing their captives in Afghanistan over to the Americans for detention and interrogation at Guantanamo Bay, possible trial before a military tribunal, and possible execution was unfortunately overshadowed by the controversy over the exact time when Minister of Defence Art Eggleton was told by the Canadian military that Canadian special forces had delivered their captives to the Americans and whether he understood what he was told. Indeed, a skilled satirist could portray the Eggleton affair as a successful "wag the dog" diversion from the real issue of whether Canada was respecting international law. Arguments made by several Canadian ministers that the Geneva Conventions are out of date when applied to terrorists are not an excuse for failing to ensure compliance with them as they exist now. The Canadian handover of captives to the Americans was also justified on the basis that Canada could join the combat operations only on the condition that it would hand over its captives to the Americans.[109] If this condition was placed on Canadian military participation, it would have been better if our troops had stayed at home. To their credit, the British military took a more independent path and refused to hand over its captives to the Americans and, instead, transferred them to the new Afghan government.[110] Nevertheless, as late as July 2002, the Canadian Navy was handing suspected al-Qaeda terrorists to the Americans for detention at an unknown location.[111] By that time, Canadian complicity in American treatment of detainees had become so engrained that the incident shamefully passed without any controversy in Canada.

In September 2002 Canadians learned that a seriously wounded Canadian teenager, Omar Khadr, had been held by the Americans since his capture during a firefight on the Afghanistan-Pakistan border. The hostilities left one American soldier dead, and Khadr may have tossed the fatal grenade before he was shot by the American troops. Canada expressed concern to the Americans that Khadr might have been a "child soldier" recruited into military and terrorist activities. Canada requested, but was denied, consular access to Khadr when he was detained by the Americans in Afghanistan. American officials responded that

Khadr was a "person under control," a designation not recognized under international law. A spokesperson for the Pentagon explained that the usual right of consular access for criminal suspects did not apply because "these folks have not been arrested, they have been detained, and there are no Geneva Conventions or other international laws" providing for such access. Khadr was subsequently designated as an enemy combatant, transported to Guantanamo Bay, and interrogated. An American soldier involved in Khadr's capture was quoted as saying that, after the teenager was wounded, "he was begging us to kill him. I'm glad we didn't though. Since then he's been squealing like a pig."[112]

Omar Khadr has been detained and interrogated in a manner not in accord with the Geneva Convention rules for the treatment of prisoners of war. No tribunal has determined that he is not a prisoner of war. Six months after his initial detention, Canadian officials, despite continued requests, are still denied consular access to Khadr. There have, however, been reports that the Americans are willing to allow the RCMP and CSIS to interrogate Khadr. Such an interrogation, should it occur, might violate the Charter, given that Canadian officials can be bound by the Charter when acting outside Canada and that Khadr is subject to indefinite detention at Guantanamo Bay without charges, judicial review, or access to a lawyer – all conditions that violate the Charter.[113] Like so many other captives from Afghanistan, Khadr has fallen between the laws governing crime and war. He has not been granted the right of a prisoner of war not to be interrogated, and he has not been afforded the right of a criminal suspect to legal assistance, knowledge of the charges he faces or access to the courts by way of *habeas corpus* or other legal remedies.

Even if Khadr is eventually charged in relation to the death of the American soldier, there are questions about the quality of justice he will receive. He could be tried before an American military tribunal that would not have all the safeguards of a civilian court. In contrast, the American citizen John Walker Lind, who was also captured in Afghanistan, was tried in an American court before he pled guilty and received a sentence of twenty years' imprisonment. Khadr, however, will not likely see the inside of an American courtroom. A US Justice official explained: "The big thing is we're talking about a U.S. soldier who was killed in battle. I think it's going to be more of a military proceeding."[114] Khadr could be subject to execution if found guilty before a military tribunal. Even in the unlikely event that Khadr will be tried by a regular American court, the teenager could still face the death penalty. The United States, along with Iran, Nigeria, Pakistan, Saudi Arabia, and Yemen, still allows executions for crimes committed by juveniles, and it is responsible for over half of such executions since 1990. In a display of its insularity, the United States Supreme Court has concluded that the ban on these executions under the *International Covenant on Civil and Political Rights* is not relevant because "it is American concepts of decency" that are at issue.[115] American officials are not shy about seeking the death penalty for teenaged terrorists. They are seeking the death penalty against a seventeen-year-old American citizen charged with sniper killings under a Virginia anti-terrorism statute. It seems likely that they will eventually seek the death penalty for Omar Khadr.

Like the Canadian handover of captives to the Americans, the treatment of Khadr shamefully did not generate serious controversy in Canada. Commentators urged Canadians "not to stand on guard" or to plea for "special status" for the teenager. Even civil libertarians seem resigned to the idea that the treatment of Khadr would not be "legal. It's political, geopolitical. The United States is going to do, at this point, whatever it wishes or decides is in its interests."[116] Canadians were complicit in American violations of international law in the detention and interrogation of captives in Afghanistan. The captives at Guantanamo Bay include a Canadian teenager implicated in the death of an American solider. He has been interrogated and may possibly be executed in violation of international law.

THE DANGERS OF LINKAGE

How did Canada, a nation that prides itself on its role in developing international law, get into a situation in which it participated in American violations of international law without a note of protest? One reason may be that Canadian leaders believed that a failure to send troops to Afghanistan would result in American economic retaliation. Although commentators such as Jack Granatstein and Michael Bliss advocate greater integration with the United States and deride anti-Americanism, their own arguments suggest that the United States will bully Canada and not hesitate to link trade matters with Canadian support for American foreign and military policy. An important principle for preserving Canadian sovereignty is for Canada to resist any attempts to link anti-terrorism measures and other aspects of Canadian-American relations.

One problem with linkages is that they are not made in a transparent or democratic manner. A senior Liberal source was quoted as saying that both Prime Minister Chrétien and Foreign Affairs Minister Manley "were particularly reluctant to water down [Bill C-36, the *Anti-terrorism Act*] or provide for a comprehensive sunset clause for fear the Americans would see such a move as a retreat." The fear seemed to be that such amendments would affect on-going negotiations leading to the smart border agreements announced in December 2001. If the Americans were actually trying to dictate the details of our domestic criminal law and tie this compliance to the border deals, these ministers should have publicly criticized such American incursions on Canadian sovereignty. Canadians should also not make linkages that the Americans may be reluctant to make. The Canadian business community was overeager to link the *Anti-terrorism Act* with trade issues. Although she confessed that she was not aware of the details of the legislation, the president of the Canadian Chamber of Commerce was convinced that "we're not going to get anywhere with our American friends in terms of improving border security unless we can show we've got good, strong anti-terrorism legislation and that we intend to enforce it."[117] The worries of many Canadians that they would suffer economically if they did not adopt strong anti-terrorism policies were not lost south of the border. They did not make Canada look particularly strong or sovereign.[118]

President Bush hinted at linkage between the smart border agreement and Canadian support for an American invasion of Iraq when, in the lead-up to his September 2002 meeting with Prime Minister Chrétien on the implementation of the agreements, he commented: "We'll talk about how to make our borders work, but at the same time, I'll talk to him about this subject" – namely, Iraq.[119] Although it is understandable that busy leaders would use infrequent personal meetings to discuss more than one matter, these comments also raise the disturbing possibility that the United States would link a controversial attack on Iraq with the separate issue of border security. If linkage occurs, it is likely to happen only at the highest levels and behind closed doors because different officials usually work on trade, border, foreign, and military policies. Linkage between border issues and Canadian support for an American war against Iraq without a UN mandate would ignore the views of a majority of Canadians who oppose such actions.[120] Canadian leaders should make public any American attempts at linkage so they can be subject to democratic debate. Blackmail behind closed doors is the antithesis of democracy.

The real fear that seems to motivate Bliss and Granatstein is that the Americans will somehow shut the borders to trade with Canada if our foreign, military, immigration, and criminal justice policies do not please our southern neighbours. Recent experience with softwood lumber and agricultural subsidies certainly demonstrate the economic suffering that American protectionism can cause in Canada. But these post-September 11 developments also reveal that Canadian compliance in America's war against terrorism at the expense of Canada's generous refugee policy or its reputation for respect for international law is no guarantee of open markets. In preventing linkages, Canada has an interest in maintaining strong international instruments to review trade barriers. For example, Canada has engaged in successful litigation over softwood lumber before panels for the General Agreement on Tariffs and Trade, the North American Free Trade Agreement, and, most recently, the World Trade Organization.[121] This litigation provides a direct and constructive means to fight linkage and trade retaliation, should it occur.

CONCLUSION

The irony of the pressures placed on Canadian sovereignty since September 11 is the way legitimate concerns about maintaining open borders, necessitated by our close economic integration with the United States, have been translated into questionable immigration, foreign, military, and criminal justice policies that have failed to ensure free trade. Increased integration – including even economic integration on the European Union model – would pay off if it allowed Canada more confidence to craft policies in non-economic areas that were less punitive and more respectful of international law than the comparable American policies.

In its attempts to keep the border open, Canada has been too quick to accept the restriction on refugee applications that is implicit in the new safe third-country agreement with the United States. With respect to compliance with the Geneva Conventions in their treatment of captives at Guantanamo Bay, American officials are unlikely to complain that Canada has been acting as the "the Stern Daughter of the

Voice of God,"[122] as they did when Canada warned the United States not to use nuclear arms during the Korean War and insisted on peacekeeping through the United Nations, even when it was not in American geopolitical interests in containing communism. A Canadian lecture to the Americans on international law would not have been gratuitous moralizing because both the Canadian Army and the Canadian Navy gave their captives in Afghanistan to the Americans for safe keeping, and a Canadian teenager is one of the captives being detained and interrogated at Guantanamo Bay. Canada should have insisted more strongly that its captives be treated in accordance with international law. If the Americans refused, Canada should have made alternative arrangements for captives, as the British did. If that was not possible, our troops should not have gone to Afghanistan. If this refusal had resulted in American trade retaliation, it should have been challenged by Canada under the various trade agreements.

Although Canada may be unsuccessful in moderating American policy and making it more sensitive to international law and institutions, it is important for Canada's identity both at home and abroad that it make visible efforts to achieve this difficult task. Disagreeing with the Americans over the Geneva Conventions or the safe third-country agreement or the possible execution of Omar Khadr would not have been a case of picking a fight with the Americans for the sake of picking a fight. It would not have been a case of puffed-up or overblown claims of sovereignty. Canada's generous treatment of refugees and its commitment to international law and international peacekeeping are not abstract matters of sovereignty, but important matters that lie near the core of Canada's identity. Canada's reputation on these matters is worth defending, even at the price of angering the Americans and risking economic harm through American trade retaliation.

But the story is not over. With some troubling exceptions,[123] Canada has so far insisted it will assist the United States with respect to weapons in Iraq only if the Americans act as part of the United Nations. The issue for Canada should be weapons and compliance with the UN's resolutions, not America's geopolitical interests. Despite repeated American requests, Canada has not dramatically increased military spending, but it has raised spending on international development. Canada has not joined the American Northern Command. Canada opposed American immigration policies that discriminated against Canadian citizens because they were born in the Middle East and Pakistan. The pendulum may swing away from integration and back towards sovereignty as Canadians realize the precise implications of following American immigration, military, and foreign policies. Many in Canada value its reputation as a multicultural country that is open to newcomers and that acts through the United Nations in peacekeeping, development, and democracy-building exercises.

It should not be forgotten that Lester Pearson's opposition to the escalation of the Vietnam War – an event that caused President Johnson to complain that the Canadian prime minister was not sufficiently house-trained[124] – came after Pearson's acceptance of nuclear weapons in Canada in the wake of the Cuban Missile Crisis. The subsequent policies of Pearson and Trudeau demonstrate that George Grant's declaration of the death of Canadian sovereignty was premature. Nationalist tracts like *Lament for a Nation* were part of the perpetual Canadian push and pull between integration with and separation from the Americans. September 11 pulled Canada uncomfortably close to the United States, and the Canadian record on issues such as the safe third-country agreement and the Canadian handover of captives to the Americans is not a proud one. Canadians and their governments can, however, move in the direction of asserting their rights to more autonomous and distinctly Canadian immigration, foreign, and military policies. The final question remains, however, whether adequate steps have been taken since September 11 to preserve the security of Canadians.

7

The Challenges of
Preserving Canadian Security

The thousands of deaths and lasting trauma that occurred on September 11 make it clear that Canada must do what it can to prevent such acts both at home and abroad. But we must oppose terrorism in our own way. Canadian nationalists such as George Grant would argue that Canada should develop its own distinctive anti-terrorism policies, ones that respect Canadian domestic and international traditions. Because anti-terrorism policy will likely be one of the major issues for the foreseeable future, the stakes are high. Indeed, the survival of Canada as an independent nation could depend in part on its ability to develop effective and creative security policies that do not mimic the American tendency to rely on imprisonment and military force.

Since September 11 Canada has placed too much emphasis on the "big bang" of reforming the criminal law and using military force in an attempt to prevent terrorism by targeting terrorists. Canada has not paid enough attention to the less glamorous role of administrative measures that target places and substances vulnerable to terrorism, as opposed to terrorists. We have been so fixated with denouncing the evil of the September 11 attacks that we have not yet placed terrorism in a rational list of the many threats to our security and well-being. We have neglected the need for a strong public health system and emergency preparedness to respond not only to mass terrorism but to accidents, diseases, and disasters that may affect our security and well-being.

TERRORISM AND OTHER DISASTERS

Ursula Franklin, a famed Canadian scientist and pacifist, has argued that, in responding to September 11, "much could be gained from using an earthquake model rather than a war response." In her view, the harm of both natural and man-made disasters "can be understood and – at times – mitigated, but neither can be eliminated." Wars fought in the name of combatting terrorism will produce only "more enemies and more suffering."[1] A disaster-based approach would reconceptualize threats to national security "to cover emergencies that range from natural disasters and industrial accidents to military attacks."[2] Although some people have criticized a disaster-based approach for blurring lines between military and civilian responsibilities and between national and local governments, it seems to be a sensible approach. It provides a means to make rational risk assessments and to allocate resources efficiently to the multiple risks faced by citizens.

A disaster-based approach to terrorism is consistent with recommendations made after September 11 by the prestigious American National Research Council. In a 400-page book, the council examines the role of science and engineering in responding to mass terrorism. It urges preventive engineering and controls on nuclear sources, biohazards, toxic chemicals, explosives, information technology, energy systems, and transportation systems, along with better fire and blast standards for buildings. It concludes: "Most of the recommendations in this report, if acted on, will not only make the nation safer from terrorist attacks but can also make it safer from natural disasters, infectious diseases, hackers disrupting the Internet, failures in electric power distribution and other complex public systems, and human error causing failures in such systems."[3] As we will see, a disaster-based approach that relies on technology, better emergency responses, and the control of weapons and other hazardous substances also poses less of a threat to liberty, privacy, and equality than one that relies on criminal investigations and prosecutions. It may also avoid some of the threats to human security that are caused by the use of war as a blunt and bloody instrument against terrorism.

The Haddon Matrix

One tool that may assist in the development of effective and rational anti-terrorism policies is to apply the Haddon Matrix to terrorism and other threats to security. This matrix was designed by William Haddon Jr, an epidemiologist, to provide a conceptual framework for thinking about the prevention and reduction of injuries arising from traffic accidents. It is divided into interventions at the pre-crash, crash, and post-crash stages which are directed at the driver, the vehicle, or the physical and socio-cultural environment. Most criminal laws (for instance, laws against speeding, drunk driving, and other forms of dangerous driving) are directed at changing human behaviour before a crash occurs. Reliance on the criminal law falls far short of a comprehensive approach to traffic safety because it affects only one of the twelve cells in the Haddon Matrix. Moreover, most studies have suggested that it is difficult to change driver behaviour, even through the threat of severe sanctions.[4] Still, society continues to focus on the "nut behind the wheel" and the "killer drunk," in part because of an understandable need to denounce such wrongful conduct.[5]

Haddon persuasively argued that society had placed "undue emphasis" on the difficult task of changing human behaviour, as opposed to "using more effective measures to reduce injuries and their results" such as better road design, better car design, reduced use of cars and alcohol, and better emergency response. "The choice of countermeasures should not be determined by the relative importance of causal or contributing factors or by their early occurrence in the sequence of injury-producing events ... Rather, priority and emphasis should be given to the measures that will most effectively reduce losses from injury."[6] Haddon is probably best known for calling attention to the "second crash" in automobile accidents and the use of devices such as padded dashes and airbags to lesson the harm of the second crash. His matrix, however, is widely used in the field of injury prevention and can usefully be applied to terrorism and other threats to human security.

In figure 1, the Haddon Matrix is modified and applied to terrorism. Interventions are divided among those that affect behaviour before the act of terrorism, during the act of terrorism, and after the act of terrorism. This pattern mirrors Haddon's distinctions between pre-crash, crash, and post-crash interventions. As in the Haddon Matrix, distinctions are also made among interventions aimed at humans, the physical environment, and the social-cultural environment. Unlike the original, however, the interventions focused on humans are divided between those aimed at terrorists and those aimed at others. Some recent criminological literature draws a similar distinction between governance strategies that target the criminal directly and those that target third parties, who may have more influence over the direct target and may be more amenable to persuasion.[7] Anti-terrorism laws enacted since September 11 in Canada and elsewhere follow this pattern, with

Figure 1: Terrorism and Security Matrix Inspired by the Haddon Matrix

	Human (Agent)	Human (Third Parties)	Environment (Physical)	Environment (Social –Political)
BEFORE TERRORISM	Criminal law to deter terrorists (attempts, conspiracy, counselling, participation, etc.) Preventive detention Immigration restrictions Selective screening and profiling Security intelligence	Criminal law to deter financing and support of terrorists Vaccinations for smallpox and anthrax* Screen all air passengers*	Weapons control* Reduction of nuclear and chemical materials* Sensors for weapons Monitor water and food supplies* Surveillance and barriers for vulnerable sites (e.g., water supplies)* No potential weapons on airplanes*	Non-violent outlet for grievances* Stigmatization of terrorism "Regime-change" for state sponsors of terrorism*
TERRORISM	Apprehension by law enforcement Armed sky marshals	Training of first responders* Passenger self-defence	Target hardening* Fire and blast standards* Location of nuclear reactors away from cities* Secure cockpits*	Stigmatization so political objectives not achieved Measured response that does not undermine the stigmatization of terrorist violence
AFTER TERRORISM	Apprehension and punishment	Criminal law to deter harbouring of terrorists Public health* (monitor and respond to bio-terrorism threats) Emergency response*	Evacuation routes* Public health infrastructure (hospitals, infectious disease labs, etc.)* Antibiotics and potassium iodide to limit damage of nuclear and bio-terrorism*	Response to grievances* Stigmatization of terrorism

* denotes broader security objectives that respond to more than the threat of terrorism

new crimes directed not only at terrorists but at third parties who finance terrorists or deal with the property of terrorists. These laws may be more effective because they are aimed at third parties who may be more rational than politically or religiously motivated terrorists.

Figure 1 also highlights those interventions in each cell of the matrix that can advance a broader security agenda by lessening the harm not only of terrorism but of other disasters as well. For example, public health measures and responses to grievances that create an environment conducive to terrorism may also advance a broader human security agenda. Target-hardening responses may make buildings more resistant to fires and blasts that are caused by accidents as well as terrorism. The control of various weapons as an intervention that affects the physical environment may also help reduce other crimes or harms caused by accidents or suicide.[8] This system builds on the insight of the National Research Council that many engineering and science-based responses to terrorism can also help prevent a wide range of harms, including natural disasters and diseases. It provides a means to allocate resources rationally between measures that respond only to the risk of terrorism and those that also respond to the more frequent risk of accidents. Such comparisons are crucial if society is to attempt to respond to terrorism in a rational manner that does not ignore other threats to human security.

The implications of this terrorism and security matrix are not that we should dispense with criminal laws that attempt to deter and punish terrorists, but that we should not rely on such measures alone. The actions of committed terrorists are likely to be at least as difficult to deter as the actions of drivers.[9] The stigmatization of terrorism so that its political objectives backfire may influence terrorists, but the threat of punishment and apprehension – the main objectives of most anti-terrorism legislation – do not seem to deter those prepared to die for their cause. Following Haddon, this conclusion should encourage policy-makers to explore interventions that alter the physical and social environment in which the terrorist operates. Interventions such as controls on nuclear and biological substances and weapons become more important, as do those such as better buildings that can limit the damage from bombs and explosions. This matrix, when applied to the bombing in Bali, Indonesia, on October 12, 2002, raises issues not only about the adequacy of Indonesian law in deterring terrorism but also about the way terrorists gained access to explosives and whether lives could have been saved by better fire and blast standards.

Greater emphasis should be placed on interventions that affect both the physical and the socio-political environments. Examples include the control of weapons and of hazardous nuclear and chemical substances, both at the source and through the use of various sensors. This focus also directs attention towards surveillance and barriers protecting sites that are particularly vulnerable to terrorists. Public health measures such as vaccinations for smallpox and anthrax are also possible anti-terrorism measures. More controversially, responses to the grievances of terrorists,[10] combined with the stigmatization of the use of violence for political and religious ends, may affect the political and social environment in which terrorists operate. Disproportionate punishment of terrorists and their supporters may backfire if it makes terrorists into martyrs and undermines the stigmatization of terrorist violence. Another controversial response that alters the socio-cultural environment in which terrorism operates are sanctions or even more forceful attempts at "regime change" for states that sponsor and support terrorism.

The matrix also directs attention to another, sometimes sensitive, issue: responses to limit harm after an act of terrorism has occurred. Better fire and blast standards for buildings probably could have saved lives in the terrorist attacks on both the World Trade Center and the Bali nightclub. Better training and technology for emergency responders may also limit the harm of mass terrorism. Better communications systems may have prevented some of the deaths of firefighters and police officers in the New York attacks. In addition, strong public health systems will be necessary to contain the effects of nuclear and bioterrorism, through monitoring outbreaks and providing drugs to limit the damage. There is a tendency to discount the importance of these post-terrorism measures because they seem to accept the inevitability of evil acts and may re-enforce people's sense of insecurity. Nevertheless, the harm-reduction approach of public health and the Haddon Matrix insist that policy-makers invest in such measures if they produce cost-effective reductions of the harm of terrorism. If the policy calculus includes non-terrorist threats to human security, such interventions may be particularly attractive, given their ability to reduce the harm of natural disasters, diseases, accidental fires, and explosions. Finally, harm-reducing interventions may have a normative edge because, compared with the use of the criminal law to deter and apprehend terrorists, they minimize threats to liberty, privacy, and equality.

The terrorism and security matrix is not an end in itself and must be supplemented by normative analysis. For example, it could be argued that drastic measures such as the preventive detention of suspected terrorists, widespread monitoring of private conversations, racial or religious profiling, collective punishment, or immigration restrictions on certain groups may perhaps help prevent terrorism. Such measures would, however, be unacceptable because of normative concerns about fairness, privacy, and equality. At the very least, the over-inclusive nature of such responses and their harmful effects on those who have no intent to commit acts of terrorism must be considered. Regime change may not be justified if it causes suffering to innocent people or subverts a democratically elected regime. The precautionary principle that requires public health officials to take all welfare-maximizing steps, such as vaccinations or the treatment of possibly infected blood, should not, in the absence of conclusive evidence, be applied in cases where particular individuals are subjected to the coercive powers of state detention or military force.[11]

ALTERNATIVES TO THE CRIMINAL SANCTION

Canada's most significant anti-terrorism initiative, the *Anti-terrorism Act*, has been justified on the basis that it aims to prevent terrorism before it occurs. Nevertheless, the preventive vision of the act is impoverished. Its interventions are limited to four of the twelve cells of the terrorism and security matrix: human interventions targeting the terrorist and third parties that assist the terrorist both before and after the act of terrorism. The *Anti-terrorism Act* is largely restricted to new offences directed against terrorists and those who finance terrorists, as well as some new investigative powers, trial procedures, and increased punishment for terrorists. It does not attempt to regulate the physical environment before, during, or after terrorism or to provide a better public health and emergency response to terrorism that has occurred. Some of these shortcomings may reflect limits on the jurisdiction of the federal government and on the scope of even a massive omnibus bill. Nevertheless, the limited vision of the *Anti-terrorism Act* remains relevant to Canadians who want their governments to take a comprehensive and coordinated response to terrorism and other security threats.

Even within its area of jurisdiction, the federal government can be criticized for not devoting more attention to alternatives to the criminal sanction which may be more effective in preventing terrorism. *The Anti-terrorism Act*, with its focus on deterring and punishing terrorists, was the government's first priority. *The Public Safety Act,* which focuses on administrative and regulatory responses to terrorism, was a very distant second. *The Public Safety Act* was introduced after the *Anti-terrorism Act* and has not yet been enacted – well over a year after September 11. As we saw in chapter 2, the *Anti-terrorism Act*, with some exceptions in the financing area, largely made criminal conduct that was already criminal before September 11, and most of its new investigative powers and offences were not even used during the first year of the law's existence. In contrast, the *Public Safety Act* would provide new powers to ministers with mandates over transportation, the environment, health, food and drugs, energy, and hazardous biological, chemical, and explosive substances. It relies less on the heavy and reactive hand of the criminal law and prosecutions and more on the gentler and pro-active hand of administrative regulation. It attempts less to deter terrorists and more to increase the security of sites and material that can be used or targeted by terrorists. It addresses practical issues such as the security of airports and pipelines and the control of explosives and biological agents.

Many of the new administrative powers in the *Public Safety Act* relating to the screening of airline passengers, the establishment of better airport security, and the import, export, and manufacture of biological agents, explosives, and other potentially hazardous goods may have a greater chance of preventing terrorism than the broad offences and enhanced punishments of the *Anti-terrorism Act*. This argument is especially true in light of the fact that what the September 11 terrorists did was already criminal long before they boarded the four airliners. An administrative approach that relies less on the heavy hand of the criminal sanction and more on encouraging private actors to take their own security measures also has a greater potential to manage the insecurity created by our reliance on risky technology such as nuclear power, computer systems, energy supplies, airplanes, and high buildings.

This is not to say that an administrative response to terrorism may not threaten important values. As originally drafted, the *Public Safety Act* gave the minister of defence too broad a discretion to declare military security zones around the sites of summits and other places. When the *Public Safety Act* was introduced by the government for a third time on October 31, 2002, these powers for security zones were scrapped.[12] As we saw in chapter 2, the federal privacy commissioner has raised concerns that, even after the new restrictions, the police can still use passenger information obtained under the *Public Safety Act* for general crime control purposes. He has expressed even stronger objections to plans to keep a database on the foreign travel of all Canadians.[13] Administrative measures, like the criminal law, can infringe civil liberties and privacy. To be fair, however, the government has responded to many of the civil liberties concerns raised about previous versions of the *Public Safety Act*. The value of the act's multi-department approach to regulating materials that can be used for terrorism and sites that are vulnerable to terrorist attacks should be recognized. The dangers of "thinking outside the box" and taking new and creative approaches to anti-terrorism policies are less when administrative measures are used that will not imprison people in boxes.

The failure to make the administrative regulation of the *Public Safety Act* a priority over the additions to the *Criminal Code* in the *Anti-terrorism Act* is unfortunate. Administrative measures may be more effective in preventing terrorism while, at the same time, providing less of a threat to liberty, privacy, and equality than the criminal law. Two concrete examples concerning the protection of vital infrastructure and aviation security will help make this point. They suggest that we may be more secure if we devote our limited resources to protecting places, as opposed to targeting people, and if we enlist the private sector and technology, as opposed to the public police, in our quest for increased security.

The Security of Vital Infrastructure

Given our need for power and heat, it is vitally important that we protect hydro transmission lines and oil and gas pipelines from possible terrorist attacks. A criminal law approach to this task, found in the *Anti-terrorism Act*, is to define terrorist activities to include intentional and serious disruptions of essential public and private services. One of the government's justifications for this provision held that it was necessary to protect critical infrastructure such as pipelines and hydro towers. One problem, however, is that the new criminal offence may be overbroad. As originally introduced, it would have made some illegal strikes and protests acts of terrorism. Even if the amendments to the *Anti-terrorism Act* solved this problem, another problem is that the threat of extra punishment, preventive arrests, and investigative hearings under the act may not stop determined and elusive terrorists. Finally, it was already a crime to destroy a pipeline or a hydro tower, or to attempt or conspire to do so, long before the new terrorism offences of the *Anti-terrorism Act* were enacted.

An alternative administrative law approach to the same problem is contemplated in the yet to be enacted *Public Safety Act*.[14] It authorizes an administrative agency, the National Energy Board, to require companies to take safety and security measures to protect pipelines.[15] This regulatory approach of requiring corporations to take responsibility for their own security measures – whether through private police, risk surveillance strategies, environmental design, technology, or the construction of barriers[16] – is more in line with contemporary security strategies than the older state-based deterrence and criminal law model of the *Anti-terrorism Act*.[17] It provides a fail-safe system should the criminal law fail. As Janice Stein has suggested, old top-down approaches may be inadequate to deal with multicentred terrorist networks that can strike in unlikely ways.[18] By enlisting the private sector in its quest for security and by focusing on vulnerable places as opposed to people, the *Public Safety Act* may provide better security than the state-dominated deterrence model of the *Anti-terrorism Act*.

The *Public Safety Act*, to the extent that it enlists companies to make vulnerable sites more secure, also poses much less of a threat to civil liberties than the criminal-based approach of defining disruptions of essential services as terrorism. Increasing the surveillance and security of sites vulnerable to terrorism also may present less of a threat to equality values. The emphasis would be not on police surveillance of people or groups who might be suspected of terrorism, but on the protection of their likely targets. Increasing the safety and security of pipelines and transmission towers may also improve response times in cases of accidents or natural disasters, such as ice storms or earthquakes, that may more frequently affect the delivery of gas and light to Canadian homes than acts of terrorism.

The Security of Airplanes

A criminal law approach to the prevention of hijackings relies on stiff penalties against hijacking and on punishing killings committed during a hijacking as first-degree murder. Such criminal laws were already in place before September 11. The *Anti-terrorism Act* deemed the commission of a terrorist crime as an aggravating factor at sentencing and included killings during all terrorist activities as first-degree murder. A moment's reflection will reveal that such strategies will not deter those such as the September 11 terrorists who are prepared to give their lives for their cause. A toughened criminal law approach would place a police officer on each plane as protection against hijackers. After initial controversy, including threats that the United States would not accept Canadian flights into Washington, armed RCMP officers now are on Canadian flights into Washington, as well as on some other flights. This is a costly strategy, not least because the Canadian air marshals fly first class to be near the cockpit, which is estimated to be open at least eight times during a flight.[19] The United States has many more police officers per capita than Canada and probably many more armed marshals. Still, even the Americans cannot place armed marshals on every plane. Just as it is impossible to place a cop on every corner, it is impossible to put a cop on every plane. For enthusiasts of the criminal law, the next best thing is to deputize pilots by giving them firearms, a practice the United States is moving towards. Although there is a pilot on every flight, pilots are not trained to be police officers. As the Canadian minister of transport has recognized, arming pilots introduces "a new element of danger" on airplanes.[20] The arming of sky marshals or pilots could provide terrorists with access to weapons that could otherwise be screened out. It is a risky and desperate criminal law strategy. It could quite literally backfire.

A better approach to aviation security, one achieved largely through administrative and regulatory law that regulates the physical environment, is to ensure that all passengers are deprived of access to weapons, explosives, and the cockpit. Although travellers in Canada pay more in security surcharges than travellers in the United States, there are real questions whether Canada has done enough to make air travel more secure. A year after September 11, the chair of a Senate Committee worried that box-cutters of the type used by the September 11 terrorists to gain control of the planes could still be brought onto airplanes at Canada's busiest airport.[21] Air Canada pilots have also demanded double security doors for their cockpits or taser weapons.[22] There are even greater concerns about the security of the bottom half of planes. One Canadian official has indicated that it may take until 2006 for all baggage on Canadian flights to be screened, even though over four hundred US airports have new equipment to detect bombs in luggage loaded on planes.[23]

A new Crown corporation, the Canadian Air Transport Security Authority, has been created and mandated with responsibility for pre-board screening, as well as the management and training of those who conduct such screening. Nevertheless, concerns have been raised that not all airport personnel with access to planes have adequate security clearances. Not all baggage placed on airplanes is screened. As the *Calgary Herald* commented: "Equipping Canada's 89 airports with simple X-ray devices on baggage ramps, and the personnel to analyze the images, should have been the first purchases from the $2.2 billion air security budget."[24] The new agency has ordered $50 million of equipment to scan bags and passengers for explosives, but this amount still marks a relatively small portion of the $416 million it will spend in its first year of operation.[25] Better technology in airports and ports could provide a means to screen all passengers, all baggage, and all containers for weapons. It should avoid any temptation to engage in profiling practices that may not catch all terrorists, but may inconvenience and harm of the dignity of many people who are thought to look like terrorists or come from the same country as terrorists. Technology can also be designed to allow people to be screened for hidden objects while not unnecessarily invading a person's privacy by allowing the operator to see all the person's unclothed features.[26] Better technology can minimize risks to equality, privacy, and liberty while providing better security than the old-fashioned criminal law methods of increased punishment and armed sky marshals.

A preventive approach to terrorism that draws on the fields of regulation, engineering, and public health will build in multiple systems in its attempts to prevent terrorism. If technology fails and terrorists are able to gain access to weapons while on planes, a second system should attempt to prevent them from gaining access to the cockpit. One risky fail-safe system is armed sky marshals or armed pilots. A better fail-safe approach than relying on fallible people with arms is to design the physical environment to be more secure. The cockpit could have double doors with bullet proofing and special locks. Communications systems could be upgraded to minimize the need for the cockpit door to be open during flights. About $35 million has been allocated by the federal government to assist airlines in re-enforcing cockpit doors at an estimated cost of $100,000 a plane, but most travellers have yet to see dramatic changes with respect to the security of the cockpit. Modern technology should be able to design more effective means of preventing planes from being used as flying bombs than the old-fashioned ideas of armed or deputized sky marshals. Weapons screening and secure cockpits may also have benefits beyond the threat of terrorist hijackings because they could provide protection from mentally disturbed or intoxicated passengers who can present a danger to aircraft safety just as surely as terrorists can.

Prevention and Profiling

The use of technology to secure cockpits and to screen all passengers and all baggage on airplanes in an efficient manner also avoids the ethical and legal harms of profiling passengers on the basis of colour, country of origin or religion, or even by more precise and less discriminatory means such as travel patterns. Ashton Carter has argued since September 11 that surveillance of means, such as crop dusters, germ culture, bomb ingredients, airports, and pilot instruction, "raises far fewer civil liberties issues than does surveillance of persons, and it might be much more effective. A group that evades surveillance becomes subject to *prevention* by efforts to keep destructive means out of their hands." A preventive approach does not rely on targeting individuals in a manner that may be expensive or fallible or that raises serious issues about discrimination.

Support for racial and religious profiling in the wake of September 11 ignores the fact that profiling is a crude and inefficient law enforcement technique, especially when compared with either the surveillance of vulnerable sites for terrorism or the use of technology to screen all people boarding airplanes or crossing borders. As Professor Carter has observed:

Placing all Middle Eastern male non-citizens resident in the United States under surveillance, for example, is both objectionable and impractical. But inquiring after all those persons, of whatever nationality, who take flying lessons but are not interested in learning to take off or land, who rent crop dusters, or who seek information on the antibiotic resistance of anthrax strains or the layout of a nuclear power plant is feasible and might be extremely useful.[27]

A preventive approach to terrorism should focus on the surveillance and hardening of vulnerable sites and the use of technology to screen all people. Such an approach minimizes the likelihood of both human error and discriminatory profiling.

Avoiding Terror Traps while Taking Security Seriously

Cracking down on terrorism with tough criminal laws may not only fail to prevent terrorism but result in a "terror trap" in which society devotes disproportionate attention to a few widely publicized acts of terrorism and produces repressive conditions that make violent terrorists look like heroes or martyrs to some people. Gwynne Dyer has taken a particularly hard-headed approach to this issue by arguing that the harms of terrorism – including September 11 and the Bali bombings – are "statistically and strategically insignificant," even though "it goes against every instinct of human sympathy and every rule of practical politics to say so."[28] One reservation about Dyer's observations is that they discount the ability of successful acts of biological and nuclear terrorism to cause much greater death and suffering than the world wars that Dyer uses as his baseline. But there is something to Dyer's argument that the greatest danger of September 11 is that governments, driven by the media and an alarmed public, will overreact in a heavy-handed and ineffective way that will hurt many innocent people and groups and perhaps inspire more terrorism. Tougher criminal laws will not prevent terrorism, but they may threaten civil liberties, equality, and robust democratic processes. A free and democratic society that respects rights may be necessary to produce the type of social structures that can produce the needed ingenuity to manage the many risks of modern life, including terrorism.[29]

An administrative and disaster-based approach to terrorism allows it to be taken seriously while minimizing the risk of a terror trap that infringes democratic values and produces collateral damage. Although there are no guarantees, an administrative, as opposed to a criminal, law approach is less likely to produce the conditions of repression and stereotyping under which terrorism may grow as an alternative to peaceful politics. It also provides the greatest opportunity for terrorism to be integrated and prioritized into the range of environmental, safety, and health risks to human security that governments must face and manage. The criminal law approach to terrorism that Canada has taken makes Canada vulnerable to a non-rational and even counter-productive allocation of resources to terrorism.

In the abstract, Canada should be better positioned than the United States to take a comprehensive approach to human security which does not rely on the criminal sanction. Canada relies much less than the

United States on the criminal sanction. The United States has an incarceration rate six times Canada's and it can attempt to deter terrorists
by the death penalty. It is generally much easier to enact legislation
within the Canadian parliamentary system than the American congres-
sional system. The federal division of powers adds complexities in both
countries, but the courts and the public in Canada seem less suspicious
than in the United States of increased federal power, especially with
respect to security, health, and the environment.[30] Canada's universal
public health-care system gives the state both the responsibility and a
means to deal with the health consequences of mass terrorism and
other disasters. Canadians are much less resistant to stringent controls
on weapons than are Americans. As George Grant and many others
have pointed out, the tory and socialist strains in Canadian political
culture should produce a greater tolerance for the state assuming
responsibility for more aspects of public well-being. Toryism can also
produce a confidence in traditional criminal law, and socialism can
produce a scepticism about using the criminal law to control all social
problems.

Despite this potential, Canada at present has a much less comprehensive and integrated anti-terrorism policy than the United States.
One factor may be a hollowing out of the state since Grant's time,
including significant inroads by American-style "neo-conservatism" or
what Grant recognized were "old-fashioned liberals" calling themselves conservative.[31] Another factor may be that Canadians still feel
comparatively safe from terrorism and are more inclined to spend
governmental monies on other goods. For whatever reason, the Canadian approach to terrorism is much thinner than the American. The
United States did not stop at the criminal law reforms of the *Patriot
Act*, but enacted other laws on airline security, insurance, and public
health measures to respond to the risk of biological terrorism. The
American plans for "Homeland Security" recognize the need to protect
critical infrastructure, to defend against catastrophic nuclear, chemical,
or biological terrorism, to augment emergency preparedness, to
improve the coordination of multiple intelligence agencies, and to
ensure border and transportation security, as well as the enforcement
of new criminal laws against terrorism.[32] A Canadian response to
terrorism should be no less comprehensive than the American response.
Given the greater role of Canadian governments in health and environmental issues, the Canadian response should aspire to be more
comprehensive and holistic. Unfortunately, it is not.

Preventing Nuclear and Biological Terrorism (and Accidents)

The *Public Safety Act*, like new British legislation enacted after September 11, contains provisions for licensing and for controlling access to dangerous chemical and biological materials. This approach is especially compelling, given reports that Iraq may have received its original supplies of various strains of anthrax and the bacteria that causes gas gangrene from the United States and that a number of countries, including perhaps Iraq, may have access to the deadly smallpox virus. The *Public Safety Act*'s approach of tightly regulating access to dangerous materials recognizes that "the most immediate legal reform to reduce the risk of catastrophic terrorism is comprehensive and effective regulatory controls to govern production, acquisition and possession of relevant materials and technologies," as opposed to criminal laws to deter nuclear or biological terrorism.[33] The harm of biological and nuclear terrorism is so catastrophic that it dwarfs the harm of September 11. We must take even a remote risk of such terrorism seriously.

The scary scenario of nuclear or biological terrorism should not blind us to the more likely threats of nuclear or biological accidents.[34] When the harm is truly catastrophic, we should not rely on attempts to change human behaviour through increased penalties and new police powers, but instead engineer the environment to make it safer from both human error and malfeasance. This approach is suggested by public health experts such as William Haddon. It is also the approach advocated by a judicial inquiry into the contamination of water in Walkerton, Ontario. That inquiry proposed the use of modern risk management techniques, multiple barriers, and multiple systems to protect water supplies.[35] A similar approach can be applied to the harm of terrorism. The criminal law should be seen as only one system, and a highly imperfect one at that, to prevent terrorism and to respond to its harms.

The focus in public health is not on identifying, deterring, or denouncing the cause of harm. It is simply on preventing and lessening the harm. The philosophy of public health is pragmatic. Whatever means are available and cost effective in preventing and reducing harm should be used. From a public health approach, one of the more positive steps taken by the Canadian government after September 11 was the October 18, 2001, announcement by Minister of Health Alan Rock that $11.5 million had been dedicated to health measures to deal with terrorism, including $5.6 million to increase the stockpile of antibiotics to deal with biological accidents, $2.2 million to better detect radioactive material, $2 million to better control biological agents, and $1.6 for better training for emergency response teams.[36] The focus was not on deterring and denouncing the evil of terrorism, but in preventing terrorists from having access to biological and nuclear materials and in reducing the harm that could occur should they obtain access to such materials. Such investments are modest compared to the billions that have been allocated to policing, security intelligence, and screening immigrants.

Since that time, however, the Canadian response to the threats of bio-terrorism has lagged behind the American response. There is an effective and safe vaccination against the anthrax poisoning that killed five Americans after September 11. The vaccination is presently given to the American military. Unfortunately, only one company makes the vaccine and it is struggling to produce just under 5 million dosages, all of which are destined for the American Department of Defense. Smallpox is an even more deadly threat than anthrax. Canada, like other countries, has stopped vaccinating its population for smallpox because of concerted international efforts to stop the deadly disease. But there are concerns that the Soviet Union may have developed smallpox as a biological weapon and that this strain may have been acquired by other countries. Even before September 11, the Americans had modelled the devastating effects of a quick-spreading smallpox outbreak. Vaccinations for smallpox carry greater risks than vaccinations for anthrax, but the United States has started programs to vaccinate military and emergency workers for smallpox and has ordered enough free smallpox vaccinations for every American. The Center for Disease Control has also developed detailed emergency response plans to track and, it hopes, contain any outbreak. Canada lags behind. For well over a year after September 11, Canada was content to rely on its existing stockpile of 365,000 doses of smallpox vaccine. It was only in November 2002 that Canada decided to spend the $30–$40 million required to contract for 10 million doses of the vaccine, which, when diluted, could provide enough vaccine for the entire Canadian population. There are no plans, however, to offer the vaccine to the population and Canada had plans to inoculate only 500 emergency workers, compared with 1 million emergency and military personnel who will be vaccinated in the United States.[37] Canada cannot afford to ignore even small threats of biological terrorism. Even if people were deliberately infected only in the United States, the disease could easily spread to Canada.

There have been some Canadian responses since September 11 to the threat of nuclear terrorism. The Canadian Nuclear Safety Commission has required companies that operate nuclear plants to provide the capability for an armed response on site, barriers to protect against car and truck bombs, and better security screening and searches of personnel and vehicles.[38] It is not clear, however, what responses have been taken to the danger that suicide terrorists could crash an airplane into a nuclear reactor, an act that the September 11 terrorists apparently contemplated. September 11 has not caused Canadians to rethink decisions to locate two nuclear plants right next to Toronto, the country's largest city. Certain public health measures can be taken to limit some of the harmful effects of radiation: for instance, there has been increased private sale of low-cost potassium iodide tablets, which can limit the harmful effects of radiation, but no widespread public distribution of the drugs.[39] There may be political resistance to public health measures to respond to the dangers of biological and nuclear terrorism or accidents, as these measures often alarm or even panic people. They may suggest that biological and nuclear terrorism or accidents are inevitable. This fear, however, does not excuse governments from taking steps to protect the security and health of their populations. The Canadian state, with its universal health system and history of intervention, should be in a better position than the privatized American system to develop and implement such public health measures. Unfortunately, Canada appears to have done less than the United States since September 11.

The threat of biological terrorism suggests that we should think twice about cutting back on public health systems that can monitor and treat such harm. Unfortunately, governments seemed slow to learn the public health lessons of both accidents and mass terrorism. A month after September 11, the Ontario government fired five scientists who were experts on biohazards. Even in the wake of seven deaths in Walkerton and criticism from the public inquiry, Ontario has yet to increase the monitoring of rural water supplies.[40] These events unfortunately fit into a pattern of the neo-liberal state cutting back on expenditures that affect human well-being, while increasing expenditures on the criminal justice system. The threat after September 11 that water supplies can be deliberately, not just accidentally, poisoned only increases the need for governments to maintain strong public health systems and infrastructures. The same is true with food supplies. The threat after September 11 that some terrorist group might deliberately poison food supplies underlines the importance of monitoring and inspection that will also detect accidental contamination.[41] Such preventive approaches can achieve a true economy because they are directed against accidental as well as deliberate contamination. An administrative approach based on public health principles of harm reduction can be expanded to a broader concern about the multiple risks to human security faced in our complex society.

The G8 and the Reduction of Nuclear Material

The G8 summit hosted by Canada in the summer of 2002 dealt with the issue of terrorism in a preventive and generally productive manner that focused on engineering the environment to be less risky. Foreign ministers meeting before the formal summit at Kananaskis issued directives on transport security that included both airline and container security. These directives also committed the G8 countries to improve controls on explosives and firearms, mentioning in particular better technology to detect potentially lethal devices and better export controls. The formal G8 summit also took a similar preventive approach by focusing on the control of weapons of mass destruction such as nuclear, radioactive, chemical, and biological materials. The countries committed themselves to spending $20 billion over the next ten years "to address non-proliferation, disarmament, counter-terrorism and nuclear safety issues ... initially in Russia ... Among our priority concerns are the destruction of chemical weapons, the dismantlement of decommissioned nuclear submarines, the disposition of fissile materials and the employment of former weapons scientists." Attention was directed to the need to "develop and maintain appropriate effective measures to account for and secure such items in production, use, storage and domestic and international transport."[42] This plan responded to the danger of terrorists obtaining "loose nucs" in Russia and elsewhere. As the Economist has editorialized, short of rogue state assistance, "the likeliest source" for terrorists to acquire nuclear, chemical, or biological weapons is "the sprawling weapons complex of the former Soviet Union ... Skimping on nuclear security was always a false savings. [Since September 11] it has been outrageous folly."[43] The G8, often criticized for its elitist nature, took a multilateralist stance on nuclear safety by indicating its willingness to cooperate with other countries. It also committed itself to the development of a nuclear safety and security group by the time of the next summit. The evil irrationality of those who would resort to nuclear terrorism is obvious, and the G8 appropriately addressed the more pressing issue of reducing access to nuclear weapons.

Canada, as host of this summit, deserves credit both for the preventive approach taken to terrorism and, in particular, the emphasis placed on reducing nuclear supplies. Canada, of course, learned important lessons about the dangers of nuclear proliferation when its CANDU nuclear reactors were used by India to explode a nuclear device in 1974.[44] Canada also deserves credit for the fact that the entire G8 summit itself was not taken over by terrorism. John Kirton observed that, in the lead-up to the summit, Canada "worked to make broader linkages, in finance, global growth, the natural environment, African poverty reduction, post-conflict reconstruction and elsewhere that would prevent the threat from recurring once the current anti-terrorism campaign was won."[45] A more holistic approach to global justice and a broad human security agenda may help prevent terrorism. The G8 experience, in contrast to Canada's inconsequential military contribution in Afghanistan, provided a brief glimpse of how Canada might be able to reclaim its internationalist middle-power role in moderating American preoccupations.

Target Hardening

Target hardening is a delicate subject because, to some extent, it proceeds on the pessimistic assumption that some attacks (or accidents) cannot be prevented. The issue of target hardening, however, must be addressed because of its potential to save lives. It is possible that lives might have been saved by better structural design and fireproofing of the twin towers of the World Trade Center. The north tower, which had 4-centimetre-thick fireproofing, fell in 104 minutes, while the south tower, which had only a 2-centimetre-thick fireproofing, fell in just 56 minutes, far below the minimum 2 hours that should be provided to allow for evacuation of such buildings.[46] The collapse of buildings and the spread of fire also probably contributed to the almost two hundred deaths in the nightclub bombings in Bali. Tougher fire-proofing standards for both buildings and their contents have the potential to limit some of the damage from terrorist attacks, but also the more likely occurrence of accidental fires. An architect who specializes in forensic investigations of building disasters commented that the fire that destroyed the World Trade Center "could happen anywhere ... The situation at the Trade Center wasn't the worst that I've seen." A retired New York City fire chief and fire safety consultant argued that "the fire service has seen a consistent weakening in fire safety" and that the spray-on fireproofing used in much of the World Trade Center is often quickly consumed in fires.

Although concerns about building safety and other forms of target hardening do not focus on the evil of terrorist attacks or the punishment of terrorists, they are relevant to some of the victims of September 11. A mother who lost her son in the attack has taken an interest in better building and fire safety standards. She commented: "I can't tell you what it's like for a mother to see the building hit, knowing your child is in the building. We're all at risk today ... I do not want 3000 people to lose their life and have it be in vain."[47] A public health approach to reducing harm does not mean that we should accept that people will hijack airliners and fly them into buildings or plant high-power bombs. Nevertheless, it does suggest that consideration should be paid to minimizing the harm of fires and blasts regardless of their cause.

Emergency Preparedness

September 11 revealed weaknesses in emergency preparedness in both the United States and Canada. Sadly, it appears that the lives of many firefighters might have been saved by better coordination between the New York Fire and Police departments and by better communication systems.[48] The Canadian approach to emergencies caused by terrorism, accidents, or natural disasters is even less sophisticated than the American approach, which involves a powerful and visible federal agency that can intervene and coordinate activities after a disaster.[49] Thomas Axworthy has warned that local first responders to emergencies in Canada are underprepared and inadequately coordinated with the provincial and federal governments. Noting that an anthrax or smallpox outbreak starting in Buffalo would soon spread to Toronto, he has argued that the federal government should immediately provide resources for emergency plans to be drawn up for Canadian cities. "The Prime Minister should then meet with the premiers and mayors in a closed session to review the results ... The military's capacity to respond to national emergencies – a flood in the Fraser Valley, a biological crisis in Montreal, etc – is also badly lacking."[50] The province of Ontario responded to September 11 by enacting a new *Emergencies Readiness Act* that requires each municipality and provincial ministry to prepare and review on an annual basis emergency plans that address hazards, public education, and training.[51] Problems of coordination and resources, however, remain. A post-September 11 report prepared by the Defence Science Advisory Board concluded that a disaster like September 11, "which created 3,000 urgent or critical cases, would break the entire system." It concluded that existing emergency responses will fail because there is no national command structure that would bring federal, provincial, and municipal governments and the private sector together to deal with a large-scale disaster.[52]

One of the most compelling justifications for increased spending on the military has been the important role that the military can play in responding to natural disasters such as the Winnipeg Flood or the Quebec Ice Storm and to man-made disasters such as search and rescue missions or chemical and nuclear accidents. In his attempts to secure more funding for the military, the minister of defence would be well advised to remind Canadians and his colleagues of the military's role in responding to such disasters, rather than attempting to make the difficult case that more soldiers or the technology required to operate in combat with American forces will somehow prevent terrorism.[53]

One of the great values of increased spending on emergency preparedness is that it responds to a broad range of threats to the security of Canadians and is not limited to the threat of catastrophic terrorism. In creating a new emergency management centre for firefighters and other emergency workers, the Ontario government recognized not only that "the events of last Sept. 11 accelerated our desire to review Ontario's fire and emergency response training and equipment,"[54] but also that the end result would be a better response to accidents caused by fire, nuclear and chemical materials. Unfortunately, emergency preparedness has not yet had the same political appeal to most governments as criminal law measures that promise to disrupt and punish terrorists, even though they respond to a much broader range of security needs.

The 2001 Security Budget

The 2001 security budget should be evaluated on the basis of the most cost-effective means to prevent and limit the harm of terrorism and other threats to the security of Canadians. The budget allocated $7.7 billion over the next five years to enhancing security. The largest category of that budget, $2.1 billion, was devoted to airline security. This amount is not intended to be new money, because $2.2 billion in revenues from a new air travellers security charge had already been projected. As we saw above, more of this money should be directed at improved technology to screen all passengers and baggage rather than to selective screening by airport security personnel. There should be more emphasis on engineering secure cockpits than on the risky strategies of arming sky marshals or pilots. An additional $1.6 billion was devoted to policing and security, with another $0.5 billion targeted for the military. Although the hiring of more people to work in security intelligence may be justified and the military could use more funds for peacekeeping abroad and emergency preparedness at home, it is doubtful that more police and soldiers will in themselves help prevent terrorism. They may also make it more likely that Canada will continue to focus on using the criminal sanction and military force to prevent terrorism.

The budget allocated $1.2 billion to "a secure, open and efficient border." Again, the emphasis here should be more on technology, including scanners and sensors that screen all traffic crossing the border for weapons and radio-active material, rather than simply adding more custom officials to ask a few more perfunctory questions in routine screening or to engage in more intensive selective screening. The reliance on human screening strategies, as opposed to technological strategies, runs the risk of human error and discriminatory forms of profiling. The budget allocated $1 billion to increased screening of entrants to Canada. If these funds are spent on administering wholesale exclusionary policies, such as the safe third-country agreement with the United States, their benefits in preventing terrorism will not be great, given that few terrorists enter into Canada or the United States as refugees. The costs of excluding refugees who may enrich Canadian society are also likely to be significant.

The preventive and environmental approach urged here lagged behind in the 2001 security budget, with $396 million dedicated to emergency preparedness and $513 million to chemical, biological, and nuclear threats.[55] It is a positive sign that these items were included in the budget and that non-trivial sums were devoted to them. Some of these funds have already been spent on useful research into developing drugs to combat the Ebola virus and acute radiation syndrome, and into production of hand-held detectors of biological agents, detectable markers for explosives, and protection for first responders from biological and chemical agents.[56] Nevertheless, the total amount of spending on such environmental and preventive measures remains relatively small in relation to the amount of money that was dedicated to policing, border security, and increased screening of entrants to Canada. It also remains small given the value of emergency preparedness and nuclear and chemical safety in responding to accidents and disasters, as well as terrorism.

The 2001 security budget and the 2002 Throne Speech have both been severely criticized for not providing more resources to the military. Jack Granatstein, for example, has called for staged increases in military spending of $2.5 billion in 2003, $3.5 billion in 2004, $4.5 billion in 2005, $5.5 billion in 2006, $6.5 billion in 2007, and $1.5 billion each year after for at least five more years. He acknowledges that "such sums would slow down the paying of the debt, but they are absolutely necessary."[57] Not only would such staggering sums slow the paying of the debt but they would also decrease spending on social, economic, and health matters that affect the immediate security of Canadians much more than the ability of the Canadian military to fight alongside the high-tech American military. Some more modest increases on military spending may be justified. Some have suggested that an additional $1.2 billion a year is needed to maintain the existing complement and ensure that the military can respond to a broad range of disasters.[58] Expenditures on the military, like all public expenditures, must ultimately be determined on the basis of their ability to contribute to the security and well-being of Canadians.

Coordinating the Prevention of Terrorism

A preventive approach to terrorism will require a multidisciplinary and multi-agency approach. In the Canadian context, the multi-departmental approach of the *Public Safety Act* may be more effective in preventing terrorism than the criminal justice approach of the *Anti-terrorism Act*, which makes various police forces and federal and provincial attorneys general departments the lead agencies in combating terrorism. The

Americans have responded to the challenges of preventing terrorism by creating a huge new agency with the mandate to ensure "homeland security." One danger with such an approach is that the multiple departments brought together to achieve homeland security may focus their mandate on terrorism and downplay other threats to security such as transportation, nuclear, and food safety accidents. In turn, departments outside of the new agency may devote less attention to efforts to prevent terrorism. All departments of government should consider what they can do to prevent and respond to terrorism and disasters, but they should not allow anti-terrorism mandates to swamp their other responsibilities in regulating multiple risks to their security and well-being.

There is a need for effective coordination of security and emergency preparedness measures across ministries within governments and among federal, provincial, and local governments. The federal approach has been a new ad hoc Cabinet committee with responsibility for anti-terrorism policy. The committee includes not only the criminal justice ministries of the attorney general and the solicitor general but also Immigration, Health, Transport, Customs, and Foreign Affairs. The Canadian approach of retaining established departments, but providing for coordination at the Cabinet level, may allow for coordination when necessary, while established departments retain the freedom to integrate and prioritize anti-terrorism efforts within their own responsibilities. At the same time, one Cabinet committee may not be strong enough to coordinate all the security responsibilities of the federal government, let alone coordinate with provincial and local governments. Emergency response in particular requires better coordination, given the diffusion of responsibilities among all three levels of government.

Security Intelligence

September 11 has widely been seen as an "intelligence failure." Despite this failure, intelligence agencies in both Canada and the United States have had their budgets substantially increased. In Canada there was an immediate 30 per cent raise in the budget of the Canadian Security Intelligence Service (CSIS). It has plans to hire almost three hundred new people. Some of the new funds have already been spent on dealing with dramatic increases in requests for security clearances in relation to Canada's military operations in Afghanistan.[59] Beyond routine security clearances, security intelligence agencies can provide information on threats to Canada's security through the use of electronic surveillance and both open and human sources. Modern technology allows a vast amount of information to be collected and stored. Nevertheless, there is no guarantee that the information will provide advance intelligence that can be used to prevent terrorism. Much depends on how the intelligence is collected, analyzed, and transmitted to various parts of the government, as well as the level of detail in the information. One of the dangers of post-September 11 increases in security intelligence budgets is that even more raw data will sit on desks, waiting for the analysis that makes the intelligence usable for governments. The collection of increased data can also create risks to privacy and civil liberties.

The emphasis must be on usable information. The Central Intelligence Agency (CIA) and the Federal Bureau of Investigation (FBI) had plenty of early warnings of September 11 sitting on their desks and stored in their filing cabinets. As early as 1996, there was intelligence that an al-Qaeda operative was planning a suicide attack by flying a plane into the White House. In 2000 a source who passed a polygraph told the FBI that he learned hijacking techniques at an al-Qaeda training camp and that he was supposed to meet five or six others, including a pilot, to assist in a hijacking in the United States. In the months and weeks leading to September 11, there were also reports that Osama bin Laden was planning a spectacular and massive attack on American interests.[60] This information, combined with other reports about suspicious people taking flying lessons, did not prevent September 11. CSIS had also been investigating al-Qaeda and similar groups before September 11. The Canadian security intelligence agency had issued a general warning, but not "of a threat sufficient in time or place to have alerted government authorities" to the actual attacks.[61]

Even when intelligence is subject to proper analysis, agencies are notoriously reluctant to share information. In the United States, the CIA and the FBI did not always share important information. Intelligence gathering in Canada is also quite fragmented. It is done in the military, in the civilian security agency (CSIS), and in the Communication Security Establishment (CSE), which was first recognized in Canadian law in the *Anti-terrorism Act* and given a statutory mandate to obtain foreign intelligence involving conversations in Canada. There are also intelligence units in a wide range of governmental departments and agencies. Martin Rudner has observed that Canada's "organizational

proliferation can be a recipe for a diffusion, if not confusion, of effort."
He warns that "compartmentalization, inadequate co-ordination and
turf battles all militate against effective utilization of intelligence."[62]
There is definitely a need for more coordination of Canadian intelligence both at the operational and the oversight levels. It now appears
that a lack of coordination between the FBI and the CIA contributed
to the intelligence failure of September 11. This insight should raise
questions about the degree of coordination among Canada's intelligence agencies. If the FBI and the CIA had trouble talking to each
other, there is a significant likelihood that Canada's multiple intelligence agencies also have the same problem. The challenge of coordination has been increased by the decision in the *Anti-terrorism Act* to
give anti-terrorism powers to officers in hundreds of police forces. The
investigation of the terrorism that killed 329 people in the Air India
bombing has been hindered by problems of coordination among CSIS
and multiple police forces. Overlap and confusion about the respective
roles of the police and CSIS will likely only increase now that the police
have been given the explicit responsibility to investigate crimes of
terrorism. The dividing line between new crimes of terrorism, which
may be committed by participation in or financing of a terrorist group,
and the collection of intelligence about potential terrorists is a fine one.
There may be disputes and turf battles between Canada's various police
forces and security intelligence agencies over the exact location of this
rather fuzzy line and whether prosecutions should be foregone in order
to continue to collect intelligence.

The *Anti-terrorism Act* was a bigger win for the police than for CSIS.
It gave CSIS no new powers. It did not include controversial proposals
that CSIS undercover agents, like the police, should be given powers
to break some laws.[63] Peace officers, and not CSIS agents, were given
the new anti-terrorism powers of preventive arrests and investigative
hearings. CSIS was created after a 1981 royal commission concluded
that the RCMP had engaged in extensive wrongdoing in their anti-
terrorism efforts after the October Crisis. CSIS has a mandate, civilian
expertise, and oversight mechanisms that are designed to minimize the
risk of targeting legitimate dissent. It can more easily than the police
develop the specialized political knowledge and language skills often
necessary to detect sophisticated international terrorists. In contrast,
the police have no special expertise in distinguishing dissent from
terrorism, and they do not have civilian specialists in foreign politics
and foreign languages. Moreover, the police have a broad mandate to

enforce all laws, not just anti-terrorism laws. Once information is received by the police for anti-terrorism purposes, there is a danger that it will be used for more general crime control purposes.

There is a good case for extending the unique oversight and audit provided by the Security Intelligence Review Commission (SIRC) over CSIS to Canada's other intelligence agencies and to any anti-terrorism squads within the RCMP. SIRC is composed of respected privy councillors with a mandate to monitor and audit the performance of CSIS, as well as investigate complaints. It issues annual reports, which have at times been critical of CSIS. It also monitors CSIS closely to see if it is drifting beyond its limited mandate and investigating dissenters. SIRC's composition and mandate compare favourably with the more limited mandate of the oversight provided for the CSE. SIRC also compares favourably to the complaints procedures of most Canadian police forces, procedures that are reactive and often not independent from the police. Even the chair of the RCMP Public Complaints Commission has publicly complained that although the RCMP has received new powers and resources to investigate terrorism, the complaints commission has not received new powers and resources.[64] There may also be a place for a greater legislative role in the oversight of intelligence gathering.[65] Strong oversight and audits of intelligence agencies can help ensure that they do not stray into the investigation of legitimate dissent, but also that they produce information that is useful to both Canada and its allies in helping to prevent terrorism.

Although its increased budget may be justified and CSIS may already have had some anti-terrorism successes since September 11,[66] security intelligence remains only a small part of a comprehensive and preventive security strategy. Intelligence gathering shares many of the limitations of the criminal law because it focuses on what suspected terrorists do before an act of terrorism. Intelligence, like policing, is subject to human error and it may harm values of equality, liberty, and privacy. There is a need for a comprehensive anti-terrorism policy that regulates the physical and political environment that gives terrorists access to weapons and victims. There is a need to screen all airline passengers for weapons, not only those who may be under surveillance or identified as a security risk. Finally, steps should be taken to minimize the harms of terrorism once it has been committed. Although security intelligence agencies and the police obviously have a role to play in preventing and responding to terrorism, it is also important to invest in other means to prevent terrorism.

A BROAD HUMAN SECURITY AGENDA

Too much of the response to September 11 has been based on a criminal justice paradigm of apprehending and punishing terrorists. Even the military response has often been justified on the basis of the criminal law concepts of catching and punishing the evil doers and their accomplices,[67] as opposed to controlling weapons of mass destruction and building democracies.[68] Both domestically[69] and now internationally, we are placing increasing emphasis on viewing harm through the lens of retributive criminal justice and of offering the criminal law and its threat of punishment as the primary response to well-documented harm and risks. It is not a coincidence that this increased stress on crime coincides with less emphasis on and less consensus about the need for reforms to achieve greater social, political, and economic justice. One is much more likely today to hear discussions of the evil of crime rather than its "root causes." Indeed, there is a danger that discussion of the causes of terrorism will become a taboo subject because they are vulnerable to being portrayed as an attempt to excuse terrorism.[70] Domestic politics and international relations are being narrowed and made harsher by the emphasis placed on punishing crime. The Americans are the experts at "governing through crime" and relying on the criminal sanction at home and military intervention abroad. Canada should be cautious about accepting such coercive, expensive, and ultimately ineffective patterns of governance.

One antidote to a criminalization of politics and its narrow focus on issues of individualized intent and evil is to place crime in its larger political, economic, and social context. It is heartening that leaders of eleven countries, including Canada and the United Kingdom (but not the United States),[71] agreed on this statement at the Progressive Summit: "We must be resolute in fighting terrorism and equally resolute in tackling its causes ... For the only lasting answers lie in justice, more effective international cooperation, peace and freedom, democracy and development."[72] Although these are platitudes, they are platitudes that counterbalance platitudes about capturing and punishing the evil doers. As we saw in chapter 5, Prime Minister Chrétien also pursued the "root causes" approach to terrorism in controversial comments made on the one-year anniversary of September 11 and repeated at the United Nations. Chrétien linked the terrorist attacks with global disparities in wealth and power and with failed states. It is unfortunate that many people in Canada and the United States criticized his comments as "anti-American," "blaming the victim" and somehow condoning terrorism. Chrétien's words did not blame the victims of September 11, and they did not excuse the terrible crimes committed by the September 11 terrorists. They simply attempted to place both September 11 and the threat of terrorism into a broader perspective of other threats to security. "It does not dishonour those murdered in New York, Washington and Pennsylvania to point out ... that the dead that day numbered less than half the total of children who die somewhere in the world each day from diarrhea (caused by the lack of clean water)."[73] It also does not dishonour the thousands of victims of September 11 to note that, while Canada and the United States are spending billions on the war against terrorism, they are under-contributing to a $10 billion international fund to help prevent the almost 6 million deaths each year from AIDS, tuberculosis, and malaria. The fund is $8 billion short, with Canada pledging only $25 million of an expected $104 million, and the United States pledging less than $200 million of an expected $1.4 billion in 2003.[74] Jeffrey Sachs has estimated that the projected $100 billion cost of a war against Iraq could, if spent on development, avert about 30 million premature deaths from disease.[75]

Blame and punishment for criminals is due, and some wars are justified. But society needs to place the threat of terrorism in the perspective of other threats to human security. Canada should resist the urge to take an exclusively punishment-based approach to terrorism because it, with its dual conservative and socialist traditions, is well placed to integrate crime into the larger context of social, economic, and political justice. As historian Kenneth McNaught observed, the Canadian tradition can combine the use of the traditional criminal law to punish violence as an unacceptable means to advance political causes with a more lenient political response to the underlying grievance.[76] The dominance of crime on the American public agenda, as well as that country's dramatic and harsh reliance on incarceration and the death penalty, may reflect the inability of the United States's decentralized system of government to deliver social, economic, or political justice. Recent figures indicate that one in every thirty-two adult Americans is subject to that country's $46 billion prison system and that its incarceration is six times the rate of Canada's.[77] Such massive spending on criminal justice does not seem to contribute to the well-being and security of Americans.

A practical way to avoid excessive reliance on the criminal sanction is to ask difficult questions about whether the criminal law reforms of the *Anti-terrorism Act* will actually make us more secure. Formal reforms to the criminal law are often a cheaper and more visible substitute for more expensive preventive measures. Can "peace bonds for terrorists"[78] actually prevent terrorism? Are preventive arrests more effective than other means of prevention, such as increased security for sites vulnerable to terrorism? Will those with knowledge about terrorism tell the truth when compelled to testify before investigative hearings? Do rewards encouraging cooperation work better than punishing people for refusing to cooperate at an investigative hearing?[79] Can enhanced penalties deter suicide bombers? These are all practical and empirical questions that should have figured prominently in our debates about the *Anti-terrorism Act*.

A practical way to avoid excessive reliance on military force in the war against terrorism is to ask difficult questions about whether the use of military force will actually make us more secure. Did American assistance in arming Islamic militants in the conflict with the Soviet Union in Afghanistan increase or decrease security? Has the war in Afghanistan made the West safer from terrorism? Will groups like al-Qaeda find new regimes or means to undertake their activities? Is the primary objective in Iraq to eliminate weapons of mass destruction or to change the regime? Would a war against Iraq make us safer from terrorism and the use of weapons of mass destruction? Would a war against Iraq alienate those in the Arab and the Muslim world who might be in a position to discourage terrorist violence against civilians? The actual contributions of military force to human security should be critically assessed. The threat of force inherent in both the criminal sanction and military intervention remains necessary, but over-reliance on such blunt instruments can harm human security.

There is some hope that Canada may pursue a broader human security agenda in the future. The throne speech after Chrétien's controversial comments placing September 11 in a larger context committed more funds to international development, but not to the military. This decision was made despite a strong domestic lobby for more military spending and repeated public hints by the American ambassador that Canada must increase its spending on the military. The weakness of the Canadian military could inspire Canada to approach terrorism and other threats to security with "soft power" strategies based on international cooperation, development, and diplomacy rather than "hard power" strategies based on the use of force. Before

September 11, Canada prided itself on a foreign policy that recognized that security involved more "than the absence of military threat" and included "security against economic privation, an acceptable quality of life and a guarantee of human rights."[80] To be sure, there were concerns even before September 11 that Canada was doing a better job at developing multilateral responses to crime than at promoting "the economic dimension of human security."[81] September 11 could encourage Canada to pursue a narrow crime-based security agenda at home and abroad, yet Chrétien's controversial remarks suggest some willingness to take a broader approach to the issue of human security. Former foreign affairs minister Lloyd Axworthy has also stressed the need to use soft power to achieve a broader security agenda. He argued: "Military responses feed the anger, poverty, rhetoric – the climate of grievance – which create and sustain terrorist intentions. Terrorism will never be eliminated, but its attraction can be signifi-cantly diminished by addressing causes: poverty, despair, disenfran-chisement, religious fanaticism, absence of effective and meaningful democracy."[82] Canada could play a role in helping to make a global alliance against terrorism not "just an alliance against evil, but an alliance for something positive – a global alliance for reducing poverty and for creating a better environment, an alliance for creating a global society with more social justice."[83] Such an approach recognizes that Canada's comparative advantage is not in military power, but in "nation-building, the development of a civic society, economic progress, democracy, the rule of law."[84] Canada could be a vital North American link in the multilateral pursuit of a broad human security agenda that goes beyond a narrow focus on terrorism or crime.

There is some reason to believe that the public would support a broader approach to security than Canada has taken since September 11. A July 2002 poll taken on the "personal security" of Canadians found low levels of concerns about terrorist threats and much higher levels of concerns over the state of health care and the economy. The report's authors speculated that their findings might reflect increased government spending on and attention to anti-terrorism efforts since September 11. Nevertheless, the poll acknowledged that the govern-ment's spending on security "could perhaps be seen as disproportionate to the increased sense of risk among Canadians, particularly in light of their other, ongoing sources of insecurity."[85] This result suggests that there should have been increased emphasis in the 2001 security budget on those measures that would respond not only to terrorism but to other threats to security. Such spending might include more on the budgeted items of emergency preparedness and nuclear and chemical safety as well as on excluded items such as food and water safety, anti-pollution measures, health care, and international development. Democratic debate and engagement about anti-terrorism policy may actually have a moderating impact if citizens are allowed to evaluate the consequences of focusing on terrorism as the prime threat to human security.

CONCLUSION

Canadian law, democracy, sovereignty, and security have faced difficult challenges since the terrorist attacks of September 11, 2001. The consequences of September 11 for Canada have been significant. But the idea that September 11 changed everything must be rejected. It must be rejected in part to do justice to the world that existed before that awful day. Well before September 11, we had entered a realm in which it was clear that neither fundamental principles of the law nor the courts, the border, or modern technology would save us from ourselves. Before September 11 we lived in a risky world that could turn on us in a flash. The lack of guarantees does not mean that the struggle to preserve legal principles, a healthy democracy, Canadian sovereignty, and a sense of security is futile; rather, it makes the struggle more pressing and vital. That we have seen similar threats to our law, our democracy, our sovereignty, and our security in the past provides some grounds for cautious optimism that we can respond to the challenges of September 11.

The pessimistic conclusion that September 11 has set us inevitably on the fast road to assimilation with the United States should be rejected. George Grant was wrong when he declared Canadian sovereignty to be dead after Canada accepted nuclear arms in the wake of the Cuban Missile Crisis. At various times in our history, Canada has pulled closer to the United States, often to step back or find other means to differentiate itself. Since Grant's time, Canada has often taken a different approach from the United States to many issues of foreign policy, criminal justice, immigration, and international law. Nevertheless, angry nationalists like Grant play an important role in remembering and imagining a distinctive path for Canadian democracy. Canadians must recognize that the struggle to differentiate ourselves from the Americans has become more difficult since September 11. Rather than lamenting a nation lost, however, we should struggle to recreate a nation that may be found, in part, by relying less than the Americans on the criminal sanction and military force in responding to the risks of terrorism and other threats to human security. It is important that Canada take smart and even small stands to differentiate its anti-terrorism, security, and foreign policies from those of the United States.

There are signs that most Canadians are determined to affirm the distinctiveness of Canadian values. A survey released on July 1, 2002, showed that, while 58 per cent believed Canada had become more like the United States over the past decade, 52 per cent said they wanted Canada to become less like the nation to the south. Only a small minority – 12 per cent – want Canada to become more like the United States.[86] Subsequent surveys indicated that 94 per cent of Canadians believe they live in one of the best countries of the world; 77 per cent would be born in Canada if they had the choice; and only 19 per cent would favour Canada becoming part of the United States.[87] If anti-terrorism policy is democratic and responsive to the wishes of the public, it should not move Canada towards integration of its criminal justice, immigration, military, and foreign policy with that in the United States. A democratic policy should also move Canada towards a broader human security agenda both at home and abroad. Canadians are rightly concerned about terrorism, but they know it is not the only threat to their security and well-being.

Canada could have more liberal anti-terrorism laws and policies than the United States and a more open democratic debate about the causes and consequences of terrorism. It could also have a more liberal refugee and entry policy and a more internationalist and multilateral foreign policy, one that places less reliance on the use of military force and insists that terrorist threats be integrated into a broader human security agenda and separated from American geo-political interests. Canadian courts could be more concerned than American courts about the rights of suspected terrorists. Canadian courts should be more respectful of international law standards and less deferential to executive claims of national security than American courts. But all these locations of potential difference will require effort and even courage to create and maintain – indeed, more effort and more courage than has generally been displayed since September 11, 2001.

Canadians may pay an economic price for differentiating our anti-terrorism, immigration, military, and foreign policies from American policies. Nevertheless, since September 11, we have been too quick to sacrifice such differences simply in the hope that their elimination will ensure the open border that is necessary for Canadian prosperity. Concessions such as an overbroad *Anti-terrorism Act*, a safe third-country agreement, and military participation in Afghanistan, including Canadian involvement in violations of the Geneva Conventions, have not guaranteed free markets and open borders, as witnessed by the present trade disputes on softwood lumber and farm subsidies. Moreover, such Canadian concessions threaten to harm Canada's reputation as a leader in respect for international law, peacekeeping, and a generous refugee policy. They may also have made Canada a more likely target for international terrorists. My point is not that Canada should stubbornly refuse all cooperation with the United States on anti-terrorism measures, but rather that each measure should be carefully considered on its own merits and in relation to Canada's commitment to domestic and international law, democracy, sovereignty, and broad concerns about human security.

At home, Canadians should be heartened by the robust (albeit too rushed) process of public and legislative debate that accompanied the enactment of the *Anti-terrorism Act*. Many groups in civil society, assisted by the media, the bar, and the academy, voiced their concerns about legislative overreaction. This sort of vigilant and critical democratic debate made some difference in the final product and compared favourably to the fevered process that resulted in the American *Patriot Act*. Such vigilence in civil society is necessary if the extraordinary state powers that have been accepted to combat terrorism are not to spread to attempts to control other serious crimes and other governmental uses. Both the independent judiciary and groups in civil society should stand on guard to ensure that the erosion of liberty, privacy, and equality are not consequences of September 11.

We can and we must do better. We should not have disparaged the strength of our existing criminal law – including its bedrock principle that no motive excuses violence – to respond to terrorism. We must be candid about the limited ability of the criminal law to prevent terrorism, and we must be creative in searching for more effective means to prevent terrorism and to integrate the threat of terrorism into the many other risks we face to our security and well-being. We should not have shut down debate on the *Anti-terrorism Act*. We should accept an overtly anti-majoritarian judicial role that may disrupt some anti-terrorism efforts as not only consistent with but crucial to our democracy. We should make it crystal clear that Canada will never send even the worst terrorists to face torture and that violations of privacy, equality, and fair trial rights will not be easily justified even in the context of national security.

Our democratic debate about terrorism and security must take care to avoid the temptation of blame, divisiveness, and an "us versus them" mentality. The multicultural nature of Canadian society should be a source of strength and pride, not alarm or division, and we should do all we can to avoid making any group in Canadian society feel it is presumptively suspected of terrorism – or, indeed, any crime. We should have paid more attention to the anti-discrimination principle in the debates about the *Anti-terrorism Act* and to international law in our treatment of captives in Afghanistan. Let us hope that these principles, as well as practical considerations of the limited efficacy of the criminal law, military force, and restrictions on refugees in actually preventing terrorism, will prevail as Canadians continue their democratic debates about terrorism and other threats to human security.

Notes

CHAPTER ONE

1 I. Peritz, "Never to be heard from again," *Globe and Mail*, 1 Nov. 2001.
2 On the October crisis, see J. Saywell, *Quebec 70* (Toronto: University of Toronto Press, 1971); W. Tarnopolsky, *The Canadian Bill of Rights*, 2nd ed. (Toronto: McClelland & Stewart, 1975), 331–48. For arguments that the ordinary criminal law was sufficient to deal with the crisis, see D. Schmeiser, "Control of Apprehended Insurrection: Emergency Measures v. The Criminal Code," *Manitoba Law Journal* 4 (1971): 359.
3 C. Freeze, "1971 Air Canada hijacker arrested in U.S.," *Globe and Mail*, 11 Sept. 2001.
4 W. Orme, "Response to terror: In Canada, a sea change follows wave of terrorism," *Los Angeles Times*, 28 Jan. 2002.
5 J. Defede, *The Day the World Came to Town* (New York: Regan, 2002).
6 Stephen Jay Gould, "An ode to human decency," *Globe and Mail*, 20 Sept. 2001.
7 J. Moller, "Stranded travellers grateful to Halifax," ibid., 17 Sept. 2001.
8 J. Ibbitson, "The aftermath," ibid., 15 Sept. 2001; "There will be no silence from Canada, PM says," *Toronto Star*, 15 Sept. 2001.
9 C. Sands, "Fading Power or Rising Power: 11 September and Lessons from the Section 110 Experience," in N. Hillmer and M. Molot, *A Fading Power* (Toronto: Oxford, 2002), 72.
10 J. Sallot, "Canadian connection suspected in hijacking," *Globe and Mail*, 13 Sept. 2001; D. Leblanc, "No evidence of Canadian link," ibid., 14 Sept. 2001.

11 As quoted in J. Ibbitson, "The war on terror: U.S. points the finger due north, Americans starting to criticize Canada as a terrorist haven," ibid., 27 Sept. 2001. See also S. Bell, "Preparing for war: The enemy within," *National Post*, 17 Sept. 2001.

12 C. Krauss, "Canada alters security policies to ease concerns of U.S.," *New York Times*, 18 Feb. 2002.

13 W. Immen and G. Abbate, "The brink of war, prayers offer many quiet comfort," *Globe and Mail*, 17 Sept. 2001.

14 David Frum, a Canadian who was a speechwriter for President Bush at the time, has subsequently reported that references to Canada in Bush's speech were cut: "The speech had been running long, and somebody had reasoned that if we mentioned Canada, we'd have to praise all the other NATO countries by name, too, and many of them had been quicker than Canada to offer aid and assistance." "Canada was purposely cut from 2001 speech, Frum says," ibid., 8 Jan. 2003. The "aid and assistance" must have been military aid, because Canada was helping the United States within forty-five minutes of the attacks.

15 J. Sallot, "The Aftermath: The Strategic Response," ibid., 14 Sept. 2001.

16 See, for example, L. Axworthy, "Liberals at the Border: We Stand on Guard for Whom?" 6th Annual Keith Davey Lecture, 11 March 2002.

17 See, for example, J. Granatstein, *A Friendly Agreement in Advance: Canada-US Defence Relations, Past, Present and Future* (Toronto: C.D. Howe Institute, June 2002).

18 A voice that is apparently bin Laden's stated that Australia ignored the warning not to assist the Americans in Afghanistan, but "it was awakened by the echoes of explosions in Bali. Its government subsequently pretended, falsely, that its citizens were not targeted. If you suffer to see your [people] killed ... Remember our dead in Afghanistan ... For how long will fear, massacres, destruction, exile, orphanhood and widowhood be our lot, while security, stability and joy remain your domain alone? It is high time that equality be established to this effect." P. Cheney, "Terrorist tape names Canada," *Globe and Mail*, 13 Nov. 2002.

19 D. Halbfinger, "Court-martial hearing begins for U.S. pilots," *New York Times*, 15 Jan. 2003.

20 D. Leblanc, "Navy seizes al-Qaeda suspects," *Globe and Mail*, 15 July 2002.

21 A. Thompson, "Toronto teen held for terror role," *Toronto Star*, 6 Sept. 2002.

22 M. Mackinnon and C. Freeze, "Canadian teen may be U.S. source," *Globe and Mail*, 30 Oct. 2002; C. Freeze, "Canadian teen held at Guantanamo," ibid., 31 Oct. 2002.

23 *Suresh v. Canada*, [2002] SCC 1. In a companion case, however, the Court held that the deportation of an assassin to Iran was acceptable because the minister's decision that he would not be tortured on his return was not unreasonable. *Ahani v. Canada*, [2002] SCC 2.

24 A. Dershowitz, *Why Terrorism Works* (New Haven: Yale University Press, 2002), chap. 4.

25 Chief Justice McLachlin has recognized that the "unique horror of Sept. 11" will place challenges on courts "to maintain our freedoms and our democracy and the rule of law, while maintaining security." C. Schmitz, "Security-rights conflict lies ahead: Chief Justice," *National Post*, 7 Jan. 2002). See also R.S. Abella, "Judging in the 21st Century," *Advocates Quarterly* 25 (2002): 138–9.

26 Hon. D. O'Connor, *Report of the Walkerton Inquiry* (Toronto: Queen's Printer, 2002).

27 L. Altman and D. Grady, "Smallpox shot will be free for those who want one," *New York Times*, 15 Dec. 2002. Canada plans to vaccinate just 500 health-care workers. T. Blackwell, "U.S. experts questions smallpox strategy," *National Post*, 30 Nov. 2002. See chapter 7 for more discussion of this issue.

28 *Smith v. Canada*, [2001] SCC 88.

29 E. Caplan, "Security and privacy: A fine balance," *Globe and Mail*, 16 Dec. 2002.

30 G. Radwanski, "A serious threat to our privacy," ibid., 18 Dec. 2002; E. Oziewicz, "Radwanski fires broadside at Caplan," ibid., 19 Dec. 2002. The opinion of Gérard La Forest dated 19 November 2002 is found at *www.privcom.gc.ca* and is discussed more fully in chapter 4.

31 C. Kenny, "Where's the justice? Pull back the veil on security," *Globe and Mail.*, 15 Aug. 2002; K. McArthur, "Air security improvements doubted," ibid., 10 Sept. 2002; "Pilots make safety demands," ibid., 12 Oct. 2002.

32 Public Law No.107–56, s. 401.

33 A. Dunfield, "Graham to push visa issue with U.S.," *Globe and Mail*, 4 Nov. 2002; "Foreign Affairs cancels U.S. travel warning," *National Post*, 7 Nov. 2002; A. Thompson, "Canadian fury as U.S. steps up border checks," *Toronto Star*, 8 Nov. 2002; G. Smith, "U.S. endorses visitor checks at border," *Globe and Mail*, 8 Nov. 2002.

34 Ekos Research Associates *Security, Sovereignty and Continentalism: Canadian Perspectives on September 11*, 27 Sept. 2001. This poll, showing significant numbers of Canadians, rightly or wrongly, seeing American foreign policy as one of the causes of September 11, is discussed in chapter 5.

35 S. McCarthy, "PM's September 11 remarks disgraceful, Mulroney says," *Globe and Mail*, 13 Sept. 2002; S. McCarthy, "Fox hounds P.M. over remarks," ibid., 14 Sept. 2002; T. Nichols, "Chrétien's state of denial is dangerous," *National Post*, 25 Sept 2002; R. Fife, "Chrétien soft on terrorism, Wall Street Journal readers told," ibid., 27 Sept. 2002.

36 R. Fulford, "U.S. bashing no longer a game," *National Post* 14 Sept. 2001.

37 M. Bliss "September 11: The End of Canadian Nationalism," ibid., 29 Sept. 2001. See also M. Bliss, "Sovereignty means the freedom to say 'me too,'" ibid., 21 Sept. 2001.

38 L. Axworthy, "Watch your step, Mr. Chrétien," *Globe and Mail*, 4 Feb. 2002.

39 *Lament for a Nation: The Defeat of Canadian Nationalism* (Toronto: McClelland & Stewart, 1965). Grant himself took issue with the concept of pessimism and argued that "it would be the height of pessimism to believe that our society could go on in its present directions without bringing down upon itself catastrophes" (xii).

40 Ibid., 31. On the eve of the 1963 election, Pierre Berton wrote: "National sovereignty is on the wane. If this election proves anything it proves that anti-Americanism is finished as a political issue. We have cast our lot with this continent for better or worse and the people know it." Quoted in R. Bothwell, I. Drummond, and J. English, *Canada since 1945* (Toronto: University of Toronto Press, 1981), 249.

41 M. Bliss, "Sept 11: The end of Canadian nationalism," *National Post*, 29 Sept. 2001; M. Bliss, "Sovereignty means the freedom to say 'me too,'" ibid., 21 Sept. 2001.

42 C. Krauss, "Canada alters security policies to ease concerns of U.S.," *New York Times*, 18 Feb. 2002.

43 In a preface to the second edition of *Lament for a Nation*, Grant acknowledged that "it is certainly much easier in 1970 than it was in 1963 for Canadians not to want to be swallowed by the U.S. ... It does not take much intelligence or patriotism to be glad that one's children are not drafted for that war ... Even the Canadian bourgeoisie can see the perhaps unresolvable racial conflict, the expansion and decay of its

cities, the increase of military influence in constitutional life ... In such a situation, Canadians are less impelled to rush headlong towards continental integration." Nevertheless, Grant still argued that "below the surface the movement towards integration continues." G. Grant, *Lament for a Nation* (Ottawa: Carleton Library, 1970), vii-ix.

44 J. Simon, "Governing Through Crime," in L Friedman and G. Fisher, eds., *The Crime Conundrum: Essays on Criminal Justice* (New York: Westview Press, 1997), 171.

45 K. Roach, *Due Process and Victims' Rights: The New Law and Politics of Criminal Justice* (Toronto: University of Toronto Press, 1999), 4, 312–13.

46 K. Roach, *The Supreme Court on Trial: Judicial Activism or Democratic Dialogue* (Toronto: Irwin Law, 2001).

47 C. Cobb, "Canadians want to elect court," *National Post*, 4 Feb. 2002. Compare J.F. Fletcher and P. Howe, "Public Opinion and Canada's Courts," in P. Howe and P.H. Russell, eds., *Judicial Power and Canadian Democracy* (Montreal and Kingston: McGill-Queen's University Press for the Institute for Research on Public Policy, 2001), 255, finding high levels of support for the Court, but less for the method of appointment.

48 Part I of the *Constitution Act, 1982,* being Schedule B to the *Canada Act* 1982 (UK), 1982, c. 11 [Charter].

49 See, for example, W.W. Pue, ed., *Pepper in Our Eyes: The* APEC *Affair* (Vancouver: UBC Press, 2000).

50 M. Valpy, "Ottawa's security bill runs roughshod over rights," *Globe and Mail,* 1 Dec. 2001.

51 *Report of the Commission on Systemic Racism in the Ontario Criminal Justice System* (Toronto: Queen's Printer for Ontario, 1995), 349–60; *Report of the Aboriginal Justice Inquiry of Manitoba: The Justice System and Aboriginal People,* vol. 1 (Winnipeg: Queen's Printer, 1991), 595 (A.C. Hamilton and C.M. Sinclair, commissioners). The Manitoba inquiry found that J.J. Harper was stopped by the police before his fatal shooting "simply because [he] was a male Aboriginal person." *Report of the Aboriginal Justice Inquiry of Manitoba: The Deaths of Helen Betty Osborne and John Joseph Harper,* vol. 2 (Winnipeg: Queen's Printer, 1991), 32 (A.C. Hamilton and C.M. Sinclair, commissioners). On the linkage of crime and immigration policy, including legislative amendments to allow permanent residents of Canada to be deported as a result of the "Just desserts" murder in Toronto, see

J. Dent, "No Right of Appeal: Bill C-11, Criminality and the Human Rights of Permanent Residents Facing Deportation" *Queen's Law Journal* 27 (2002): 749.

52 See M. Tonry, *Malign Neglect: Race, Crime, and Punishment in America* (New York: Oxford University Press, 1995); R. Kennedy, *Race, Crime and the Law* (New York: Vintage, 1998); D. Cole, *No Equal Justice: Race and Class in the American Criminal Justice System* (New York: New Press, 1999).

53 *Canada-United States Free Trade Agreement Implementation Act*, SC 1988, c. 65. See generally S. Clarkson, *Uncle Sam and Us* (Toronto: University of Toronto Press, 2002).

54 Drawing on the work of Ulrich Beck, my colleague David Schneiderman has observed that "modernity has moved from a phase where it safely could ignore the 'side-effects' of industrialization – the threat of radioactive fallout, cancer-causing toxins, and pollutants – to a new phase called 'risk society.'" In this phase, society is better at calculating risks to human security than controlling them. There is also a tendency to overrely on "expert and professional knowledge" and "overreach in response to the threat of risk. Legislation is broadly drafted to promote feelings of security, but other priorities, like the exercise of rights and freedoms, are, in turn, threatened." D. Schneiderman, "Terrorism and the Risk Society," in R. Daniels, P. Macklem, and K. Roach, eds., *The Security of Freedom: Essays on Canada's Anti-terrorism Bill* (Toronto: University of Toronto Press, 2001), 64, 70. See also U. Beck, *Risk Society: Towards a New Modernity* (London: Sage Publications, 1992); T. Homer-Dixon *The Ingenuity Gap: Can We Solve the Problems of the Future?* (Toronto: Vintage, 2000).

55 T. MacCharles, "Tough anti-terrorism measures still on shelf," *Toronto Star*, 19 Dec. 2002.

56 On a broader human security agenda, see R. Conway, ed., *Ethics and Security in Canadian Foreign Policy* (Vancouver: UBC Press, 2001); Axworthy, "Liberals at the Border."

CHAPTER TWO

1 Work had been done before 11 September 2001 on those parts of the bill that relate to the *Official Secrets Act*, the deregistration of charities involved in terrorism, and amendments to the *Canada Evidence Act*, but "nothing on ... the core elements of this Bill," including the definition of terrorism that was debated in the Department of Justice "right

up until two days before the Bill was introduced." See the remarks of Richard Mosley, assistant deputy minister of justice, in R. Daniels, P. Macklem, and K. Roach, eds., *The Security of Freedom: Essays on Canada's Anti-terrorism Bill* (Toronto: University of Toronto Press, 2001), 436–7.

2 T. MacCharles, "Tough anti-terror measures still on shelf," *Toronto Star*, 19 Dec. 2002.

3 Notes for her 20 November appearance before House of Commons Justice Committee.

4 *R. v. Cotroni*, [1979] 2 SCR 256 at 276, 45 CCC (2d) 1.

5 See *Director of Public Prosecutions for Northern Ireland v. Maxwell*, [1978] 3 All ER 1140, [1978] 1 WLR 1350 (HL) (accomplice liability in a terrorist operation when the accused did not know the exact means of the attack).

6 *R. v. Deutsch*, [1986] 2 SCR 2 at 28, 27 CCC (3d) 385.

7 D. Paciocco, "Constitutional Casualities of September 11: Limiting the Legacy of the New Anti-Terrorism Act," *Supreme Court Law Review* 16 (2002)(2d), 185.

8 D. Stuart, "The Dangers of Quick Fix Legislation in the Criminal Law: The Anti-Terrorism Bill C-36 Should Be Withdrawn," in Daniels, Macklem, and Roach, eds., *The Security of Freedom*, 206.

9 S. Cohen, "Law Reform, the Charter and the Future of Criminal Law," in Jamie Cameron, ed., *The Charter's Impact on the Criminal Justice System* (Toronto: Carswell, 1996), 347–8.

10 Writing in 1997, Jonathan Simon observed that "every U.S. presidential campaign since Goldwater-Johnson in 1964 has been fought partly on the turf of crime. Since the reaction to the 'Willie Horton' ad on behalf of George Bush in 1988, the salience of crime and its interconnection with race have been taken as given features of American politics." J. Simon, "Governing through Crime," in L. Friedman and G. Fisher, eds., *The Crime Conundrum* (New York: Westview Press, 1997), 174.

11 Grant argued both that Canadian "nationalism had to go hand in hand with some measure of socialism" and that "the impossibility of conservatism in our era is the impossibility of Canada." G. Grant, *Lament for a Nation* (Toronto: McClelland & Stewart, 1965), 15, 68. The classic statement that the Canadian political tradition has tory and socialist touches that distinguish it from the American political tradition is found in G. Horowitz, *Canadian Labour in Politics* (Toronto: University of Toronto Press, 1968), chap. 1.

12 For an argument that the traditional Canadian reaction to political trials (from the rebellions of 1837 to the October Crisis of 1970) demonstrated both a tory faith in order and a socialist inclination to leniency and response to the underlying grievances behind political crimes, see K. McNaught, "Political Trials and the Canadian Political Tradition," in M.L. Friedland, ed., *Courts and Trials: A Multidisciplinary Approach* (Toronto: University of Toronto Press, 1975), 137.

13 *Criminal Code*, s. 231(6). A similar combination of media and political pressure led to the creation of the criminal harassment or stalking offence itself in 1993. See R. Cairns Way, "The Criminalization of Stalking: An Exercise in Media Manipulation and Political Opportunism," *McGill Law Journal* 39 (1994): 379.

14 *Criminal Code*, s. 231(6.1). For further discussion of the media and the political pressures that led to these *Criminal Code* amendments, see D. Stuart, "Politically Expedient but Potentially Unjust Legislation against Gangs," *Canadian Criminal Law Review* 2 (1997): 207.

15 *Criminal Code*, s. 231(6.2).

16 *Criminal Code*, s. 231(6.01), as amended by Bill C-36, s. 9.

17 Note that the Law Reform Commission of Canada would have defined murders as first-degree murder if committed "for terrorist or political motives" and "by means which the accused knows will cause the death of more than one person." Law Reform Commission of Canada, *Recodifying Criminal Law* (Ottawa: Supply and Services, 1987), 58.

18 See, for example, N. Kasirer, "Honour Bound," *McGill Law Journal* 47 (2001): 237; R.A. Macdonald, "The Fridge-Door Statute," ibid., 47 (2001): 11; P. Noreau, "Comment la législation est-elle possible? Objectivation et subjectivation du lien social," ibid., 47 (2001): 195; K. Roach, "The Uses and Audiences of Preambles in Legislation," ibid., 47 (2001): 129; L.B. Tremblay, "La justification de la législation comme jugement pratique," ibid., 47 (2001): 59.

19 *Criminal Code*, s. 83.01(1)(*b*)(i)(A).

20 *United States v. Dynar*, [1997] 2 SCR 462 at para. 81, 115 CCC (3d) 481. See also Justice Dickson's statement: "The mental element of a crime ordinarily involves no reference to motive." *R. v. Lewis*, [1979] 2 SCR 821 at 831, 47 CCC (2d) 24. In *R. v. Latimer*, [2001] 1 SCR 3 at para. 82, the Supreme Court even denied the relevance of motive to the issue of whether mandatory punishment was cruel and unusual. An international criminal law scholar has recently observed: "A motive is generally irrelevant in criminal law, except at the sentencing stage when

it might be relevant to mitigation or aggravation of the sentence. That an accused committed a crime with 'purely personal motives or reasons' does not exonerate him from being guilty of a crime against humanity if his act fits into the pattern of crimes against humanity as described above." K. Kittichaisaree, *International Criminal Law* (Oxford: Oxford University Press, 2001), 92.

21 In 1997 Parliament amended the existing crime of aggravated assault to provide that wounding or maiming includes female genital mutilation. The amendment makes no mention of political or religious motives for such acts. See *Criminal Code*, ss. 268(3)-(4).

22 *Criminal Code*, s. 83.01(1.1). Note, however, that threats to commit terrorist acts would be excluded from this protection because they would themselves constitute terrorist activities.

23 As examined below, such expression may constitute terrorism if they amount to threats to commit terrorism.

24 The motive requirement is not necessary to restrict the new offences to the terrorism context because of the separate requirement of proof of an intent to intimidate the public with regard to its security or to compel actions. *Criminal Code*, s. 83.01(1)(b)(i)(B). The American *Patriot Act*, Public Law No. 107-56, ∞ 808, 115 Stat. 272 at 378-9 (2001), relies on a similar but narrower requirement of intimidation of the public or compelling governments to act by means of coercion, intimidation, and crime – to distinguish crimes of terrorism from other crimes without requiring proof of religious or political motive. Some international conventions provide that political or ideological consider-ations do not justify terrorism, but such provisions are consistent with the traditional criminal law principle that motive is not relevant to crime and they do not make political or religious motive an essential part of international crimes of terrorism.

25 Even requirements of high forms of subjective intent for war crimes in *R. v. Finta*, [1994] 1 SCR 701, 88 CCC (3d) 417, and hate crimes in *R. v. Buzzanga and Durocher* (1979), 25 OR (2d) 705, 49 CCC.(2d) 369 (CA), have frequently been criticized for making prosecutions more difficult.

26 P. Edwards, "Judge grapples with motive of Lackawanna Six," *Toronto Star*, 4 Oct. 2002.

27 As Ziyaad Mia has argued: "The unseemly and inappropriate ques-tions that could arise in the course of investigations, interrogations and prosecutions to establish a political or religious motive for 'terrorist

activity' can easily be imagined." Z. Mia, "Terrorizing the Rule of Law: Implications of the Anti-terrorism Act," *National Journal of Constitutional Law* (forthcoming).

28 Hansard, 16 Oct. 2001, 1025.

29 It is only when debate matures over a period of time – time that was not available in the enactment of Bill c-36 – that Canadians will learn "not to equate Islam with fundamentalism" and that "not all Muslims support keeping women locked up in the house; not all Muslims support talaq divorces and clitoridectomy; not all Muslims support killings authors who criticize Islam." W. Kymlicka, *Finding Our Way: Rethinking Ethnocultural Relations in Canada* (Toronto: Oxford University Press, 1998), 69.

30 *Criminal Code*, s. 430(4.1).

31 Ibid., s. 718.2(*a*)(i).

32 People behind a veil of ignorance, who would not know whether they had a religion or politics different from the majority, could agree to laws prohibiting intentional murder. Nevertheless, they might hesitate before agreeing to terrorism crimes based in part on proof of religious or political motive. See J. Rawls, *A Theory of Justice* (Cambridge: Harvard University Press, 1971).

33 P. Macklem, "Canada's Obligations at International Criminal Law," in Daniels, Macklem, and Roach, eds., *The Security of Freedom*, 362.

34 I. Cotler, "Thinking Outside the Box: Foundational Principles for a Counter-Terrorism Law and Policy," ibid., 113.

35 M. Drumbl, "Judging the 11 September Terrorist Attack," *Human Rights Quarterly* 24 (2002): 336–8; M. Fry, "Terrorism as a Crime against Humanity and Genocide: The Backdoor to Universal Jurisdiction," UCLA *Journal of International and Foreign Affairs* 7 (2002): 169.

36 *Suresh v. Canada* (2002), 208 DLR(4th) 1 at para 94 (SCC).

37 A. Cassese, "Terrorism Is Also Disrupting Some Crucial Legal Categories of International Law," *European Journal of International Law* 12 (2001): 993; R. Mosley "Preventing Terrorism: Bill c-36, the *Anti-terrorism Act, 2001*," in D. Daubney et al., *Terrorism, Law and Democracy: How Is Canada Changing after September 11* (Montreal: Les Éditions Thémis, 2002), 148.

38 M. Gee, "Frontiers: Defining terrorism," *Globe and Mail*, 24 Nov. 2001.

39 G. Levitt, "Is 'Terrorism' Worth Defining," *Ohio Northern University Law Review* 13 (1986): 97.

40 R. Morden, "Finding the Right Balance," *Policy Options*, September 2002, 48.

41 *Suresh v. Canada*, para 95.

42 UN Security Council Resolution 1373 of 28 September. R. Mosley, "Concluding Comments from the Department of Justice," in Daniels, Macklem, and Roach, eds., *The Security of Freedom*, 438.

43 (1994) 88 CCC (3d) 417 (SCC).

44 A. Ashworth, *Human Rights, Serious Crime and Criminal Procedure* (London: Sweet and Maxwell, 2002), 30.

45 The preamble of Bill C-36 amplifies this concern by stating that terrorism threatens "the stability of the economy and the general welfare of the nation." On the role of preambles in legislation, see Roach, "The Uses and Audiences of Preambles in Legislation."

46 D. Stuart, *Canadian Criminal Law*, 4th ed. (Toronto: Carswell, 2001), 704.

47 K. Roach, "The New Terrorism Offences and the Criminal Law," in Daniels, Macklem, and Roach, eds., *The Security of Freedom*, 160.

48 *Hunter v. Southam*, [1984] 2 SCR 145.

49 *Criminal Code*, s. 83.05(6)(d).

50 C. Clark, "Canada outlaws Hamas, but not Hezbollah," *Globe and Mail*, 28 Nov. 2002.

51 G. Smith, "Canada asked to drop Hezbollah ban," ibid., 26 Dec. 2002; J. Sallot, "Hezbollah ban attacked as biased," ibid., 12 Dec. 2002.

52 *Criminal Code*, s. 83.02.

53 Stewart Bell has argued that blending of funds to support both legitimate causes and violence "is a deliberate tactic designed to throw investigators off the scent of blood money." S. Bell, "Blood Money, International Terrorist Fundraising in Canada," in N. Hillmer and M. Molot, *A Fading Power* (Toronto: Oxford University Press, 2002), 175–6.

54 *Criminal Code*, s. 83.02.

55 Kevin Davis, "Cutting Off the Flow of Funds to Terrorists," in Daniels, Macklem, and Roach, eds., *The Security of Freedom*, 301, 303.

56 *Criminal Code*, s. 83.04(b).

57 Ibid., s. 83.08.

58 Ibid., s. 83.1.

59 Ibid., s. 83.14.

60 Ibid., s. 83.14(9)(b).

61 A. Dershowitz, *Why Terrorism Works* (New Haven: Yale University Press, 2002), 175. Following his instrumental logic, Dershowitz's proposals to reform Israel's house destruction practices revolved around increasing their deterrent value by announcing "clearly, in advance,

exactly what the response to future terrorist attacks would be." Ibid., 177.

62 Davis, "Cutting Off the Flows of Funds to Terrorists," 315.

63 *Criminal Code*, s. 83.18.

64 D. Stuart, "The *Anti-terrorism Bill* (Bill C-36): An Unnecessary Law and Order Quick Fix that Permanently Stains the Canadian Criminal Justice System," in Daubney et al., *Terrorism, Law and Democracy*, 180.

65 *Public Order Regulations* 1970, SOR/70–444 s. 8.

66 *Criminal Code*, s. 83.19.

67 E. Machado, "A Note on the Terrorism Financing Offences," *University of Toronto Faculty of Law Review*, 105.

68 Mosley, "Preventing Terrorism," 165.

69 Paciocco, "Constitutional Casualities in the War against Terrorism."

70 *Criminal Code*, s. 83.21.

71 Roach, "The New Terrorism Offences and the Criminal Law," 164.

72 *Criminal Code*, s. 83.22.

73 Roach, "The New Terrorism Offences and the Criminal Law," 164.

74 House of Representatives 3162, s. 803, amending s. 2339 of the United States Code.

75 *Criminal Code*, s. 431.2.

76 Ibid., s. 430(4.1).

77 Ibid., s. 718.2(a)(I).

78 *R v. Morrisey*, [2000] 2 SCR 29. On the Court's new deference to mandatory minimum penalties, see K. Roach, "Searching for *Smith*: The Constitutionality of Mandatory Sentences," *Osgoode Hall Law Journal* 39 (2001): 367.

79 The act does not give Canada's civilian security intelligence agency new powers, but it recognizes the Communications Security Establishment for the collection of foreign intelligence.

80 *Criminal Code*, s. 185(1.1), 186.1, 196(5). See also M.L. Friedland, "Police Powers in Bill C-36," in Daniels, Macklem, and Roach, eds., *The Security of Freedom*. 269.

81 O. Gross, "Cutting Down Trees: Law-Making under the Shadow of Great Calamities," in Daniels, Macklem, and Roach, eds., *The Security of Freedom*, 39.

82 C. Hill, S. Hutchinson, and L. Pringle, "Search Warrants: Protection or Illusion?" *Criminal Reports* 28 (5th series) (2000): 89l.

83 Ipsos Reid, "Majority (58%) say terrorism threats outweigh protection of individual right," 5 Oct. 2001.

84 T. MacCharles, "Tough anti-terror measures still on shelf," *Toronto Star*, 19 Dec. 2002.

85 In response to law enforcement concerns, provisions to enable ongoing investigations to continue were also included in the sunset provisions. *Criminal Code*, s. 83.32, 83.33.

86 Ibid., s. 83.3.

87 Ibid., s. 495, as interpreted in *R. v. Storrey*, [1990] 1 SCR 241.

88 Ipsos Reid, "Majority (58%) say terrorism threats outweigh protection of individual rights."

89 G. Trotter, "The Anti-Terrorism Bill and Preventive Restraints on Liberty," in Daniels, Macklem, and Roach, eds., *The Security of Freedom*, 239.

90 *R. v. Heywood*, [1994] 3 SCR 761.

91 *Criminal Code*, s. 83.28(10).

92 *R v. S (RJ)* (1995), 96 CCC (3d) 1 (SCC); *British Columbia (Securities Commission) v. Branch* (1995), 97 CCC (3d) 505 (SCC). The courts might, however, halt an investigative hearing as violating the Charter if it was demonstrated that the state's sole objective was to compel the accused to engage in self-incrimination. In almost every case, however, the state would be able to argue that its objective was to obtain information about terrorism, not to compel the subject of the investigative hearing to engage in self-incrimination.

93 The electronic surveillance and participation offences in the *Anti-terrorism Act* are themselves taken from earlier *Criminal Code* amendments designed to deal with organized crime. Similarly, the peace bond provisions follow from the expansion of peace bonds throughout the 1990s to apply to sexual offences and criminal organizations crimes. Provisions in the *Anti-terrorism Act* for the deletion of hate propaganda from the internet are similar to other new provisions relating to child pornography.

94 D. Dyzenhaus, "The Permanence of the Temporary: Can Emergency Powers Be Normalized?" in Daniels, Macklem, and Roach, eds., *The Security of Freedom*, 22.

95 Gross, "Cutting Down Trees," ibid., 39.

96 Ashworth, *Human Rights, Serious Crime and Criminal Procedure*, 30, 95.

97 R. Seguin and C. Freeze, "Al-Qaeda may have infiltrated diamond sector," *Globe and Mail*, 24 Aug. 2002. Despite the provocative headline of the last article, no evidence was actually provided that al-Qaeda had indeed infiltrated the Canadian diamond industry, even though such

involvement would arguably run afoul of the new offences against financing terrorism.

98 T. Walkom, "War on terror being used a fig leaf," *Toronto Star*, 20 Aug. 2002.

99 S. Bell, "The black Muslim connection," *National Post*, 25 Oct. 2002; M. Wente, "Once again, terrorism comes to America," *Globe and Mail*, 26 Oct. 2002; D. Frum, "Western Muslims are on the front lines," *National Post*, 28 Oct. 2002.

100 J. Blair, "Sniper case will be the first test of Virginia antiterrorism law," *New York Times*, 17 Dec. 2002.

101 K. Lunman, "Air-travel database plan alarms rights advocates," *Globe and Mail*, 28 Sept. 2002. The database will also be used for tax investigations. C. Clark, "Travel files a threat, watchdog says," ibid., 27 Sept. 2002. There were also reports that it would be expanded to include rail, bus, and train travel. B. Gorham, "Anti-terror database to expand," *National Post*, 28 Oct. 2002.

102 K. Lunman, "MacAulay misled public, privacy commissioner says," *Globe and Mail*, 18 May 2002.

103 Backgrounder Highlights of the *Public Safety Act*, 2002, 5. See also Bill C-17, *The Public Safety Act*, s. 4.82(11), as introduced for first reading, 31 Oct. 2002.

104 *Smith v. Canada* 2001 SCC 81 at para 2. See chapter 4 in this book for further discussion of how this decision fits into the trend for the Court to take a more empirical and less normative approach to defining a reasonable expectation of privacy. It also demonstrates the Court's tendency to see almost every difficult issue as a question of the appropriate balance of competing values.

105 The privacy commissioner did, however, obtain a legal opinion from retired Supreme Court Justice Gérard La Forest which concluded that plans by customs officials to keep a database on the foreign travels of all Canadians for a six-year period would violate the Charter. La Forest stressed that while individuals have a diminished expectation of privacy when crossing the border, the proposed database would allow a wide range of governmental agencies to have access to detailed travel information "of millions of innocent Canadians" "without either prior judicial authorization or individualized suspicions." La Forest argued that the Supreme Court's recent decision in *Smith v. Canada* 2001 SCC 81 should be limited to the unemployment insurance context because of the self-reporting nature of the scheme. He also stressed that the

proposed database would contain more detailed information on more people and could be accessed by government for a broad range of governmental and crime control purposes. Opinion of Gérard La Forest, 19 Nov. 2002, available at *www.privcom.gc.ca*. These distinctions are plausible, but as discussed in chapter 4, Justice La Forest's expansive approach to privacy did not always win favour with the majority of the Supreme Court.

106 Privacy Commissioner News Release, 1 Nov. 2002.

CHAPTER THREE

1 The phrase "country of minorities" is from J. Ralston Saul, *Reflections of a Siamese Twin* (Toronto: Penguin, 1997), 127. See also C. Taylor, *Multiculturalism* (Princeton: Princeton University Press, 1994).

2 K. Roach, *Due Process and Victims' Rights: The New Law and Politics of Criminal Justice* (Toronto: University of Toronto Press, 1999), chaps. 4–7.

3 A. Alan Borovoy, *The New Anti-Liberals* (Toronto: Canadian Scholars' Press, 1999).

4 A comprehensive review of the law and its operation by a committee of Parliament is mandated in the law by the end of 2004. See *Anti-terrorism Act*, Statues of Canada, 2001, c. 41, s. 145.

5 G. Grant, *English Speaking Justice* (Toronto: Anansi, 1985), 5.

6 This is the phrase used by Michael Ignatieff to describe the danger of justifying wars as necessary to protect human rights. M. Ignatieff, *Virtual War* (Toronto: Viking, 2000), 213.

7 T. Tyler, "Law societies seek changes to terror bills," *Toronto Star*, 4 Dec. 2001.

8 Special Senate Committee on Bill C-36, 6 Dec. 2001.

9 Ibid., 24 Oct., 6 Dec. 2001.

10 Ibid., 6 Dec. 2001.

11 S. McIntyre, "Redefining Reformism: The Consultations That Shaped Bill C-49," in J. Roberts and R. Mohr, eds., *Confronting Sexual Assault: A Decade of Legal and Social Change* (Toronto: University of Toronto Press, 1994). Many of the groups that spoke against Bill C-36 in the legislative committees might be seen as "post-materialistic elites" and minorities associated with the so-called Court Party. See F.L. Morton and R. Knopff, *The Charter Revolution and the Court Party* (Peterborough: Broadview Press, 2000). For criticisms that the label Court

Party ignores the status of many of these groups as vulnerable minorities, as well as the role they play in the legislative process, see K. Roach, *The Supreme Court on Trial* (Toronto: Irwin Law, 2001), chap. 8.

12 Standing Committee on Justice and Human Rights, 1 Nov. 2001, 1540.

13 Ibid., 1545.

14 Ibid., 6 Nov. 2001, 1000.

15 Ibid., 5 Nov. 2001, 2020.

16 Ibid., 7 Nov. 2001, 1540, 1600.

17 Ibid., 1545

18 Special Senate Committee on Bill c-36, 6 Dec. 2001.

19 D. Schneiderman and B. Cossman, "Political Association and the Anti-Terrorism Bill," in R. Daniels, P. Macklem, and K. Roach, eds., *The Security of Freedom: Essays on Canada's Anti-terrorism Bill* (Toronto: University of Toronto Press, 2001), 178–80.

20 Special Senate Committee on Bill c-36, 6 Dec. 2001.

21 A. Macklin, "Borderline Security," in Daniels, Macklem, and Roach, eds., *The Security of Freedom*, 383.

22 Standing Committee on Justice and Human Rights, 5 Nov. 2001, 2005, 2010.

23 Ibid., 6 Nov. 2001, 1000.

24 Canadian Arab Federation, Brief to Standing Committee on Justice and Human Rights on Bill c-36, Oct. 2001.

25 Standing Committee on Justice and Human Rights, 31 Oct. 2001, 1650.

26 Coalition of Muslim Organizations, Brief to Standing Committee on Justice and Human Rights on Bill c-36, 8 Nov. 2001, 3.

27 Standing Committee on Justice and Human Rights, 6 Nov. 2001, 0935. See also 30 Oct. 2001, 1535.

28 D. Martin, "Extradition, The Charter and Due Process: Is Procedural Fairness Enough?" *Supreme Court Law Review* 16 (2nd series) (2002): 161; A. Ashworth, *The Criminal Process*, 2nd ed. (Oxford: Oxford University Press, 1999), 11–12.

29 See Privacy Commissioner of Canada, News releases, 8 Nov., 21 Nov. 2001.

30 T. MacCharles and A. Thompson, "Anti-terrorism bill worries Dhaliwal," *Toronto Star*, 30 Oct. 2001.

31 D. Leblanc and S. McCarthy, "Terror bill worries Dhaliwal," *Globe and Mail*, 30 Oct. 2001.

32 S. McCarthy and D. Leblanc, "PM orders cabinet ministers to present a united front," Ibid., 31 Oct. 2001.

33 I. Cotler, "Thinking Outside the Box: Foundational Principles for a Counter-Terrorism Law and Policy," in Daniels, Macklem, and Roach, eds., *The Security of Freedom*, 121–9.

34 D. Savoie, *Governing from the Centre* (Toronto: University of Toronto Press, 1999).

35 Special Senate Committee on Bill C-36, *First Report*, 1 Nov. 2001.

36 Hansard, 27 Nov. 2001, 1000, per House Leader Don Boudria.

37 Ibid., 26 Nov. 2001, 1220.

38 Ibid., 27 Nov. 2001, 1025.

39 D. Leblanc, "Terror bill passes Commons," *Globe and Mail*, 29 Nov. 2001.

40 C. Hebert, "Opponents didn't win but fight was inspiring," *Toronto Star*, 21 Nov. 2001. See also the comments of Reid Morden that Bill C-36 had been debated extensively across the country and represented a healthy spectrum of views, intellectually yet passionately argued. R. Morden, "Finding the Right Balance," *Policy Options*, Sept. 2002, 45.

41 *The Anti-terrorism Act*, s. 145.

42 *Criminal Code*, s. 83.31. For criticisms, see E. Mendes, "Between Crime and War: Terrorism, Democracy and the Constitution," in D. Daubney et al., eds., *Terrorism, Law and Democracy: How Is Canada Changing Following September 11* (Montreal: Les Éditions Thémis, 2002), 262–5.

43 A case can be made that new powers should not have been given to every police officer, but only to the Canadian Security Intelligence Service, which is subject to special forms of accountability. See M.L. Friedland, "Police Powers in Bill C-36," in Daniels, Macklem, and Roach, eds., *The Security of Freedom*, 270–4.

44 A. Borovoy, "Watching the Watchers: Democratic Oversight," in Daubney et al., *Terrorism, Law and Democracy*, 409; S. Heafey, "Civilian Oversight in a Changed World," ibid., 401.

45 B. Rae, "Notes for an Address," in ibid., 405–6. On the rationale for placing security intelligence functions in the hands of a civilian agency subject to special civilian and parliamentary oversight, as opposed to the RCMP, see Canada, Commission of Inquiry Concerning Certain Activities of the Royal Canadian Mounted Police, *Certain R.C.M.P. Activities and the Question of Governmental Knowledge* (Ottawa: Minister of Supply and Services Canada, 1981).

46 Bill C-35, *An Act to amend the Foreign Missions and International Organizations Act*, 1st Session, 37th Parliament, 2001, cl. 10.1(2) (passed by House of Commons, 29 Nov. 2001).

47 *Tremblay v. Québec (Procureur général)*, [2001] RJQ 1293, para. 92.

48 J. Bronskill, "Good fences make good summits: RCMP," *National Post*, 25 Feb. 2002, citing Minister of Foreign Affairs Bill Graham; Alan Borovoy, "Protest Movements and Democracy," *Policy Options*, Sept. 2002, 54.

49 Irwin Cotler also criticized the *Public Safety Act* for giving ministers excessive powers without requiring legislative or judicial approval. S. McCarthy, "Liberal MP slams security bill for too much ministerial powers," *Globe and Mail*, 6 Dec. 2001.

50 M. Valpy, "Ottawa's security bill runs roughshod over rights," ibid., 1 Dec. 2001.

51 R. Seguin, "Antiterror bill worries Quebec," ibid.

52 "The danger zone," ibid., 7 Dec. 2001.

53 S. Choudhry, "Protecting Equality in the Face of Terror: Ethnic and Racial Profiling and s. 15 of the Charter," in Daniels, Macklem, and Roach, eds., *The Security of Freedom*, 367.

54 Ekos Research Associates, "Security, Sovereignty and Continentalism: Canadian Perspectives on September 11," 27 Sept. 2001; "Canadians moving on," *Toronto Star*, 9 Sept. 2002.

55 "Nuclear plant offers fired Muslim his job back," *Toronto Star*, 23 Nov. 2001.

56 K. Donovan, "Also a victim of Sept. 11," ibid., 18 Aug. 2002.

57 A. Thompson, "Can Canada still lay claim to being glorious and free," ibid., 9 Sept. 2002.

58 E. Quinn, "Anti-U.S. comment no reason for firing, board rules," ibid., 24 Aug. 2002.

59 G. Fraser, "Controversial art exhibit opens," ibid., 18 Oct. 2001.

60 H. Levy, "U.N. panel knocks Canada over racism, rights," ibid., 27 Aug. 2002.

61 Profiling has been defined both as a decision to subject a person to further investigation solely on the basis of race or ethnicity or as a decision to use race or ethnicity in conjunction with other factors. There is much to be said for the latter definition, which would cover American immigration practices of using a person's national origin as one factor in deciding whether to fingerprint or photograph. See Choudhry, "Protecting Equality in the Face of Terror," 368–70.

62 As George Grant argued: "One distinction between Canada and the United States has been the belief that Canada was predicated on the rights of nations as well as on the rights of individuals." G. Grant, *Lament for a Nation* (Toronto: McClelland & Stewart, 1965), 21–2.

63 The government has committed itself to ending Aboriginal overrepresentation in jail within a generation. See House of Commons, *Debates*, 30 Jan. 2001, 14–15 (Speech from the Throne). It has also included provisions in s. 718.2(e) of the *Criminal Code* and s. 38(2)(d) of the *Youth Criminal Justice Act* (Bill C-7, *An Act in respect of criminal justice for young persons*, 1st Session, 37th Parliament, 2001 (assented to 19 Feb. 2002, SC 2002, c. 1)), requiring judges to pay particular attention to the circumstances of Aboriginal offenders when considering whether sanctions other than imprisonment are reasonable in the circumstances. For a defence of this provision, see J. Rudin and K. Roach, "Broken Promises," *Saskatchewan Law Review* 65 (2002): 3.

64 *R. v. Gladue*, [1999] 1 SCR 688, 133 C CC (3d) 385 (need to consider Aboriginal overrepresentation in sentencing).

65 *Patriot Act*, Public Law No. 107–56, ∞102(a)(3). These statements are unenforceable "findings of Congress."

66 Amnesty International has said "that many of the 1,200 people swept up in the post-Sept. 11 investigation have been detained arbitrarily and deprived of basic human rights." E. Oziewicz, "Many foreign nationals still imprisoned in U.S.," *Globe and Mail*, 18 March 2002. American officials have also interviewed young male visitors from Arab and Muslim countries, and some police forces have refused to cooperate because of their own policies prohibiting racial profiling. S. Ashar, "Immigration Enforcement and Subordination: The Consequences of Racial Profiling after September 11," *Connecticut Law Review* 34 (2002): 1185, 1192–4. Canadians should also not be complacent as there are reports of immigration centres containing large number of detainees of Arab origin since September 11. S. Toope, "Fallout from '9–11': Will a Security Culture Undermine Human Rights?" *Saskatchewan Law Review* 65 (2002): 281, 286.

67 J. Sallot and S. McCarthy, "Tougher border checks anger Ottawa," *Globe and Mail*, 1 Nov. 2002.

68 C. Freeze, "Mistry cancels U.S. tour over racial profiling," ibid., 2 Nov. 2002.

69 A. Thompson, "Canadian fury as U.S. steps up border checks," *Toronto Star*, 8 Nov. 2002; "Foreign Affairs cancels U.S. travel warning," *National Post*, 8 Nov. 2002.

70 K. Roach and S. Choudhry, "Brief to the Special Senate Committee on Bill C-36," Nov. 2001. See also S. Choudhry, "Laws needed to ban racial profiling," *Toronto Star*, 25 Nov. 2002.

71 Some of this support is described and criticized in Choudhry, "Protecting Equality in the Face of Terror."

72 Standing Committee on Justice and Human Rights, 20 Nov. 2001, 1320.

73 Victims of discriminatory profiling will have few effective remedies. If incriminating evidence is found and a Charter violation is established, it may possibly be excluded under s. 24(2) of the Charter. Courts are, however, reluctant to exclude improperly obtained evidence or throw a case out of court if a fair trial is still possible. The vast majority of victims of profiling who are factually innocent will not have any incriminating evidence to exclude. They may, at best, receive modest financial compensation, but only after paying a lawyer and having to pay the lawyers representing the defendant if they lose. Courts may also be reluctant to order governments to take steps to ensure that profiling does not occur again. See S. Choudhry and K. Roach, "Racial and Ethnic Profiling: Statutory Discretion, Constitutional Remedies and Democratic Accountability," *Osgoode Hall Law Journal* 41 (2003) (forthcoming); K. Roach, "Hard to prove racial profiling," *Toronto Star*, 25 Nov. 2002. See also chapter 4 of this book for further discussion of the difficulties of litigating profiling claims. Complaints to human rights commissions may be a less expensive alternative to litigation in the courts, but few complaints result in a public hearing – and then often after much delay.

74 "We don't do racial profiling: RCMP," *Toronto Star*, 28 Sept. 2002. Commissioner Zaccardelli told the Senate Special Committee on Bill C-36 that "we profile modes of transportation but never racial profiling. That is unacceptable, in my view, in this country and I will never accept that as part of a policy of the RCMP." Special Senate Committee on Bill C-36, 23 Oct. 2001.

75 D. Leblanc, "Anne McLellan's new ideas," *Globe and Mail*, 22 Oct. 2001.

76 When asked, 56 per cent of the sample of 1228 said prevention was most important, 20 per cent said punishment, and 24 per cent said both prevention and punishment equally. Ekos Research Associates, "Security, Sovereignty and Continentalism: Canadian Perspectives on September 11," 27 Sept 2001.

77 As Minister of Justice Anne McLellan did when, in response to criticism of Bill C-36, she stated: "Sometimes when I read something from someone: Gosh, you know, I wish you were in my shoes for 24 hours. I wish you knew what I know, in terms of how hard it is to detect these guys and get these guys and stop their fundraising or whatever."

S. McCarthy, "Anne McLellan's new ideals," *Globe and Mail,* 22 Oct. 2001.

78 Hansard, 15 Oct. 2001, 1110.

79 Notes for appearance before the Justice Committee, 18 Oct. 2001.

80 Ipsos Reid, "Majority (58 per cent) say terrorism threats outweigh protection of individual rights, freedom and due process of law," 5 Oct. 2001.

81 Remarks of Stanley Cohen in "Concluding Comments from the Department of Justice," in Daniels, Macklem, and Roach, eds., *The Security of Freedom,* 435, 440. The *Department of Justice Act,* RSC 1985, c. J-2, s. 4.1, requires the attorney general of Canada to examine legislation for consistency with the Charter and empowers the attorney general to report to Parliament that proposed legislation would be unconstitutional. On the failure of the attorney general to use this power in several recent cases of "in your face" parliamentary replies to Supreme Court decisions, see K. Roach, "The Attorney General and the Charter Revisited," *University of Toronto Law Journal* 50 (2000): 1, 30–8.

82 *R. v. Mills,* [1999] 3 SCR 668, upholding an effective legislative reversal of *R. v. O'Connor,* [1995] 4 SCR 1411. For different approaches to the complex issues of dialogue between courts and legislatures implicated by this decision, see K. Roach, "Common Law and Constitutional Dialogues between the Supreme Court and Canadian Legislatures," *Canadian Bar Review* 80 (2001): 481, and *R. v. Hall,* [2002] SCC, per Iacobucci J. (in dissent), paras 123–8.

83 R. Dworkin, "The Threat to Patriotism," *New York Review of Books,* 28 Feb. 2002, 44, 47.

84 For concerns that the Charter may inhibit democratic debate open to all, see M. Mandel, *The Charter of Rights and the Legalization of Politics in Canada* (Toronto: Thomson, 1994), and A. Hutchinson, *Waiting for CORAF* (Toronto: University of Toronto Press, 1995).

85 Some concerns were raised on federalism grounds, but they raise the larger issue of whether it was necessary to give these new anti-terrorism measures to every police officer in the country as opposed to only federal agencies such as the RCMP or CSIS.

86 Hansard, 16 Oct. 2001, 1015.

87 *Criminal Code,* s. 320.1.

88 Ibid., s. 430(4.1).

89 Roach, *Due Process and Victims' Rights,* chaps. 5–8.

90 A survey conducted in late September found 50 per cent of respondents prepared to accept that airline and customs officials and the police

should give special attention to individuals of Arabic origin. T. Harper, "Canadians feel closer to U.S. since attacks: poll," *Toronto Star*, 29 Sept. 2001; Ekos Research Associates, "Security, Sovereignty and Continentalism: Canadian Perspectives on Sept. 11," 27 Sept. 2001.

91 Ipsos Reid, "Strong majority (82 per cent) worried that people of Arab Decent or Muslims in Canada may become the target of unwarranted racism or personal attacks because of terrorist attacks," 24 Sept. 2001.

92 In Toronto, this increase was first directed "against anyone who was perceived to be of the Muslim (Islamic) religion," but "then evolved to include occurrences targeting U.S. and Canadian interests and the Jewish community." J. Quinn, "Spike in hate crimes followed Sept. 11," *Toronto Star*, 26 Feb. 2002; Peter Ray, "Arabs, Muslims still live in fear of attacks," ibid., 23 March 2002.

93 Minister's notes for appearance before Senate Special Committee on Bill C-36, 29 Oct. 2001.

94 I. Cotler, "Towards a Counter-Terrorism Law and Policy," *Terrorism and Political Violence* 10 (1998): 1.

95 I. Cotler, "Thinking Outside the Box: Foundational Principles for a Counter-Terrorism Law and Policy," in Daniels, Macklem, and Roach, eds., *The Security of Freedom*, 112.

96 L. Chwialkowska, "Human rights lawyer unlikely ally of terror bill," *National Post*, 25 Oct. 2001.

97 See, generally, K. Roach, "Four Models of the Criminal Process," *Journal of Criminal Law & Criminology* 89 (1999): 671; Roach, *Due Process and Victims' Rights*.

98 *Criminal Code*, s. 83.14(5.1), and *Patriot Act*, ∞ 621–24.

99 The issue of victim compensation can, however, raise complex issues of distributive justice. The generosity of the *Patriot Act* to the families of the victims of September 11 may create inequities in the treatment of the families of other crime victims. A focus on victim compensation through fines and mandatory restitution may constitute a highly regressive tax that compensates for an inadequate social safety net that should catch not only the victims of crime but the victims of other misfortunes.

100 On the role that the families of victims of terrorism have played in law reform in the United States, see M. Crenshaw, "Counterterrorism Policy and the Political Process" *Studies in Conflict & Terrorism* 24 (2001): 329, 334.

101 M. Friscolanti, "Ottawa warns Sept. 11 widow to pay taxes," *National Post*, 5 Sept. 2002.

102 I. Cotler, "Does the anti-terrorism bill go too far? No: we need powerful new legal tools to fight the new global terror threat," *Globe and Mail*, 20 Nov. 2001.

103 D. Stuart, "The Anti-terrorism Bill (Bill C-36): An Unnecessary Law and Order Quick Fix That Permanently Stains the Canadian Criminal Justice System," in Daubney et al., *Terrorism, Law and Democracy*, 185.

104 Note, however, that the Supreme Court has endorsed such a relational approach to competing rights in a number of cases, including *R. v. Mills*, [1999] 3 SCR 668, and *R. v. Mentuck*, 2001 SCC 76.

105 Professor Cotler and I agree about the importance of ensuring that jurors are not racially prejudiced against either the accused or the victim in a criminal trial. See I. Cotler, "War Crimes and the Finta Case," *Supreme Court Law Review* 6 (2nd series) (1995): 577; K. Roach, "Using the Williams Question to Ensure Equal Protection for Aboriginal Crime Victims," *Criminal Reports* 38 (5th series) (2001): 335.

106 Bill C-24, *An Act to amend the Criminal Code (organised crime and law enforcement) and to make consequential amendments to other Acts*, 1st Session, 37th Parliament, 2001 (assented to 18 Dec. 2001, SC 2001, c. 32), served as a blueprint of sorts for some of the new offences in Bill C-36. Even temporary anti-terrorism legislation in Britain has served as a model for restrictions on the right to silence in that country. See O. Gross, "Cutting Down Trees: Law-Making under the Shadow of Great Calamities," in Daniels, Macklem, and Roach, eds., *The Security of Freedom*, 49–50.

CHAPTER FOUR

1 *Re Gray* (1918), 57 SCR 152 at 160. Chief Justice Fitzpatrick added: "It is our clear duty to give effect to their patriotic intention." See also *Japanese Canadians Reference*, [1947] AC 87; *Fort Frances Pulp and Power Co. v. Manitoba Free Press*, [1923] AC 695, for similar deference to what the government determines is necessary in wartime. For a contemporary defence of this last case on the basis that the question of "when a wartime emergency ends is not prone to judicial analysis" or "deductive reasoning" and is "not based on an open evidentiary record but on information that only the government knows," see E. Morgan, "No 'proof' needed to go after Iraq," *National Post*, 24 Oct. 2002. Under the Charter, however, the Supreme Court has rejected such a

hands-off-political-questions approach when reviewing the decision to test cruise missiles, and it would have intervened if such testing resulted in proven harm to some particular group. *Operation Dismantle v. The Queen*, [1985] 1 SCR 441.

2 *Gagnon v. Vallieres* (1971), 14 CRNS 321 at 350 (Que. CA), dismissing an argument articulated in N. Lyon, "Constitutional Validity of Public Order Regulations," *McGill Law Journal* 18 (1971): 136.

3 R.S. Abella, "Judging in the 21st Century," *Advocates' Quarterly* 25 (2002): 138-9.

4 R. Bork, *Coercing Virtue: The Worldwide Rule of Judges* (Toronto: Vintage, 2002), 2.

5 Grant was an opponent of *Roe v. Wade*, 410 US 113, 93 S. Ct. 705 (1973), but more for its failure to recognize fetal rights than for its judicial creation. G. Grant, *Technology and Justice* (Toronto: Anansi, 1986), 117-30.

6 K. Roach, *The Supreme Court on Trial: Judicial Activism or Democratic Dialogue* (Toronto: Irwin Law, 2001), chap. 3.

7 Many, however, trace the start of the Cold War to the Igor Gouzenko affair immediately after the Second World War, in which two justices of the Supreme Court acted as an inquisitorial commission that questioned suspected spies without counsel being present. Even Prime Minister Mackenzie King had private misgivings that "the whole proceedings are far too much like Russia itself." See R. Whitaker and G. Marcuse, *Cold War Canada: The Making of a National Insecurity State*, 1945-1957 (Toronto: University of Toronto Press, 1994), 67.

8 Compare *Dennis v. United States*, 341 US 494, 71 S. Ct. 857 (1951), with *Boucher v. R.* (1950), [1951] SCR 265, 99 CCC 1, on freedom of speech and sedition; *American Communications Association v. Douds*, 339 US.382, 70 S. Ct. 674 (1950), with *Smith & Rhuland Ltd. v. R. ex rel. Andrews*, [1953] 2 SCR 95, 107 CCC 43, on unions and communists; and *Adler v. Board of Education of the City of New York*, 342 US 485, 72 S. Ct. 380 (1952), with *Switzman v. Elbling*, [1957] SCR 285, 117 CCC 129, on the treatment of subversive organizations. In each case, the Canadian court, even without a constitutional bill of rights, took an approach more accepting of freedom of speech.

9 The Court of Appeal in the United Kingdom upheld, under the *Human Rights Act of* 1998 and the European Convention, indefinite detention of foreign nationals who could not be deported because they would be tortured in their home states. *A, X, Y v. Secretary of State for the Home Department*, [2002] ECWA Civ. 1502. The Court of Appeals for the Fourth Circuit in the United States upheld the indefinite detention

of an American citizen captured in Afghanistan as an enemy combatant, with the judges emphasizing that judicial review of "battlefield
captures overseas is a highly deferential one." *Rumsfeld v. Hamdi*,
No. 02–7338, 13 Jan. 2003.

10 See J. Hiebert, *Charter Conflicts? What Is Parliament's Role* (Montreal:
McGill-Queen's University Press, 2002).

11 T. MacCharles, "Sweeping anti-terror powers introduced," *Toronto
Star*, 16 Oct. 2001.

12 *Gagnon v. Vallieres* (1971), 14 CRNS 321 at 350 (Que. CA).

13 D. Paciocco, "Constitutional Casualties of September 11: Limiting the
Legacy of the *Anti-terrorism Act*,' *Supreme Court Law Review* 16 (2nd
series) (2002): 199, in reference to the definition of terrorist groups in
section 83.01(b) of the *Criminal Code*.

14 Lyon, "Constitutional Validity of Public Order Regulations," 136.

15 *R. v. Whyte*, [1988] 2 SCR 3 (drunk driving); *R. v. Downey*, [1992] 2
SCR 10 (pimping); *R. v. Keegstra*, [1990] 3 SCR 697 (hate propaganda); *R. v. Daviault*, [1994] 3 SCR 63 (sexual assault); *R. v. Stone*,
[1999] 2 SCR 290 (violent offences).

16 *R. v. Keegstra*; *R. v. Butler*, [1992] 1 SCR 452.

17 *Criminal Code*, s. 264.1, 423(1)(b).

18 *Hunter v. Southam*, [1984] 2 SCR 145.

19 *Smith v. Canada* 2001 SCC 81 at para 2.

20 *R. v. Plant*, [1993] 3 SCR 281; *R. v. Edwards*, [1996] 1 SCR 128; *R. v.
Belnavis*, [1997] 3 SCR 341; *R. v. M (M.R.)*, [1998] 3 SCR 393. See,
generally, L. Austin, "Is Privacy a Casualty in the War against Terrorism?" in R. Daniels, P. Macklem, and K. Roach, eds., *The Security of
Freedom: Essays on Canada's Anti-terrorist Bill* (Toronto: University of
Toronto Press, 2001), 258–63, and D. Stuart, *Charter Justice in Canadian Criminal Law*, 3rd ed. (Toronto: Carswell, 2001), chap. 3.

21 See Justice La Forest's rejection of risk analysis, which reasons back
from the fact that the individual whom the state brings proceedings
against is guilty. *R. v. Wong*, [1990] 3 SCR 36. On Justice La Forest's
passionate commitment to privacy and the way in which the Supreme
Court has, unfortunately in my view, moved away from his vision of
privacy, see K. Roach, "Justice La Forest: A Bickelian Balance of State
and Individual Interests," in R. Johnson et al., *Gérard V. La Forest at
the Supreme Court of Canada, 1985–1997* (Winnipeg: Canadian Legal
History Project, 2000), 167–73.

22 See Legal Opinion of Gérard La Forest, 19 Nov. 2002, at www.priv-
com.gc.ca. The privacy commissioner also obtained legal opinions that
the travel database may violate the Charter from Roger Tasse, who

helped draft the Charter, and Marc Lalonde, a former minister of justice. M. Higgins, "Ottawa will re-examine customs database," *National Post*, 16 Jan. 2003.

23 P. Waldie, "Customs to gather racial data," *Globe and Mail*, 16 Dec. 2002.

24 S. Choudhry, "Protecting Equality in the Face of Terror: Ethnic and Racial Profiling and S. 15 of the Charter," in Daniels, Macklem, and Roach, eds., *The Security of Freedom*, 367. This paragraph draws on Professor Choudhry's analysis.

25 *Little Sisters Book and Art Emporium v. Canada (Minister of Justice)*, [2000] 2 SCR 1120 at para 121.

26 *Law v. Canada*, [1999] 1 SCR 497.

27 Choudhry, "Protecting Equality in the Face of Terror," 376.

28 See S. Choudhry and K. Roach, "Racial and Ethnic Profiling: Statutory Discretion, Constitutional Remedies and Democratic Accountability," *Osgoode Hall Law Journal* 41 (2003) (forthcoming).

29 *Little Sisters Book and Art Emporium v. Canada (Minister of Justice)* [2000] 2 SCR 1120 at para 157-8. See also K. Roach, *Constitutional Remedies in Canada* (Aurora: Canada Law Book, as updated), chap. 11; K. Roach, "Remedial Consensus and Dialogue under the Charter," *University of British Columbia Law Review* 35 (2002): 232-5.

30 R. Salhany, *The Origins of Rights* (Toronto: Carswell, 1986), 95.

31 *British Columbia (Securities Commission) v. Branch*, [1995] 2 SCR 3.

32 R. Mosley, "Preventing Terrorism: Bill C-36 *The Anti-terrorism Act, 2001*," in D. Daubney et al., *Terrorism, Law and Democracy: How Is Canada Changing after September 11?* (Montreal: Les Éditions Thémis, 2002), 167.

33 Our allies may be able to use compelled statements if the terrorist is extradited from Canada to face trial in other country. See Paciocco, "Constitutional Casualties of September 11," 231.

34 It has been argued that the provisions still offend the Charter because the state could be acting simply for the purpose of forcing a person to incriminate himself and because the investigative hearings conscript judges into compelling the person to talk. Ibid., 230-6. The state, however, will fend off this argument by stressing that its purpose is to catch terrorists, not to compel self-incrimination, and that the court retains its independence and discretion to decide whether to compel the person to talk.

35 *R. v. Martineau*, [1990] 2 SCR 633; *R. v. Finta*, [1994] SCR 701.

36 The Court has drawn a distinction between criminal law "theory," or the "ideal" requirement (that a person accused of manslaughter had been at fault for causing the accused death), and the minimum requirements of

the Charter (which require only that the accused person acts unlaw-
fully in situations in which he or she would have recognized a threat of
non-trivial bodily harm). *R. v. Creighton*, [1993] 3 SCR 3.

37 *R. v. Sharpe*, [2001] SCC 2. For a critical assessment of the Court's
attraction to constitutional minimalism, which defines constitutional
defects narrowly and saves possibly overbroad laws, see Roach, *The
Supreme Court on Trial*, 147–52.

38 *R v. Heywood* (1994), 94 CCC (3d) 481. Legislation in the United
States and the United Kingdom is generally more precise and somewhat more limited in setting out the forms of assistance to terrorist
groups which are prohibited. The American *Patriot Act*, s. 805, for
example, excludes the provision of medicine and religious materials
from the prohibited act.

39 See, for example, M. Shaffer, "Effectiveness of Anti-Terrorism Legislation: Does Bill C-36 Give Us What We Need?" in Daniels, Macklem,
and Roach, eds., *The Security of Freedom*, 201–3.

40 *R. v. Keegstra*, [1990] 3 SCR 697; *R. v. Butler*, [1992] 1 SCR 452.
See R. Sharpe, K. Swinton, and K. Roach, *The Charter of Rights and
Freedoms*, 2nd ed. (Toronto: Irwin Law, 2002), 136–46.

41 For example, the courts have upheld Parliament's reply legislation to
the Court's 1994 decision striking down an overbroad vagrancy offence
which allows a judge to prohibit a person from doing any activity that
involves conduct with children on the basis that there are "reasonable
fears" that he or she will commit a sexual offence with a child. *R. v.
Budreo* (1998), 142 CCC(3d) 225 (Ont. CA). See, generally, Stuart,
Charter Justice in Canadian Criminal Law, 102–7.

42 *Canada Evidence Act*, s. 38.13, as amended. See H. Stewart, "Rule
of Law or Executive Fiat? Bill C-36 and Public Interest Immunity," in
Daniels, Macklem, and Roach, eds., *The Security of Freedom*.

43 The Court stated that "courts do not hold a monopoly on the protection and promotion of rights and freedoms: Parliament also plays a role
in this regard and is often able to act as a significant ally for vulnerable groups." *R. v. Mills*, [1999] 3 SCR 668, para 58.

44 *Ruby v. Canada* 2002 SCC 75 at para 44–6.

45 *R. v. Seaboyer*, [1991] 2 SCR 577; *R. v. Stinchcombe*, [1991] 3 SCR
326.

46 K. Roach, "The Dangers of a Charter-Proof and Crime-Based Response
to Terrorism," in Daniels, Macklem, and Roach, eds., *The Security of
Freedom*, 131.

47 E. Mendes, "Between Crime and War Terrorism, Democracy and the
Constitution," in Daubney et al., *Terrorism, Law and Democracy*, 257.

48 An unnamed senior civil servant quoted in R. Cleroux, "The Chattering Classes," *Law Times*, 2 Dec. 2002.

49 See, generally, Roach, *The Supreme Court on Trial*.

50 Ibid.

51 Mosley, "Preventing Terrorism," 150.

52 Roach, *The Supreme Court on Trial*, chap. 14.

53 E. Burke, *Burke's Speech on Conciliation with America* (London: Macmillan, 1961), 35.

54 K. Roach, "The Attorney General and the Charter Revisited," *University of Toronto Law Journal* 50 (2000): 1.

55 [2001] 1 SCR 283, 151 CCC (3d) 97.

56 2002 SCC 1.

57 *Burns and Rafay*, para 112.

58 *Suresh v. Canada*, paras 42–75.

59 As quoted in Roach, *The Supreme Court on Trial*, 94.

60 Hansard, 27 Nov. 2001, 1015.

61 "Staying terrorists," Editorial, *National Post*, 12 Jan. 2002.

62 In his Barbara Frum Lecture, Robert Bork criticized the Israeli Supreme Court for taking away "important means to preserve national security." Bork, *Coercing Virtue*, 12–29. To his credit, Judge Bork did recognize that the Court's decision ruling against the use of physical force in interrogations was "correct" because the legislature had not explicitly authorized such force in legislation.

63 A. Dershowitz, *Why Terrorism Works* (New Haven: Yale University Press, 2002), chap. 4. He suggests that a warrant and immunity for the person being tortured from subsequent prosecution might ensure that torture complies with due process guarantees under the American Bill of Rights. Ibid., 135. He notes, however, that the Supreme Court of Canada refused to extradite a person to the United States after an American prosecutor threatened that the fugitive would, if imprisoned in the United States, "be the boyfriend of a very bad man if you wait out your extradition." Ibid., 251, citing *United States of America v. Cobb*, [2001] 1 SCR 587.

64 D. Saunders, "US walks a fine line to make prisoners talk," *Globe and Mail*, 17 Sept. 2002.

65 Dershowitz, *Why Terrorism Works*, 137. For a Canadian decision refusing to extradite a person to the Philippines on the basis that its criminal procedure would shock the conscience of Canadians and violate the Charter, see *Canada (Minister of Justice) v. Pacificador* (2002), 60 OR(3d) 685 (CA).

66 *The Anti-terrorism, Crime and Security Act,* 2001, Part 3. For appro-
   priately critical commentary of this British legislation, see A. Tomkins,
   "Legislating versus Terror," *Public Law* [2002], 205; H. Fenwick, "The
   Anti-Terrorism, Crime and Security Act 2001: A Proportionate
   Response to 11 September?" *Modern Law Review* 65 (2002): 724.

67 "Ends, means and barbarity," *The Economist,* 9 Jan. 2003.

68 The Special Immigration Appeals Tribunal held that the derogation
   from fair trial rights was not sufficient because the indeterminate
   detention of suspected international terrorists and their supporters also
   discriminates against non-British citizens. Fenwick, "The Anti-
   Terrorism, Crime and Security Act," 762. Its decision was, however,
   reversed by the Court of Appeal, which upheld the new law. *A, X, Y v.
   Secretary of State for the Home Department,* [2002] ECWA Civ. 1502.

69 On these different understandings of dialogue, see K. Roach, "Constitutional and Common Law Dialogues between the Supreme Court and
   Canadian Legislatures," *Canadian Bar Review* 80 (2001): 481.

70 *Suresh v. Canada,* para 88. The Court adds: "It may once have made
   sense to suggest that terrorism in one country did not necessarily impli-
   cate other countries. But after the year 2001, that approach is no
   longer valid." Ibid., para 87.

71 My colleague Audrey Macklin has argued that, "thanks to *Ahani,* if the
   Minister determines that the individual has not made out a prima facie
   case of torture, there is no requirement to inform the refugee of the
   case against him or her, to provide the refugee with an opportunity to
   respond to the evidence marshalled against him or her, or to provide
   reasons for the decision." She also notes that the victorious Mr. Suresh
   was supported by eight interveners, while Ahani was much less popular and remained in detention on the day of the hearing before the
   Supreme Court. See A. Macklin, "Mr. Suresh and the Evil Twin,"
   Refuge 20, 4 (2002): 21, 17.

72 *Ahani v. Canada* (2002), 58 OR(3d) 107 at para 113, per Rosenberg JA
   in dissent. See also *Ahani v. Canada* 2002 SCC 2.

73 *Suresh v. Canada* at para. 33, quoting *Secretary of State for the Home
   Department* v. *Rehman,* [2001] 3 WLR 877 at para 62 (HL).

74 Hon. Roy McMurtry, "Speech at the Opening of the Courts, 2002."

75 See, for example, Justice Lamer's statement: "The Charter is designed
   to protect the accused from the majority, so the enforcement of the
   Charter must not be left to that majority." *R. v. Collins* (1987), 33
   CCC(3d) 1 at 17 (SCC).

76 Bill C-36, s. 95, amending the *Federal Court Act,* RSC 1985, c. F-7.

77 P.H. Russell and J.S. Ziegel, "Federal Judicial Appointments: An Appraisal of the First Mulroney Government's Appointments and the New Judicial Advisory Committees," *University of Toronto Law Journal* 41 (1991): 4.

78 D. Dyzenhaus, "The Permanence of the Temporary: Can Emergency Powers Be Normalized?" in Daniels, Macklem, and Roach, eds., *The Security of Freedom*, 33.

79 *Criminal Code*, s. 83.06, and s. 8 of the *Charities Registration (Security Information) Act*, S.C. 2001, c. 41, Part 6. This authority goes beyond the limits in the deportation case of *Chiarelli v. Canada (Minister of Employment and Immigration)*, [1992] 1 SCR 711 at 746, in which the Court held: "It is not necessary, in order to comply with fundamental justice in this context, that the respondent also be given details of the criminal intelligence investigation techniques or police sources used to acquire that information." In *Chiarelli*, the individual was given "sufficient information to know the substance of the allegations against him, and to be able to respond."

80 *Canada (Minister of Citizenship and Immigration) v. Tobiass*, [1997] 3 SCR 391 at paras 74–75.

81 J. Hugessen, "Watching the Watchers: Democratic Oversight," in Daubney et al., *Terrorism, Law and Democracy*, 384–6.

82 *Ruby v. Canada* 2002 SCC 75. As discussed above, however, this case arose not in the context of criminal or immigration proceedings or the decision to list a group or an individual as a terrorist, but in an attempt by a lawyer to gain access to CSIS files on him.

83 *Canada Evidence Act*, s. 38.13.

84 P. McMahon, "Amending the *Access to Information Act*: Does National Security Require the Proposed Amendments of Bill C-36?" *University of Toronto Faculty of Law Review* 60 (2002): 95.

85 Special Senate Committee on the Subject Matter of Bill C-36, First Report, *Journals of the Senate*, 1st Session, 37th Parliament (1 Nov. 2001), 933–4.

86 *Canada Evidence Act*, s. 38.14.

87 *R. v. Carosella*, [1997] 1 SCR 80.

88 The Supreme Court has recognized societal interests in less drastic alternatives to stays of proceedings in *R. v. O'Connor*, [1995] 4 SCR 411.

89 *Criminal Code*, s. 83.3.

90 G. Trotter, "The Anti-Terrorism Bill and Preventive Restraints on Liberty," in Daniels, Macklem, and Roach, eds., *The Security of Freedom*, 243.

91 Nevertheless, this and the other new peace bond provision in s. 810.01 will likely be held to be consistent with the Charter. See *R. v. Budreo* (2000), 142 CCC(3d) 225 (Ont. CA), upholding similar peace bond provisions under the Charter.

92 Whitaker and Marcuse, *Cold War Canada*, 65.

93 Paciocco, "Constitutional Casualities of the War on Terrorism," 233

94 *R. v. Belmas* (1985), 27 CCC (3d) 142 (BCCA).

95 Preston Manning's reply to the 1999 Throne Speech featured criticisms of the courts as being soft on crime and refugee applicants. See House of Commons, *Debates*, 13 Oct. 1999, 38–9.

CHAPTER FIVE

1 G. Grant, *Lament for a Nation* (Toronto: McClelland & Stewart, 1965), 57ff.

2 R. Dworkin, "The Threat to Patriotism," *New York Review of Books*, 28 Feb. 2002), 45.

3 T. Homer Dixon, "Now comes the real danger," *Globe and Mail*, 12 Sept. 2001.

4 J. Simpson, "Still the world's longest undefined border," ibid., 12 Sept. 2001.

5 K. Toughill, "McDonough's anti-war stance under fire," *Toronto Star*, 13 Oct. 2001.

6 N. Klein, "War isn't a game after all," *Globe and Mail*, 14 Sept. 2001.

7 M.Gee, "Stop making excuses for terrorism," ibid., 15 Sept. 2001.

8 H. Siddiqui, "It's the U.S. foreign policy," *Toronto Star*, 19 Sept. 2001, as quoted in R. Fulford, "From delusions to destruction: How Sept. 11 has called into question the attitudes by which our society lives," *National Post*, 6 Oct. 2001.

9 My focus has been on major English-language newspapers, not on other forms of media.

10 "Freedom of speech a casuality of a new war," *Toronto Star*, 3 Oct. 2001.

11 These restrictions included CNN's decision to comply with the government's request not to run a tape of Osama bin Laden and to balance any negative stories about civilian casualties in the war against Afghanistan with a reminder that more than 3000 people had been killed in the September 11 attacks. L. Hurst, "From tiger to pussycat: America's press defanged," ibid., 8 Sept. 2002.

12 The book, edited by Ron Daniels, Patrick Macklem, and Kent Roach, was published with record speed by University of Toronto Press.

13 C. Sunstein, "Why They Hate Us: The Role of Social Dynamics," *Harvard Journal of Law and Public Policy* 25 (2002): 438; R. Parker, "Homeland: An Essay on Patriotism," ibid., 407

14 See, for example, G. Fletcher, "On Justice and War: Contradictions in the Proposed Military Tribunals," ibid., 635. It is interesting that George Fletcher and Ronald Dworkin, the two most prominent American legal academics to speak out against American responses to September 11, have a comparative sensibility that remains rare in the American legal academy. Dworkin teaches at Oxford and Fletcher is an expert on continental legal systems.

15 J. Martin and A. Neal, *Defending Civilization: How Our Universities Are Failing America and What Can Be Done About It* (Washington: American Council of Trustees and Alumni, 2002), 9, 13, 14.

16 Thobani's speech, as well as responses to her critics, is widely available on the internet. See, for example, *www.terminalcity*.com:8080/terminal city/1003130821/index-html.

17 "Thobani talk 'terrible' but PM backs gathering," *Sault Star*, 4 Oct. 2001.

18 M. Hume, "RCMP now want to probe threats against Thobani," *National Post*, 12 Oct. 2001.

19 *Criminal Code of Canada*, RSC 1985, c. C-46, s. 318(4).

20 P. McMartin, "Free speech in a pristine vacuum," *Vancouver Sun*, 3 Oct. 2001; "The freedom to spew hate," *Victoria Times Colonist*, 4 Oct. 2001.

21 C. Blatchford, "A product of Chrétien's Canada," *National Post*, 3 Oct. 2001.

22 "Voices of dissent feel the heat in the wake of Sept 11" CAUT Bulletin 1 Nov 2001.

23 "No censorship," *Ottawa Citizen*, 16 Oct. 2001.

24 J. Rebick, "Assault on liberty," *Canadian Dimension*, 11 Oct. 2001.

25 Ekos Research Associates, "Security, Sovereignty and Continentalism: Canadian Perspectives on Sept 11," 27 Sept. 2001.

26 J. Kay, "Exploding the blowback fallacy in U.S. relations," *National Post*, 8 Oct. 2001.

27 S. McCarthy, "PM says U.S. attitude helped fuel Sept. 11," *Globe and Mail*, 11 Sept. 2002. On September 16, 2002, Chrétien made a speech to the United Nations that related the terrorist attacks to "failed states

in faraway places." M. Certnetig, "PM links Sept. 11 to 'failed states,'"
ibid., 17 Sept. 2002.

28 S. McCarthy, "PM's Sept. 11 remarks 'disgraceful,' Mulroney says,"
ibid., 13 Sept. 2002; M. Kennedy, "PM denies 'blaming victim' for Sept.
11," National Post, 13 Sept. 2002; "Sept. 11: Chrétien's version,"
National Post, 13 Sept. 2002.

29 S. McCarthy, "Fox hounds PM over remarks," Globe and Mail, 14
Sept. 2002; T. Nichols, "Chrétien's state of denial is dangerous,"
National Post, 25 Sept. 2002; R. Fife, "Chrétien soft on terrorism, Wall
Street Journal readers told," National Post, 27 Sept. 2002; R. Fulford,
"Chrétien talked, Canadians cringed," National Post, 14 Sept. 2002.

30 S. McCarthy, "PM's Sept. 11 remarks 'disgraceful', Mulroney says,"
Globe and Mail, 13 Sept. 2002.

31 Of the respondents, 14 per cent said the United States bore no responsibility and 15 per cent said it bore all the responsibility. S. McCarthy,
"Majority thinks U.S. partly to blame for Sept. 11," ibid., 7 Sept.
2002.

32 Prime Minister's Office Press Release, 12 Sept. 2002.

33 M. Nafik, "Antiterror war conceals global injustices," Jakarta Post,
23 Sept. 2002.

34 R. Fulford, "From delusions to destruction: How Sept. 11 has called
into question the attitudes by which our society lives," National Post,
6 Oct. 2001.

35 R. Fulford, "Chaos v. civilization? We're neutral," ibid., 24 Nov. 2001.

36 Stephen Toope has commented on the dangers of a "dichotomy of
virtuous 'us' and evil 'them' reflected in the rhetoric of 'clashing civilizations' promoted by Samuel Huntington and his followers." S. Toope,
"Fallout from 9–11: Will a Security Culture Undermine Human
Rights," Saskatchewan Law Review 65 (2002): 294.

37 R. Fulford, "US bashing is no longer a game," National Post, 14 Sept.
2001.

38 R. Fulford, "Anti-American cant a self-inflicted wound," ibid., 22 Sept.
2001.

39 P. Gzowski, "Being anti-US is like being anti-winter: In the end you
love them both," Globe and Mail, 15 Sept. 2001.

40 "Perhaps the logic of free trade and 9/11 will lead to the explicit har-
monization of continental tariff and immigration policies, security and
defence. Gradually Canada's tax policies will have to be harmonized
with those of nearby U.S. states. The debate on a common currency is

not likely to recede. As American economic influence on Canada continues to evolve, the pressure for erasing the border in every non-political way will be irrestible." M. Bliss, "Is Canada a country in decline?" *National Post*, 30 Nov. 2001.

41 M. Bliss, "The fate of U.S.'s northern suburb," ibid., 29 Jan. 2002.

42 J. Granatstein, "Our best friend – whether we like it or not," ibid., 23 Oct. 2002.

43 L. Axworthy, "Make sense, not war," *Globe and Mail*, 17 Sept. 2001. See also L. Axworthy, "How to prosecute bin Laden," ibid., 5 Dec 2001.

44 L. Axworthy, "Watch your step, Mr. Chrétien," ibid., 4 Feb. 2002.

45 L. Axworthy, "Stop the U.S. foul play," ibid., 17 July 2002.

46 L. Axworthy, "Liberals at the Border: We Stand on Guard for Whom?" The 6th annual Keith Davey Lecture, 11 March 2002.

47 See chapter 6 for further discussion of these developments.

48 M. Gee, "What rogue power?" *Globe and Mail*, 20 July 2002.

49 J. Ibbitson, "Fourscore and 253 days ago," ibid., 22 July 2002.

50 D. Frum, "Canada has earned America's suspicion," *National Post*, 2 Nov. 2002. Frum was commenting on Canada's opposition to American profiling of Canadian citizens born in the Middle East. To Frum's credit, he noted that, "on the merits of the dispute ... Canada is surely right. In both Canada and the United States, foreign-born citizens are entitled to be treated as citizens, plain and simple."

51 Grant, *Lament for a Nation*, 68.

52 The analogy should not be overstated, as American universities have not required loyalty oaths, hired security officers, or fired many professors, all things that happened during the communist witch-hunt of the 1950s. R. Pells, *The Liberal Mind in a Conservative Age* (New York: Harper & Row, 1985), 288–9. With reference to a petition started by American law professors to protest the legality of American military tribunals, Stephen Toope has concluded: "So far, academic freedom to criticize the war effort and its fall-out has not been significantly muffled." Toope, "Fallout from '9–11,'" 294.

53 As under the investigative hearings of Bill c-36, the suspected spies were required to answer questions during the Gouzenko spy inquiries. "'You must answer,' reluctant witnesses were told again and again ... The suspects were trapped, anxious about self-incrimination, but told in no uncertain terms that they must testify or be punished for their refusal." R. Whitaker and G. Marcuse, *Cold War Canada* (Toronto:

University of Toronto Press, 1994), 65. Unlike Bill c-36, the suspected spies were detained longer and without access to counsel. They received immunity for further use of their compelled statements only if they requested it, whereas section 83.28(10) of the *Criminal Code* provides use and derivative use immunity for all statements compelled at investigative hearings.

54 "Within a week of Pearl Harbor, as firings and acts of vandalism continued apace, irate writers of letters to the editor were demanding that all Japanese be at once interned." After internment, Prime Minister King announced: "The government's intention would be to have these disloyal persons deported to Japan as soon as that is physically possible. Prior to deportation, British subjects, falling within this class, would be deprived of their status as such." Quoted in K. Adachi, *The Enemy That Never Was* (Toronto: McClelland & Stewart, 1976), 201, 276. This policy of deporting even Canadian citizens was upheld by the courts in *Reference re Deportation of the Japanese Canadians*, [1947] AC 87 (JCPC). No group-based profiling of this type has been implemented or even advocated in Canada in the wake of September 11. See S. Choudhry, "Protecting Equality in the Face of Terror," in Daniels, Macklem, and Roach, eds., *The Security of Freedom*, 369.

55 Canada's restrictive refugee policy was influenced by anti-Semitism and led to many Jewish refugees from Nazi Germany being denied access to Canada. I. Abella and H. Troper, *None Is Too Many* (Toronto: Key Porter, 2000). Comparisons have been drawn between this "none is too many" policy and the "safe third country" agreement initialed between Canada and the United States since September 11. The safe third-country agreement will prevent most refugees who land in the United States first from applying for refugee status in Canada, but will not prevent refugee applicants from particular countries or groups.

56 RSC 1970, c. W-2. Under the *Public Orders Regulation* 1970, SOR 70–444, it was illegal to be a member of the Front de Libération du Québec or any other association that advocates force or the commission of crime to achieve governmental change within Canada. It was also illegal to contribute to, or to solicit contributions for, an unlawful association, or to allow such an association to use one's premises. Evidence that a person attended meetings or spoke publicly in advocacy of the association, or on its behalf, was, in the absence of evidence to the contrary, proof that he or she was a member of the association. Bill c-36 does not go as far as making membership in terrorist organizations

illegal, but it makes illegal many forms of association with, and participation in, terrorist organizations. It also provides that frequent association with any of the persons who constitute a terrorist group, or the use of a name, word, or symbol associated with a terrorist group, is relevant evidence in determining whether a person has committed the new offence of participating in the activity of a terrorist group. See *Criminal Code*, s. 83.18.

57 These illegal activities included the theft of dynamite, the burning of a barn, and a break and enter to steal the membership lists of the Parti Québécois. See Canada, *Freedom and Security Under the Law* (Ottawa: Supply and Services, 1981). As a result of organized crime amendments, the *Criminal Code* now contains some powers allowing the police to commit illegal acts. See *Criminal Code*, s. 25.1–25.4.

58 *Operation Dismantle v. Canada*, [1985] 1 SCR 441.

59 K. Ramakrishna, "The US Foreign Policy of Praetorian Unilateralism and the Implications or Southeast Asia," in U. Johannen, A. Smith, and J. Gomez, eds., *September 11 and Political Freedom: Asian Perspectives* (Singapore: Select Publishing, 2002), 139, quoting Thomas Friedman.

60 On the dangers of governments conflating terrorism and separatism, see A. Acharya, "State-Society Relations: Asian and World Order after September 11," in K. Booth and T. Dunne, *Worlds in Collision* (Houndmills, Eng.: Palgrave, 2001), 201. For concerns that terrorism may be conflated with Quebec separatism in Canada, see A. Gagnon, "A Dangerously Shrinking Public Sphere," *Policy Options*, Sept. 2002, 18–19. For calls for Canada to be more active in Sri Lankan peace talks on the basis that Canada "is more relevant than most other countries to the problems we face in Sri Lanka," see A. Thompson, "Peacebroker wants helps for Sri Lanka," *Toronto Star*, 23 Sept. 2002.

61 For concerns that the new war against terrorism may have stopped the momentum for reform of internal security laws in Singapore and Malaysia which allow indeterminate detention without trial of those deemed by the government to be threats to "security" or "essential services," see M. Hor, "Terrorism and the Criminal Law: Singapore's Solution," *Singapore Journal of Legal Studies* [2002]: 30; T. Lee, "Malaysia and the Internal Security Act: The Insecurity of Human Rights after September 11," ibid., 56. See also K. Roach, "Indonesia's delicate balancing act," *Ottawa Citizen*, 16 Oct. 2002; K. Roach, "Terrorism and Democracy in Southeast Asia," *Lawyers Weekly*, 30 Oct. 2002.

62 M. Gee, "Embracing Pakistan's dictator," *Globe and Mail*, 24 Aug. 2002.

63 D. Leblanc and J. Sallot, "PM says critics are defending terrorists," ibid., 7 Feb. 2002.

64 Ibid.

65 C. Krauss, "Canada alters security policies to ease concerns of U.S.," *New York Times*, 18 Feb. 2002.

CHAPTER SIX

1 G. Grant, *Lament for a Nation* (Toronto: McClelland & Stewart, 1965), 86–7. Diefenbaker's tragic flaw, according to Grant, was that he did not recognize "that a branch-plant society could not possibly show independence over an issue on which the American government was seriously determined." Ibid., 31.

2 *The Patriot Act*, ∞ 401–2.

3 C. Krauss, "Canada alters security policies to ease concerns of U.S.," *New York Times*, 18 Feb. 2002.

4 A. Picard, "Most want PM to cede sovereignty over border," *Globe and Mail*, 1 Oct. 2001.

5 "Canadians feel closer to US since attack," *Toronto Star*, 28 Sept. 2001.

6 Former prime minister Brian Mulroney argued that "our internal borders will only be smart if our external perimeter is secure" and called for the negotiation of a new security perimeter with new joint institutions. A. Thompson, "Ex-PM pushes security accord," *Toronto Star*, 10 Dec. 2002.

7 M. Campbell, "Align with US on security, executive says," *Globe and Mail*, 15 Sept. 2001.

8 S. McCarthy, "Canada will make its own laws, PM vows," ibid., 20 Sept. 2001.

9 S. Chase, "Ottawa firm on making its own rules," ibid., 24 Sept. 2001.

10 M. Molot and N. Hillmer, "The Diplomacy of Decline," in N. Hillmer and M. Molot, *A Fading Power* (Toronto: Oxford University Press, 2002), 14; notes for an address by the Hon. John Manley to the US Foreign Policy Association, New York City, 5 Nov. 2001.

11 Molot and Hillmer, "The Diplomacy of Decline," 17

12 W. Walker, "US fails to tighten northern border," *Toronto Star*, 5 Aug. 2002.

13 CBCNews.ca, "Canada, U.S. agree to more secure border," 3 Dec. 2001.

14 C. Clark, "The border debate: The Ashcroft plan," *Globe and Mail*, 4 Dec. 2001.

15 The Standing Committee on Citizenship and Immigration, *Second Report*, Dec. 2001, New Democratic Party Dissenting Opinion.

16 Although visa policy coordination was part of the border framework agreement, the text commits the two countries only to formal consultation "during the process of reviewing a third country for the purpose of either a visa imposition or visa exemption." *Summary of Smart Border Action Plan Status*, 9 Sept. 2002.

17 The Canadian man, Michel Jalbert, had a hunting rifle in his truck and had apparently been previously warned about crossing the border without going through customs. Bill Graham indicated that the case "was reflective of the type of things we can get into if there's a problem between us," and US Secretary of State Colin Powell called it an "unfortunate incident." On his release, Jalbert told reporters: "it wasn't a pleasant experience. I wouldn't wish it on anyone ... Don't go to the United States. Don't set foot there." A. Chung, "Quebec man freed after U.S. ordeal," *Toronto Star*, 15 Nov. 2002.

18 Without success, Graham protested American actions in deporting Maher Arar, a Canadian citizen, to his native Syria when he stopped over in New York as he was returning to his Ottawa home. Graham argued that "a person travelling on a Canadian passport is a Canadian citizen and has a right to be treated as a Canadian citizen," but Paul Cellucci, the American ambassador to Canada, defended his country's actions on the basis that they "had good and sufficient reason for what they did, based on the current threat" and allegations that Arar had connections with al-Qaeda. P. Cheney, "Graham takes on U.S. over deported Canadian," *Globe and Mail*, 17 Oct. 2002. Three months later, Arar was still detained in Syria. His wife later wrote of that time: "One day, Maher was a loving husband, a devoted father and a brilliant engineer. Then, he was turned into a file number. I still cannot accept that a Canadian citizen, who left Syria at 17 – whose unused Syrian passport still shows the face of an adolescent – can be thrown in jail, interrogated at length, threatened with deportation, denied proper access to a lawyer, denied a transparent trial, and then deported to the country of his birth." M. Mazigh, "Please send my husband home," ibid., 18 Jan. 2003. Despite these pleas, the Arar case has not become a compelling controversy in Canada.

19 A. Thompson, "Manhunt 'hoax' warrants apologies, minister insists," *Toronto Star*, 8 Jan. 2003; P. Koring, "Hillary Clinton unbowed," *Globe and Mail*, 10 Jan. 2003.

20 C. Clark, "New visa rules imposed on 8 countries," *Globe and Mail*, 5 Dec. 2001; E. Oziewicz, "Canada to require entry visas for Saudis," ibid., 6 Sept. 2002; D. Leblanc, "Canada caved in on visas, Saudis say," ibid., 24 Sep. 2002; "Muslim students in limbo," *Herald Tribune*, 25 Sept. 2002; A. Thompson, "System swamped for new Canadians," *Toronto Star*, 5 Oct. 2002. Concerns were raised by American universities that the American policy was denying access to moderate and educated people who could help prevent terrorism on their return to their countries. Canada's quicker and more generous approach to the issuance of student visas provides an opportunity to attract foreign students who might otherwise have studied in the United States.

21 A. Dunfield, "Graham opposes new U.S. border requirements," *Globe and Mail*, 30 Oct. 2002. Others in the Liberal government used even stronger language to protest the American policy. See chapter 3 for the reactions of Natural Resources Minister Herb Dhaliwal and Liberal Member of Parliament Sarkis Assadourian.

22 V. Malarek, "Woman tells of humiliation by U.S. officials," *Globe and Mail*, 6 Nov. 2002; G. Smith, "U.S. endorses visitor checks at border," ibid., 8 Nov. 2002; M.Kitmitto, "New U.S. border policies cause grief for Oakville residents," *Oakville Today*, 16 Jan. 2003.

23 C. Freeze, "Detained Canadians to be freed from jail," *Globe and Mail*, 24 Dec. 2002; C. Freeze, "Jailed in U.S. snafu, man disillusioned," ibid., 26 Dec. 2002.

24 G. Galloway, "New Canadians alienated by U.S. travel indignities," ibid., 2 Jan. 2003.

25 "Buchanan calls Canada 'freeloading nation,'" ibid., 1 Nov. 2002.

26 A. Thompson, "Canadian fury as U.S. steps up border checks," *Toronto Star*, 8 Nov. 2002; "Foreign Affairs cancels U.S. travel warning," *National Post*, 8 Nov. 2002.

27 J. Vicini, "US adds five more nations to immigrant registration list," *National Post*, 17 Jan. 2003.

28 T. Harper, "Ottawa slams U.S. visa plan," *Toronto Star*, 4 Nov. 2002; A. Thompson, "Graham to fight visa battle quietly," ibid., 5 Nov. 2002; A. Thompson "Canadian fury as U.S. steps up border checks," ibid., 8 Nov. 2002.

29 Ipsos Reid, "Three-quarters (77%) of Americans believe potential terrorists have slipped into U.S. through Canada," 10 May 2002.

30 Professor Bland commented: "Canada faces no greater foreign and defence policy challenge than finding an appropriate and credible way to reassure the U.S. that Canada can live up to the 1938

Roosevelt-Mackenzie King agreement under which the Prime Minister assured the Presidency that no attack on the United States would come through Canadian territory." Douglas Bland, "Canada and Military Coalitions: Where, How and with Whom?" *Policy Matters,* Institute for Research on Public Policy, Feb. 2002, 27. See also J.L. Granatstein, *A Friendly Agreement in Advance: Canada-U.S. Defence Relations Past, Present, and Future* (Toronto: C.D. Howe Institute, 2002).

31 Prime Minister Chrétien, President Bush Release Joint Statement on Canada-US Border Cooperation, 9 Sept. 2002.

32 M. Higgins, "'Smart card' for crossing border urged by CEO's," *National Post,* 15 Jan. 2002.

33 A. Thompson, "Manley wary of border security plan," *Toronto Star,* 7 Dec. 2002; "New U.S. rules to require more data from Canadian travelers," *Globe and Mail,* 4 Jan. 2003.

34 The Standing Committee on Citizenship and Immigration, *Second Report,* Dec. 2001.

35 "Canada and the U.S. unveil border plan," CBCNews.ca, June 28, 2002.

36 Notes for an Address by Hon. John Manley to the U.S. Foreign Policy Association, 5 Nov. 2001.

37 In the 2002, 42 per cent of the sample of 1,400 Canadians opposed such restrictions and 12 per cent were neutral. M. Blatchford, "Canadian attitudes on immigration hardening against Muslims," *Ottawa Citizen,* 21 Dec 2002.

38 [1985] I SCR 177.

39 J. Hathaway and A. Neve, "Fundamental Justice and the Deflection of Refugees from Canada," *Osgoode Hall Law Journal* 34 (1996): 213, para 131.

40 Ibid., para 105.

41 Ibid., para 106.

42 R. Germain, "Rushing to Judgment: The Unintended Consequences of the USA Patriot Act for Bona Fide Refugees," *Georgetown Immigration Law Journal* 16 (2002): 505.

43 B. Frelick, "Refugee ping pong North American style," *Chicago Tribune,* 5 Sept. 2002.

44 A. Macklin, "Borderline Security," in R. Daniels, P. Macklem, and K. Roach, eds., *The Security of Freedom: Essays on Canada's Antiterrorism Bill* (Toronto: University of Toronto Press, 2001), 388.

45 H. Adelman, "Refugees and Border Security Post September 11," *Refuge* 20, 4 (2001): 11.

46 "Study finds terrorists exploit every means of immigration to enter US," *US Newswire*, 22 May 2002.

47 J. Sallot, "Canada's refugee rules superior," *Globe and Mail*, 6 Feb. 2002; C. Kraus, "Canada alters security policies to ease concerns of US," *New York Times*, 18 Feb. 2002; J. Berlau, "Canada turns into terrorist haven," *Insight on the News*, 24 June 2002.

48 Canadian Council for Refugees, 10 *Reasons Why the U.S.-Canada Refugee Deal Is a Bad Idea*, July 2002; K. Jacobs, "The Safe Third Country Agreement: Innovative Solution or Proven Problem?" *Policy Options*, Sept. 2002.

49 S. Gallagher, "The Open Door Beyond the Moat: Canadian Refugee Policy from a Comparative Perspective," in Hillmer and Molot, eds., *A Fading Power*, 117; J. Bissett, "A Defence of the 'Safe Country' Concept for Refugees," *Policy Options*, Sept. 2002, 36.

50 I. Peritz and C. Clark, "Refugees jam border fearing new policy," *Globe and Mail*. 28 June 2002.

51 C. Nickerson, "Illegal U.S. immigrants turn sights on Canada," *Toronto Star*, 4 Jan. 2003; I. Peritz, "Fears spark surge in rate of asylum seekers at border," *Globe and Mail*, 3 Jan. 2003.

52 Macklin, "Borderline Security," 388ff.

53 R. Irwin, "Unfair US trade attack on Canada," *Providence Journal*, 11 April 2001.

54 Canada has won reductions in American duties in twelve of the eighteen cases Canada has appealed under NAFTA. I. Jack, "NAFTA has helped curb US trade enforcement," *National Post*, 10 Oct. 2002.

55 S. McCarthy, "We'll back US fight, PM vows," *Globe and Mail*, 18 Sept. 2001.

56 "Canadian military awaits a plan, and orders," Canadian Press, *Cornwall Standard Freeholder*, 18 Sept. 2001.

57 W. Immen, "Would-be recruits swamping Canadian Forces," *Globe and Mail*, 26 Sept. 2001.

58 M. Campbell, "Nation's grief turns to anger," ibid., 19 April 2002.

59 D. Halbfinger, "Court-martial hearing begins for U.S. Pilots," *New York Times*, 15 Jan. 2003; W. Walker, "Truth has to come out," *Toronto Star*, 19 Jan. 2003.

60 J. Ibbitson, "US Air Force confirms it may discipline pilot," ibid., 29 June 2002; "U.S. pilot ignored 2 orders," ibid., 29 June 2002: D. Yourk, "U.S. pilots face charges in friendly fire bombing," ibid., 13 Sept. 2002; "Don't jail pilots, families of soldiers killed in April say," ibid., 14 Sept. 2002; C. Freeze, "U.S. governor fund-raising for

pilots' defence," ibid., 24 Oct. 2002; "Illinois Senate supports pilots who face charges," ibid., 7 Dec. 2002; "U.S. pilots pressured to take speed, lawyer says," ibid., 2 Jan 2003.

61 M. Ignatieff, *Virtual War: Kosovo and Beyond* (Toronto: Viking, 2000), 6, 213.

62 S. McCarthy, "We'll back US fight, PM vows," *Globe and Mail*, 18 Sept. 2001.

63 S. Toope, "Fallout from '9–11': Will a Security Culture Undermine Human Rights," *Saskatchewan Law Review* 65 (2002): 292–4.

64 P. Cheney, "Terrorist tape names Canada," *Globe and Mail*, 13 Nov. 2002.

65 M.O'Malley, "Land, Sea, and Air, Ottawa goes to war," CBCNews.ca, 9 Oct. 2001; B. Yaffe, "Queen's prof case for military spending," *Kingston Whig-Standard*, 1 March 2002.

66 "Canada's defence spending too low, U.S. says," *Globe and Mail*, 3 Sept. 2002; "U.S, ambassador again chides Canada over military spending," ibid., 26 Sept. 2002.

67 R. Fife, "Canada to U.S.: Mind your business," *Ottawa Citizen*, 21 Nov. 2002.

68 "Who needs whom?" *The Economist*, 9 March 2002, 32.

69 D. Middlemiss and D. Stairs, "The Canadian Forces and the Doctrine of Interoperability: The Issues," *Policy Matters* 3, 7 (2002): 30–1.

70 M. Byers, "Canadian Armed Forces under U.S. Command," Liu Centre, *www.liucentre.ubc.ca*, June 2002, and *International Journal* 58 (2003) (forthcoming).

71 A. Sens, *Somalia and the Changing Nature of Peacekeeping: The Implications for Canada* (Ottawa: Public Works, 1997), 98.

72 Michael Ignatieff has argued that contemporary peacekeeping requires combat capabilities. "This is the Wild West and you have the people who can go into the Wild West and say, 'You mess with us, we'll mess with you' ... That means we [Canadian Forces] have to have more armour, we have to have more firepower, we have to have better rules of engagement, we have to be able to operate in environments of great uncertainty." T. Blackwell, "Canada needs 'lethal power,' Ignatieff says," *National Post*, 7 Nov. 2002. Major-General Lewis Mackenzie, however, has drawn distinctions between peacekeeping and war skills when, in his own words, he warned Americans: "Don't touch this peacekeeping stuff with a ten-foot pole ... it will erode the warrior ethic in the minds of your citizens and it will also erode your war fighting skills." MGen (Retd) Lewis Mackenzie, "The Minnow and the Whale: Will the Canadian Forces Be Rescued by US Defence Policy?" in

D. Rudd et al., eds., *Playing in the Bush-League? Canada-U.S. Relations in a New Era* (Ottawa: Canadian Institute for Strategic Studies, 2001), 73.

73 N. Ayed, "Officer praises troops 'ready to die,'" *Toronto Star*, 15 July 2002.

74 L. Axworthy, "Liberals at the Border: We Stand on Guard for Whom?" 6th annual Keith Davey Lecture, 11 March 2002; J. Stein, "Soft Power," *Toronto Star*, 7 Sept. 2002.

75 As one analyst predicted in 1993, "our detachment as a peacekeeper and our acceptance among Third World peoples will all diminish as our alignment with the United States becomes more obvious." A. Andrew, *The Rise and Fall of a Middle Power: Canadian Diplomacy from King to Mulroney* (Toronto: Lorimer, 1993), 166.

76 Quoted in Molot and Hillmer, "The Diplomacy of Decline," 6.

77 Middlemiss and Stairs, "The Canadian Forces and the Doctrine of Interoperability," 17–18.

78 J. Jockel, "After the September Attacks: Four Questions about NORAD's Future," *Canadian Military Journal*, spring 2002, 11.

79 The Canadian deputy director of NORAD reports both to Canada's chief of defence staff and the U.S. general who heads both NORAD and Northern Command. O. Moore, "Deal would let U.S. troops operate in Canada," *Globe and Mail*, 9 Dec. 2002.

80 D. Brown, "Canada wary of U.S. anti-terror plan: Some fear a continental defence system would threaten Ottawa's sovereignty," *Washington Post*, 24 Feb. 2002.

81 M. Byers, "On guard for Uncle Sam?" *Globe and Mail*, 18 April 2002; M. Byers, "Canadian Armed Forces under U.S. command"

82 D. Leblanc, "Canada, U.S. near troop deal," *Globe and* Mail, 28 Aug. 2002.

83 A Senate committee recommended the expansion of NORAD to include maritime matters. A planning committee described by Canada's vice-chief of the Defence Staff as something short of "a maritime NORAD," but based in the Colorado headquarters of both NORAD and Northern Command, is being planned. D. Yourk, "Extend NORAD concept, Senate urges," ibid., 3 Sept 2002; R. Fife and S. Alberts, "Canada, US devise joint military units," *National Post*, 17 Sept. 2002; S. Alberts, "U.S. Canada terror team a step closer," *National Post*, 2 Oct. 2002.

84 S. McCarthy and P. Koring, "Canada opts out of American plan to defend continent," *Globe and Mail*, 18 April 2002.

85 J. Sallot, "Canada lone NATO country to oppose U.S. nuclear policy," ibid., 1 Nov. 2002.

86 D. Leblanc, "Canada open to missile-shield discussions," ibid., 10 Dec. 2002; S. McCarthy, "U.S. envoy sure Canada will join NMD plan," ibid., 21 Dec. 2002; P. Koring, "Canada may fight without U.N. support," ibid., 10 Jan. 2003; A. Thompson, "Debate on missile defence urged," Toronto Star, 14 Jan. 2003.

87 Granatstein, A Friendly Agreement in Advance, 3.

88 Bland, "Canada and Military Coalitions," 26–7.

89 Ibid., 13.

90 S. Clarkson, Locksteps in the Continental Ranks: Redrawing the American Perimeter after September 11 (Ottawa: Canadian Centre for Policy Alternatives, 2002). See also Anthony Westell's arguments that September 11 made "brutally clear the extent of Canada's dependence on and subservience to the United States – and the ruthlessness of the U.S. in pursuing its own interests. It is painfully apparent that Canada escaped from being a colony of Britain only to become a colony of the U.S." Like Grant, Westell relates the failure of Canada to a failure of true conservatism or socialism. A. Westell, "How's your mindset?" Literary Review of Canada 10, 2 (2002): 8.

91 D. Pugliese, "Details of JTF2 missions released by the U.S. Military," National Post, 28 Sept. 2002.

92 Geneva Convention relative to the Treatment of Prisoners of War, 12 Aug. 1949, 75 (United Nations Treaty Series) 135 [hereinafter Geneva Convention on Prisoners of War]; Geneva Convention relative to the Protection of Civilian Persons in Time of War, 12 Aug. 1949, ibid., 287.

93 Geneva Convention relative to the Treatment of Prisoners of War, art. 5.

94 M. Byers, "US doesn't have the right to decide who is or isn't a PoW," The Guardian, 14 Jan. 2002. See also M. Drumbl, "Judging the September 11 Attack," Human Rights Quarterly 24 (2002): 325–6.

95 19 Dec. 1966, 999 United Nations Treaty Series 171, arts. 9–14. See also J. Cerone, "Status of Detainees in International Armed Conflict, and Their Protection in the Course of Criminal Proceedings," January 2002, ASIL Insights, online: American Society of International Law <http://www.asil.org/insights/insigh81.htm> (date assessed 9 May 2002).

96 A. Freeman, "Legal expert sees trouble in war role," Globe and Mail, 15 Jan. 2002,

97 P. Knox, "For captives, Guantanamo proves harsh environment," ibid., 17 Aug. 2002; G. Miller, "Dozens detained in Guantanamo may be innocent," Toronto Star, 22 Dec. 2002.

98 E. Mendes, "Between Crime and War: Terrorism, Democracy and the Constitution," in D. Daubney et al., *Terrorism, Law and Democracy* (Montreal: Les Éditions Thémis, 2002), 242, 268.

99 *R. v. Cook*, [1998] 2 SCR 597.

100 There have been reports of American officials in Bagram Air Base in Afghanistan and on Diego Garcia engaging in techniques such as hooding, sleep deprivation, holding detainees in awkward positions, and even beatings. One American official was quoted as saying: "If you don't violate someone's human rights some of the time, you probably aren't doing your job." "Ends, means and barbarity," *The Economist*, 9 Jan. 2003.

101 US, Executive Order 66, Fed. Reg. 57,833 at 57,833–4 (13 Nov. 2001). Subsequent regulations did provide for safeguards, such as the right to counsel, and were greeted with bipartisan support. For some remaining reservations, see R. Dworkin, "The Trouble with the Tribunals," *New York Review of Books*, 25 April 2002, 10.

102 "Note: Responding to Terrorism: Crime, Punishment and War," *Harvard Law Review* 115 (2002): 1237.

103 "In Letter, 300 Law Professors Oppose Tribunals Plan," *New York Times*, 8 Dec. 2001.

104 *Sale v. Haitian Council*, 509 US 155 (1993).

105 P. Koring, "Canada, other allies blast immunity push," *Globe and Mail*, 22 June 2002.

106 P. Koring, "US edict on court decried," ibid., 7 May 2002.

107 J. Ibbitson, "Canada condemns World Court compromise," ibid., 13 July 2002.

108 Canada's actions in handing its captives over to the Americans cannot be seen as part of "our counter-terrorism activities [that] complement Canada's long-standing support for the establishment of a rules-based system of enforceable international norms as reflected in the ICC." B. Graham, "Notes for an Address," in Daubney et al., *Terrorism, Law and Democracy*, 325.

109 S. McCarthy, "Chrétien with Bush on prisoners' status," *Globe and Mail*, 7 Feb. 2002.

110 A. Freeman, "UK to hand suspects to Afghans," ibid., 18 Jan. 2002; J. Sallot, "Britain will give Afghans PoW status," ibid., 30 April 2002.

111 D. Leblanc, "Navy seizes al-Qaeda suspects," ibid., 15 July 2002.

112 M. Mackinnon and C. Freeze, "Canadian teen may be U.S. source," ibid., 30 Oct. 2002; C. Freeze, "Canadian teen held at Guantanamo," ibid., 31 Oct. 2002. Representatives of Amnesty International expressed

concerns about Omar Kahdr's detention with adults. "Anyone concerned about the treatment of juveniles will question the sending of a person to this type of facility. Because of his age, he has to be separated from the larger community. There are UN standards in terms of treatment of juveniles."

113 R. Fife and S. Bell, "U.S. lets CSIS, RCMP question Khadr," *National Post*, 31 Dec. 2002; A. Thompson, "Canada 'pressing' for access to teen," *Toronto Star*, 18 Jan. 2003. On the possible applicability of the Charter to actions of Canadian police abroad, see *R. v. Cook*, [1998] 2 SCR 597. Section 7 of the Charter provides that no persons should be deprived of their liberty except in accordance with the principles of fundamental justice which have been interpreted as the basic tenets of our legal system. Section 9 of the Charter provides that "everyone has the right not be arbitrarily detained or imprisoned." Section 10 of the Charter provides that, upon detention, everyone has the right to be informed promptly of the reasons therefore; to retain and instruct counsel without delay and to be informed of that right; and to have the validity of the detention determined by way of *habeas corpus* and to be released if the detention is not lawful.

114 J. Brean, "No POW rights for enemy combatants," *National Post*, 6 Sept. 2002; C. Freeze and C. Boyd, "U.S. holds Canadian teen as an al-Qaeda assassin," *Globe and Mail*, 6 Sept. 2002.

115 Amnesty International, *Execution of Child Offenders*, www.icomm.ca/ aiusa/abolish/juvexec.html; *Stanford v. Kentucky*, 492 US 361 at 369 n.1(1989); "The disgrace of juvenile executions," *New York Times*, 24 Oct. 2002.

116 The statements were made by John Dixon, president of the BC Civil Liberties Association. C. Freeze, "CSIS watches Islamic extremists," *Globe and Mail*, 7 Sept. 2002. See also I. Vincent, "There should be no special status for this kid," *National Post*, 6 Sept. 2002; E. Morgan, "Don't stand on guard for Omar," *National Post*, 12 Sept. 2002. For belated expression of editorial concern about Khadr's situation, see "The case of Omar Khadr," *Globe and Mail*, 5 Nov. 2002.

117 S. McCarthy, "Can Canada ease up and still please the U.S.?" *Globe and Mail*, 21 Nov. 2001.

118 In February 2002 the *New York Times* reported that Canadian changes to immigration and criminal laws and increased military and law enforcement cooperation with the Americans had "come in part from a desire to reassure the United States that Canada is not a sanctuary for terrorists exploiting this country's liberal refugee laws and porous

borders. But it also reflects the economic shock that Canada suffered late last year when long border and port delays throttled Canadian exports to the United States, by far its largest customer." C. Krauss, "Canada alters security policies to ease concerns of U.S.," *New York Times*, 18 Feb. 2002.

119 W. Walker, "Bush: Why we must attack," *Toronto Star*, 6 Sept. 2002.

120 A poll of 1,000 Canadians in mid-January 2003 showed 62 per cent said that Canada should provide military assistance to an invasion of Iraq only with UN approval, with only 15 per cent supporting such assistance if the US acts without UN approval. G. Galloway, "Canadians oppose war in Iraq without UN," *Globe and Mail*, 18 Jan 2003.

121 Molot and Hillmer, "The Diplomacy of Decline," 14, 25; T. Weber, "Canada wins key softwood bout," *Globe and Mail*, 26 July 2002.

122 The use of the phrase "Stern Daughter of the Voice of God" (taken from a William Wordsworth poem "Ode to Duty") in relation to Canada was attributed to Dean Acheson, who served as the United States secretary of state in the Truman administration. N. Hillmer and J.L. Granatstein, *Empire to Umpire: Canada and the World to the 1990s* (Toronto: Copp Clark Longman, 1994), 217. Acheson subsequently wrote an essay criticizing Canadian foreign policy under Pearson for attempting to make NATO more than a military alliance and participating in peacekeeping under the auspices of the United Nations. Acheson argued that Canada's policy was elitist and naïve, compared with the predominant American interest in containing communism. See D. Acheson, "Canada: 'Stern Daughter of the Voice of God,'" in L. Merchant, ed., *Neighbors Taken for Granted: Canada and the United States* (Toronto: Burns & MacEachern, 1966), 139–47.

123 Canada's defence and foreign affairs ministers both indicated in January 2003 that Canada might join an American war against Iraq even if the war was not approved by the UN as necessary to enforce UN resolutions against Iraq's possession of weapons of mass destruction. This apparent and surprising change in Canada's position was announced immediately after a meeting in the Pentagon with Secretary of Defense Donald Rumsfeld. The Canadian minister of defence reported that Rumsfeld was "very happy with what I said," but most Canadians opposed the possibility that Canada might contribute to a war against Iraq without a UN mandate. A few days later, Prime Minister Chrétien dismissed the ministers' comments as "speculative" and affirmed the position that, "if the international community decides that the use of force against Iraq is necessary because it is the only way to bring an

end to Iraq non-compliance (with U.N. resolutions), Canada would do its part." See J. Cienski, "Canada might not wait for U.N.," *National Post*, 10 Jan. 2003; P. Koring, "Canada might fight without UN support," *Globe and Mail*, 10 Jan. 2003; A. Thompson, "Graham opens door wider for joining war on Saddam," *Toronto Star*, 11 Jan. 2003; "Decision on Iraq should go through UN, PM says," *Toronto Star*, 15 Jan 2003; G. Galloway, "Canadians oppose war in Iraq without UN," *Globe and Mail*, 18 Jan. 2003.

124 President Johnson apparently clasped Prime Minister Pearson by the shirt collar and told him, "You pissed on my rug!" in response to Pearson's 1965 call for a halt to the bombing of North Vietnam. L. Martin, "Thank you, Mr. Nixon: It was a good time for Canada's soul," *Globe and Mail*, 19 March 2002. See also R. Bothwell, I. Drummond, and J. English, *Canada since 1945: Power, Politics, and Provincialism* (Toronto: University of Toronto Press, 1981), 277.

CHAPTER SEVEN

1 U. Franklin, "Peace," *Toronto Star*, 7 Sept. 2002.

2 M. Barkun, "Defending against the Apocalypse: The Limits of Homeland Security," *Policy Options*, Sept. 2002, 30.

3 National Research Council, *Making the Nation Safer: The Role of Science and Technology in Countering Terrorism* (Washington, DC: National Academy Press, 2002), 23.

4 H.L. Ross, *Deterring the Drunken Driver*, rev. ed. (Lexington: D.C. Heath, 1984).

5 J. Gusfield, *The Culture of Public Problems: Drinking, Driving and the Symbolic Order* (Chicago: University of Chicago Press, 1981).

6 W. Haddon and S. Baker, "Injury Control," in D. Clark and B. MacMahon, eds., *Preventive and Community Medicine*, 2nd ed. (Boston: Little Brown, 1981), 110. For an early presentation of the Haddon Matrix, see W. Haddon, "A Logical Framework for Categorizing Highway Safety Phenomena and Activity," *Journal of Trauma* 12 (1972): 193.

7 J. Braithwaite, "On Speaking Softly and Carrying Sticks: Neglected Dimensions of a Republican Separation of Powers," *University of Toronto Law Journal* 47 (1997): 296.

8 A. Picard, "Bulk of violent deaths are suicides, WHO study," *Globe and Mail*, 3 Oct. 2002.

9 Alan Dershowitz has argued that terrorists may be amenable to deterrence. See A. Dershowitz, *Why Terrorism Works* (New Haven, NJ: Yale

University Press, 2002), 21–3. He also suggests that third parties who influence, support, or benefit from terrorism should also be targeted and even punished for acts of terrorism committed by others. Ibid., 117–19, 172–81. As we discussed in chapter 4, targeting third parties becomes objectionable when it imposes criminal guilt by association or status.

10 According to Dershowitz, responding to the grievances of terrorism will only encourage more terrorism. In his view, the better approach is to delay responses to the grievances of terrorism as a means to punish terrorists and their supporters. Ibid., chaps. 1 and 2. There are normative and practical problems with Professor Dershowitz's argument. One is the ethics of effectively punishing innocent people who have acts of terrorism committed in their name. Another more practical problem is that it seems counter-intuitive to think that a response to a grievance that may have motivated terrorism, coupled with criminal prosecution and stigmatization of those who commit criminal acts of terrorism, will encourage more terrorism. As suggested in chapter 2, the criminal law has never excused crimes because they are motivated by well-founded grievances.

11 Justice Horace Krever raises the interesting and provocative question of whether the precautionary principle that governs public health should also be applied to national security matters because "national security can be imperiled by an internal or external threat of violence or by a threat to public." He questions why the public health approach, which led him to recommend that the Red Cross take actions to reduce the risk of AIDS in blood in the absence of conclusive evidence, should also not be applied to people who may be terrorists. In my view, the answer is that fairness considerations make the risk of false positives greater when the state is detaining a person or subjecting someone to intrusive forms of investigation. As Justice Krever recognized, the values of liberalism and democracy are threatened when the police investigate or detain a peaceful group that is simply out of favour with the mainstream of today. See H. Krever, "National Security and the Public Right to Know: Blood, Water and War," paper given at the Open and Controlled Society Conference, 9 May 2002.

12 Concerns about the ability of the minister of defence to create broad military security zones that could prohibit protest without legislative or judicial approval led to the withdrawal of the bill and the eventual introduction of an amended bill that would not give the minister such powers. As we discussed in chapter 2, concerns have been expressed

that some of the surveillance powers in this bill extend beyond the terrorism context to other law enforcement purposes. The bill also frequently contemplates prosecutions and penalties, as well as using more creative strategies such as the licensing of hazardous goods.

13 K. Lunman, "Privacy watchdog sounds alarm," *Globe and Mail*, 2 May 2002; "Antiterror bill opens the door to police state, watchdog says," ibid., 2 Nov. 2002; Privacy Commissioner of Canada, News release, 1 Nov. 2002.

14 Bill C-42, *An Act to amend certain Acts of Canada, and to enact measures for implementing the Biological and Toxin Weapons Convention, in order to enhance public safety*, 1st Session, 37th Parliament, 2001 (first reading, 22 Nov. 2001).

15 Ibid., s. 94. See now s. 84 of Bill C-17, *An Act to amend certain Acts of Canada, and to enact measures for implementing the Biological and Toxin Weapons Convention, in order to enhance public safety*, 2nd Session, 37th Parliament, 2001 (first reading, 31 Oct. 2002).

16 Another example would be companies qualifying for fast tracking at customs if they comply with measures to keep their products secure. B. McKenna, "U.S. firms recruited to combat terrorism," *Globe and Mail*, 16 April 2002.

17 D. Garland, "The Limits of the Sovereign State: Strategies of Crime Control in Contemporary Society," *British Journal of Criminology* 36 (1996): 445.

18 J. Stein, "Network Wars," in R. Daniels, P. Macklem, and K. Roach, eds., *The Security of Freedom: Essays on Canada's Anti-terrorism Bill* (Toronto: University of Toronto Press, 2001), 73.

19 J. Taber, "Airlines ask Ottawa to pay marshal's way," *Globe and Mail*, 26 Sept. 2002.

20 P. Brethour, "Canadian pilots flying to U.S. may have to carry cockpit guns," ibid., 7 Sept. 2002.

21 K. McArthur, "Air security improvements doubted," ibid., 10 Sept. 2002.

22 "Pilots make safety demands," ibid., 12 Oct. 2002.

23 23 S. Chase, "Screening of all luggage years away, officials say," ibid., 28 Nov. 2002; I. Jack, "Senator sees 'bizzare' gaps in airport security," *National Post*, 6 Jan. 2003.

24 Quoted in "Disturbing report on airport security," *Toronto Star*, 20 Aug. 2002. See also C. Kenny, "Where's the justice? Pull back the veil on security," *Globe and Mail*, 15 Aug. 2002.

25 K. McArthur, "Air security improvements doubted," *Globe and Mail*, 10 Sept. 2002.

26 A. Cavoukian, "Security Technologies Enabling Privacy (STEPs): Time for a Paradigm Shift," Information and Privacy Commissioner of Ontario, June 2002.

27 A. Carter, "The Architecture of Government in the Face of Terrorism," *International Security* 26, 3 (2001–2): 15, 19 (emphasis in original).

28 G. Dyer, "Falling into the terror trap," *Toronto Star*, 17 Oct. 2002. See also G. Dyer, "Terrorism, Law and Democracy," in D. Daubney et al., *Terrorism, Law and Democracy: How Is Canada Changing following September 11?* (Montreal: Les Éditions Thémis, 2002), 67.

29 See, for example, D. Schneiderman, "Terrorism and the Risk Society," in Daniels, Macklem, and Roach, eds., *The Security of Freedom*, 63; T. Homer-Dixon, *The Ingenuity Gap* (New York: Alfred A. Knopf, 2000).

30 *R.J.R. MacDonald Inc. v. Canada*, [1995] 3 SCR 199; *R. v. Hydro Quebec*, [1997] 3 SCR 213; *Firearms Reference*, [2000] 1 SCR 783.

31 G. Grant, *Lament for a Nation: The Defeat of Canadian Nationalism* (Toronto: McClelland & Stewart, 1965), 64. On the connection between retraction of the Canadian state and the issue of nationalism, see S. Clarkson, *Uncle Sam and Us* (Toronto: University of Toronto Press, 2002).

32 These are the "six critical mission areas" identified in the *National Strategy for Homeland Security* (Washington: Office of Homeland Security, 2002).

33 B. Kellman, "Catastrophic Terrorism – Thinking Fearfully, Acting Legally," *Michigan Journal of International Law* 20 (1999): 551–2; M. Kelley, "Germs for Iraq weapons supplied by U.S.," *Toronto Star*, 1 Oct. 2002.

34 The dean of the Harvard School of Public Health, Barry Bloom, commented: "The threat of bioterrorism is an opportunity to protect ourselves against all infectious diseases." He went on to observe that while five people have died in the United States from anthrax-laced letters, at least 20,000 people die there each year from influenza. Quoted in A. Picard, "Bioterrorists prey on public's anxiety," *Globe and Mail*, 18 Feb. 2002.

35 An epidemiological or public health approach to harm is often based on scepticism about the ability to control human behaviour. It focuses, rather, on regulation of both the physical and socio-cultural environment to prevent and reduce harm. See M. Friedland, M. Trebilcock, and K. Roach, *Regulating Traffic Safety* (Toronto: University of Toronto Press, 1990), 13–18. For example, a public health approach would not attempt to deter suicide bombers, but would limit their access to

explosives through centralized controls and licensing systems. It would also explore the possibility of limiting the access of potential suicide bombers to populated areas in a variety of ways, including the use of barriers and sensors for explosives. Attempting to respond to some of the grievances that produced the terrorism could also be a response suggested by a public health approach, but only if it resulted in empirically verifiable benefits.

36 Health Canada, News release, 18 Oct. 2001.

37 P. Cheney, "Ottawa to buy smallpox vaccine," *Globe and Mail*, 28 Nov. 2002; T. Blackwell, "Ottawa stockpiling smallpox vaccine," *National Post*, 28 Nov. 2002.

38 Canadian Nuclear Safety Commission, *Backgrounder Action on Nuclear Security Post Sept. 11, 2001.*

39 M. Millestaedt, "Worried about nuclear terrorism? Take a pill," *Globe and Mail*, 12 Oct. 2002.

40 T. Boyle, "Province axes key biohazard experts," *Toronto Star*, 18 Oct. 2001; R. Brennan, "Water quality control 'abandoned': Watchdog," ibid., 27 Sept. 2002. The Walkerton Inquiry concluded that, if the Ministry of the Environment "had adequately fulfilled its regulatory and oversight role, the tragedy in Walkerton would have been prevented (by the installation of continuous monitors) or at least significantly reduced in scope." Budget reductions had reduced staff at the ministry by 30 per cent despite warnings about health risks and without a risk management plan. Hon. D. O'Connor, *Report of the Walkerton Inquiry: The Events of May 2000 and Related Issues* (Toronto: Queen's Printer, 2002), 30, 35.

41 Canadian Food Inspection Agency, Enhanced biosecurity measures, News release, 12 July 2002.

42 "Statement by G8 Leaders: The G8 Global Partnership against the Spread of Weapons and Materials of Mass Destruction," Kananaskis, Alberta, 27 June 2002.

43 "Getting what you pay for," *The Economist*, 29 June 2002.

44 Canada responded with restrictions on the export of nuclear power. D. Bratt, "The Ethics of CANDU Exports," in R. Irwin, ed., *Ethics and Security in Canadian Foreign Policy* (Vancouver: UBC Press, 2001), 235.

45 J. Kirton, "Canada as a Principal Summit Power: C7/8 Concert Diplomacy from Halifax 1995 to Kananaskis, 2002," in N. Hillmer and M. Molot, eds., *A Fading Power* (Toronto: Oxford University Press, 2002), 223. For concerns about the inadequacy of American restrictions on the export of nuclear and chemical materials, given the threat of terrorism,

see R. Sievert, "Urgent Message to Congress," *Texas International Law Journal* 37 (2002): 89.

46 "Fireproofing blamed for fall of twin towers," *Calgary Herald*, 25 June 2002.

47 C. Haughney, "Fireproofing faulted in Trade Center collapse," *Washington Post*, 25 June 2002.

48 "9/11 exposed deadly flaws in rescue plan," *New York Times*, 7 July 2002.

49 The Canadian Department of National Defence has an Office of Critical Infrastructure Protection and Emergency Preparedness, which was created before September 11 in large part because of concerns about computers, but it "works under the radar screens of public consciousness." W. Wark, "Learning to live with terror," *Globe and Mail*, 15 Nov. 2002.

50 Thomas Axworthy adds: "Public health capacity to meet national emergencies requires laboratory facilities, stockpiles of vaccines, regional deployment of emergency supplies, expertise on decontamination, a national inventory of equipment and training of first responders to nuclear, biological or chemical attack." T. Axworthy, "Our lack of preparedness is the emergency," *National Post*, 8 Nov. 2002.

51 *Emergencies Readiness Act*, 2002, Statutes of Ontario, 2002, c. 14.

52 J. Monchuck, "Emergency planning is flawed, report says," *Toronto Star*, 14 Nov. 2002.

53 Council for Canadian Security in the 21st Century, *People's Defence Review*, 11 Sept. 2002. For reports of a speech in which the minister of defence related the need for increased spending to terrorism and the Bali bombings, see C. Watte, "'I will ask for more money,' McCallum says," *National Post*, 26 Oct. 2002.

54 R. Brennan, "Firefighters to get specialized 'disaster' training," *Toronto Star*, 30 Aug. 2002.

55 Canada Budget 2001, Enhancing Security for Canadians, 10 Dec. 2001.

56 T. Blackwell, "Bioterror threat sparks research," *National Post*, 17 Sept. 2002.

57 J. Granatstein, *A Friendly Agreement in Advance* (Toronto: C.D.Howe Institute, 2002), 19.

58 Council for Canadian Security in the 21st Century, *People's Defence Review*, 11 Sept. 2002.

59 Security Intelligence Review Committee, *Annual Report*, 2001–2002, 31.

60 M. Higgins, "US had warnings of plot to attack WTC," *National Post*, 20 Sept. 2002.

61 Security Intelligence Review Committee, *Annual Report 2001–2002*, 7.

62 M. Rudner, "International Terrorism Dimensions of a Security Challenge," in Daubney et al., *Terrorism, Law and Democracy*, 11–12.

63 M.L. Friedland, "Police Powers in Bill C-36," in Daniels, Macklem, and Roach, eds., *The Security of Freedom*, 280–1.

64 S. Heafey, "Civilian Oversight in a Changed World," in Daubney et al., *Terrorism, Law and Democracy*, 401.

65 See M. Rudner, "Contemporary Threats, Future Tasks: Canadian Intelligence and the Challenges of Global Security," in Hillmer and Molot, eds., *A Fading Power*, 163; W. Wark, "We must review CSE's performance, not legality," *Globe and Mail*, 29 July 2002.

66 C. Boyd and A. Woods, "CSIS hands over Canadian al-Qaeda suspect," *Globe and Mail*, 29 July 2002.

67 "The rhetoric of the current military action in Afghanistan draws largely on the rhetoric of the criminal law. The enunciated goal of the campaign is to disrupt terror networks and to 'bring [their members] to justice.' This goal is essentially identical to the primary goal of the criminal law: to prevent harm by punishing those who cause or would cause it. U.S. military action thus appears in this case to be an instrument of American criminal law: a continuation of criminal justice policy carried on by other means." Note, "Responding to Terrorism: Crime, Punishment and War," *Harvard Law Review* 115 (2002): 1224.

68 On the need for greater emphasis on these preventive and development aspects of American foreign policy, see S.M. Walt, "Beyond bin Laden: Reshaping U.S. Foreign Policy," *International Security* 26, 3 (2001–2): 56.

69 For a discussion of the concept of the "criminalization of politics," see K. Roach, *Due Process and Victims' Rights* (Toronto: University of Toronto Press, 1999), 312–13. On the related concept of "governing through crime," see J. Simon, "Governing through Crime," in L. Friedman and G. Fisher, eds., *The Crime Conundrum: Essays on Criminal Justice* (New York: Westview Press, 1997); M. Valverde, "Governing Security, Governing through Security," in Daniels, Macklem, and Roach, eds., *The Security of Freedom*, 83.

70 Some attempts to link September 11 with Palestinian grievances have been resisted. New York mayor Giuliani returned a $10 million donation from a Saudi prince who made the comment: "Our Palestinian brethren continue to be slaughtered at the hands of the Israelis while the world turns the other cheek." See K. Roach, "The Dangers of a Charter-Proof and Crime-Based Response to Terrorism," in *The Security of Freedom*, n. 41.

71 President Bush did, however, subsequently announce a $5 billion increase in development funding and stated: "We fight against poverty because hope is an answer to terror." Graham Fraser, "Fight poverty to beat terrorism: Bush," *Toronto Star*, 23 March 2002.

72 S. McCarthy, "Anti-terror coalition's fissures are showing," *Globe and Mail*, 25 Feb. 2002.

73 K. Booth and T. Dunne, "Worlds in Collision," in K. Booth and T. Dunne, eds., *Worlds in Collision: Terror and the Future of Global Order* (Houndmill, Eng.: Palgrave, 2002), 6.

74 A. Picard, "Spending on war over health 'moral delinquency,' Lewis says," *Globe and Mail*, 11 Oct. 2002; S. Nolan, "Global AIDS fund is short $8 billion," ibid., 12 Oct. 2002.

75 J. Sachs, "Weapons of mass salvation," *The Economist*, 26 Oct. 2002.

76 In his brilliant survey of Canadian political trials from the 1837 Rebellions to the October Crisis of 1970, Kenneth McNaught observed: "Few countries have witnessed the repentance of such a high proportion of political rebels. It is not impossible that a major reason for this has been the combination of firm action and succeeding lenience which seems to characterize our basically conservative political-judicial tradition. It seems unlikely, for example, that had Vallières [a terrorist associated with the FLQ] been as closely implicated in a revolutionary movement in the American republican democracy as he was in Quebec he would today not only be free but the beneficiary of a federal grant to assist community organization." K. McNaught, "Political Trials and the Canadian Political Tradition," in M.L. Friedland, ed., *Courts and Trials* (Toronto: University of Toronto Press, 1974), 139.

77 M. Cernetig, "US solidifies its ranking as the world's biggest jailer," *Globe and Mail*, 27 Aug. 2002.

78 G. Trotter, "The Anti-Terrorism Bill and Preventative Restraints on Liberty," in Daniels, Macklem, and Roach, eds., *The Security of Freedom*, 241.

79 "Ramzi Yousef, the mastermind of the first World Trade Center bombing in 1993 and the author of a plan to simultaneously attack a number of U.S. airliners crossing the Pacific, was caught by using offers of rewards on matchbooks. Alternatively, people arrested know that they can reduce their sentence or even obtain immunity by revealing information about far more serious past crimes or future dangers ... Both of these systems of rewards need better advertising." P. Heymann, "Dealing with Terrorism: An Overview," *International Security* 26, 3 (2001-2): 37. On the use of rewards, see also M.L. Friedland,

"Controlling the Administrators of Criminal Justice," *Criminal Law Quarterly* 31 (1989): 280.

80 Lloyd Axworthy, quoted in A. Latham, "Theorizing the Landmine Campaign: Ethics, Global Cultural Scripts, and the Laws of War," in Irwin, ed., *Ethics and Security in Canadian Foreign Policy*, 174.

81 R. Irwin, "Towards Human Security?" ibid., 272. Professor Irwin warns that "much of the human security agenda in Canada and elsewhere has downplayed economic and social concerns, focusing instead on the protection of individual security from violence. This limited response to the structural challenges of global distributive problems reveals a conservativeness in policy approaches." R. Irwin, "Linking Ethics and Security in Canadian Foreign Policy," ibid., 6.

82 L. Axworthy, "The Human Security Solution to Terrorism," *Winnipeg Free Press*, 5 Sept. 2002; R. Boswell, "Axworthy says Bush will lose terror war," *Ottawa Citizen*, 20 Nov. 2002; L. Axworthy, "A human approach will defeat terrorism," *Ottawa Citizen*, 21 Nov. 2002.

83 J. Stiglitz, "Globalism's Discontents," *The American Prospect* 13, 1 (2002): A21.

84 R. Gwyn, "Steering our own course," *Toronto Star*, 22 Sept. 2002.

85 T. MacCharles, "Canadians healthier, wealthier but more pessimistic, study finds," ibid., 15 July 2002.

86 P. Calamai, "Canada growing stronger, poll says," ibid., 1 July 2002. Another survey conducted in July 2002, around the same time, suggested that 35 per cent of respondents wanted more distant ties from the United States, 36 per cent wanted them to remain the same, and 28 per cent wanted closer ties. The percentage wanting closer ties with the United States was down from 33 per cent in October 2001, but up from 23 per cent in March 2001. L. Moore, "Canadians frustrated with U.S., poll finds," *National Post*, 7 Sept. 2002. A subsequent poll found that 66 per cent of respondents wanted increased economic integration with the United States. R. Fife, "66% favour stronger ties to the U.S.," *National Post*, 21 Oct. 2002. This question is different from whether Canadians want to be more like the United States.

87 D. York, "Canada is still no. 1 in the hearts of most Canadians, studies suggest," *Globe and Mail*, 27 July 2002; D. York, "Canadians overwhelmingly happy with homeland," ibid., 26 July 2002.

Acknowledgments

The origins of this book lie in the papers and talks I have given since the terrorist attacks of September 11, 2001. I have been fortunate to be asked to speak about anti-terrorism law and policy to a wide variety of Canadians – from judges and senators to anti-globalization protesters and listeners to radio phone-in shows. I have also addressed lawyers, students, and civil society groups in the United States, Singapore, and Indonesia on Canada's responses to September 11 and the challenges their countries face. All these experiences have been stimulating and have affirmed my faith in the importance of a democratic, lawful, and sovereign approach to the very real dangers of terrorism.

I thank the University of Toronto's Faculty of Law for providing support and encouragement for my initial post-September 11 work on anti-terrorism law. In particular, I thank all those who made possible the November 2001 conference on Bill C-36 and the publication a few days later of *The Security of Freedom: Essays on Canada's Anti-Terrorism Bill* by the University of Toronto Press. All my colleagues who contributed to this volume have provided a strong and collegial nucleus of interest, expertise, and support for my further work in the area, and many at the faculty generously made comments on drafts of this book.

I thank the Special Senate Committee on Bill C-36 for inviting me to speak and my colleague Sujit Choudhry, who wrote much of the brief we presented before the committee. This experience allowed me to see first hand part of the important process of parliamentary review of Bill C-36, as well as the controversies surrounding the issue of racial and religious profiling.

I thank Studio Two at Television Ontario and the Canadian Broadcasting Corporation's syndicated radio and Ideas programs for allowing me to speak about Bill c-36. These appearances enabled me to experience how the issue was covered in the media and to hear from a range of Canadians about their fears and concerns in the aftermath of September 11. Much of this book draws on a broad range of reporting in Canada's English-language newspapers, and I am grateful for all the hard work done by the many reporters covering the multiple consequences of September 11 for Canada.

I thank the National Judicial Institute and the Ontario Court of Justice for inviting me to speak to judges of both the Federal Court and the Ontario Court of Justice on the *Anti-terrorism Act*. These opportunities allowed me to reflect on the difficult position many judges will face as they administer the act, as well as to consider the reactions of some judges to their new and onerous responsibilities under the law.

I thank the Canadian Consulate in New York City and the New York Bar Association for asking me to speak on a panel there on Canadian and American responses to September 11. This event forced me to reflect on the manner in which both countries have responded to the tragic events of September 11. It also affirmed my faith that the Canadian response to September 11, while far from perfect, was in many ways more civil, productive, and inclusive than the American approach. I thank my Canadian co-panelist Richard Mosley, who, throughout the difficult debates about Bill c-36, conducted himself with exemplary courtesy and professionalism.

I thank the Canadian Institute for the Administration of Justice for asking me to speak at its conference on anti-terrorism law and policy in Montreal. This experience was especially helpful in enriching my understanding of the need for greater accountability for anti-terrorism efforts and the consequences of giving the police new responsibilities for investigating crimes of terrorism.

I thank the University of Toronto's Innovation Law and Policy Centre, the Ontario Privacy Commissioner, and the University of Waterloo's Centre for Applied Cryptographic Research for inviting me to speak at their conference on security and privacy in Toronto. This experience was helpful in enriching my understanding of privacy concerns in the wake of September 11 and the role of technology both in invading and in protecting privacy.

I also spoke about the *Anti-terrorism Act* at public forums in Hamilton, Ontario, a panel sponsored by the University of Toronto's chapter of Amnesty International, and at the G6 Billion alternative to the G8 summit in Kanaskasis, Alberta. These events helped me to understand the fears that a variety of civil society groups, including those associated with the anti-corporate globalization movement and groups of Arab and Muslim Canadians, have about Canada's anti-terrorism policy.

I thank the Faculty of Law of the National University of Singapore for inviting me to visit their law school in September and October 2002 to speak about comparative anti-terrorism laws and policies and to contribute to a special issue of the *Singapore Journal of Legal Studies* on comparative anti-terrorism law. Special thanks to Gary Bell, Michael Hor, Victor Ramraj, and Tan Cheng Han, who made my stay at their law school enjoyable, stimulating, and productive.

I also thank James Agee and the Economic Law, Institutional and Professional Strengthening Project for inviting me to Jakarta, Indonesia, in May and September 2002 to speak and work with a group drafting anti-terrorism legislation in Indonesia and with civil society groups concerned about such legislation. These visits caused me to reflect on how Canada's response to September 11 is perceived abroad and to experience the challenge of crafting anti-terrorism policies that respect legal principles, democracy, sovereignty, and the need for security. The terrorist attacks in Bali on October 12, 2002, underlined the need for effective and just anti-terrorism policies.

Special thanks to the *McGill Law Journal* and Patrick Healy for asking me to deliver the 2002 McGill Law Journal Lecture and for subsequently publishing that lecture as "Did September 11 Change Everything? Preserving Canadian Values in the Face of Terrorism" in volume 47(4) of that journal. Revised and expanded parts of that lecture are included as parts of chapters 2, 4, and 7 of this book.

A number of colleagues and friends have generously read and commented on drafts or parts of this book. I thank Jutta Brunnée, Michael Byers, Sujit Choudhry, Jan Cox, David Dyzenhaus, Marty Friedland, Patrick Healy, Horace Krever, Audrey Macklin, Patricia McMahon, Ziyaad Mia, Victor Ramraj, Howard Roach, Jonathan Rudin, David Schneiderman, Janice Stein, Don Stuart, and Gary Trotter for reading all or parts of the initial manuscript. I am also grateful to two anonymous referees for McGill-Queen's University Press for providing prompt, expert, and helpful comments on an earlier draft of the manuscript. Special thanks to David Schneiderman, who encouraged me to expand my initial lecture into a book, and to Patricia McMahon, who guided me through the analogies to the Cuban Missile Crisis and came up with the eventual title of the book. Thanks also to Lisa Allegro, who provided tireless research assistance during the summer of 2002 and responded with good cheer and efficiency to all my research requests. I was extremely fortunate that Rosemary Shipton could again provide expert editing. I also thank all those at McGill-Queen's University Press involved in the production of the book. I have tried to keep the book current to January 15, 2003, and all errors and shortcomings remain my responsibility.

Finally, I cannot thank my family enough for their continued love and support and for tolerating the time away from them that some of this work required.

Kent Roach
January 2003

Index